ROYAL
DOCKYARDS

ROYAL DOCKYARDS

PHILIP MACDOUGALL

DAVID & CHARLES
Newton Abbot   London   North Pomfret (VT)

British Library Cataloguing in Publication Data

MacDougall, Philip
  Royal dockyards.
  1. Great Britain. *Royal Navy* 2. Navy-yards and
  naval stations – Great Britain – History
  I. Title
  623.8′ 3   VA460

  ISBN 0-7153-8148-2

Photoset by Typesetters (Birmingham) Ltd,
and printed in Great Britain
by Redwood Burn Ltd, Trowbridge, Wilts
for David & Charles (Publishers) Limited
Brunel House Newton Abbot Devon

Published in the United States of America
by David & Charles Inc
North Pomfret Vermont 05053 USA

Contents

1
The Royal Dockyards:
An Introduction

The history of the royal dockyards is naturally linked closely to developments within the Royal Navy. Over the years the various dockyards have performed the essential tasks of both building and maintaining a very high proportion of all warships commissioned into the navy. Of these royal yards, only Portsmouth, Devonport, Rosyth and Chatham are still retained although the last mentioned is currently due for closure sometime in 1984. Other royal dockyards, such as Harwich, Woolwich, Deptford and Sheerness, have all ceased their associations with the Royal Navy, and the areas they once occupied are now being used for very different purposes. Royal dockyards have not been restricted to the British Isles: in earlier years, a great number of foreign yards were established, each responsible for the maintenance and repair of warships operating far from home. Amongst these yards were those of Halifax, Antigua, Bermuda, Gibraltar and Singapore. As with the home yards, their numbers have been greatly depleted over the years with only Gibraltar, due for closure in 1983, still remaining.

By definition, a royal dockyard must be a government concern, fully owned by the crown, and with facilities either for the maintenance or construction of warships. Thus a royal dockyard might have both wet- and dry-docks, building slips, numerous stores and a considerable array of workshops. Most essential, however, are the dry-docks. Usually built of timber or stone, and frequently referred to as graving docks*, they allow a vessel of any size to be completely removed from the water so that the hull might be inspected, cleaned and repaired. This cleaning of a ship's hull, a process once known as graving had, during the age of sail, to be carried out every time a vessel returned from service, or had been held in harbour for three years.

The number of dry-docks at any particular royal yard naturally varied, but the largest number was at Portsmouth where, at the

* Technical words, such as graving, are more fully explained in the glossary

beginning of the present century, there was a total of fourteen. Whilst referring to the dry-docks, it should also be noted that during the nineteenth century floating docks were developed to fulfil the same purpose as a dry-dock, but could be transferred between yards or established where the building of a dry-dock might prove uneconomic.

In addition to the royal dockyards, there were also a number of naval yards, such as those of Deal and Kinsale in Cork. Their role was that of providing store facilities for warships needing to replenish both general equipment and victuals. The one at Deal was particularly useful during the years of sail as it lay opposite The Downs, a sheltered area of water in which vessels gathered whilst awaiting more favourable winds. As a navy yard, Deal had no docking facilities, but a number of small boats and transport craft were actually built there.

Finally, at this point, reference must be made to the various merchant yards. Frequently resorted to by the Admiralty both for the repair and construction of warships, they were, of course, privately owned, and cannot be considered in conjunction with the royal dockyards. Yet the history of the Royal Navy really begins with the merchant yards. In the Middle Ages, the private shipyards of Southampton, Bursledon, and the Cinque Ports were commissioned by Henry V to build a number of ships which were to join his battle fleet. Of these, Southampton was the most important, building the *Grace Dieu* and *Holigost*, two of Henry's larger ships. In an earlier century, also, Southampton had been building and repairing vessels for King John.

With the establishment of the royal dockyards, the private yards subsequently lost their right to build warships. The rather limited size of England's sixteenth- and seventeenth-century navy could be handled by the royal dockyards working alone. In the eighteenth century, however, the situation was reversed. Constant wars with France and Spain led to a massive increase in the number of fighting ships required, and the merchant yards were once again utilized. Private yards sited along the Thames, Medway, Hamble and Solent were busily engaged in the all-important work of building fourth, fifth and sixth rates.

The story of the private yards has since turned full circle. The remaining royal yards no longer build ships of war; this role is exclusively in the hands of a group of companies, such as Vickers and Vosper Thorneycroft, who go to make up British Shipbuilders. Of these, Vickers is undoubtedly one of the largest, building at their

Barrow shipyard certain of the Polaris-carrying submarines currently in service, the first of the new Type 42 destroyers and *Invincible*, the Royal Navy's first through-deck cruiser, which was completed in 1979.

The earliest royal dockyards, by far, were those established under the Tudor monarchs: Portsmouth, Deptford, Woolwich and Chatham. Portsmouth was undoubtedly the first naval dockyard, a dry-dock being established in 1496. Distance from London, however, proved inconvenient, leading Henry VIII to establish additional yards at Woolwich and Deptford. Chatham, a relative newcomer, was not performing the duties of a dockyard until 1570. Its earlier use as an anchorage merely earned for itself the title of navy yard.

During the seventeenth century three further dockyards were founded, at Harwich, Sheerness and Plymouth. The former, established close to the confluence of the Stour and Orwell rivers, had a fine natural harbour from which warships could be quickly directed towards a raid upon the Dutch coast or any fleet then being assembled by that nation during periods of hostility. Sheerness, located at the mouth of the Medway, was designed to take pressure away from Chatham, so preventing ships in need of only small repairs having to traverse the entire length of the Medway. So useful did Sheerness prove that it was soon to replace Harwich, which fell into private hands, and subsequently built a number of successful warships for a rapidly expanding navy.

Plymouth, the last of the seventeenth-century yards, was established to service a western squadron. Originally considered to be of only temporary status, a later realization of the Atlantic's strategic value led to a permanent fleet and the consequent need for an enlarged dockyard. By the middle of the eighteenth century, Plymouth was second only to Portsmouth in both size and output.

It was not until the nineteenth century that the various royal dockyards witnessed any further major alterations to their facilities. Portsmouth, Plymouth (Devonport) and Chatham were all considerably enlarged, whilst Deptford and Woolwich were closed down. The growth of what we must now refer to as Devonport was particularly marked, the Keyham Extension belonging to these years. It was during this century also that Pembroke yard was created, specializing in the building rather than the maintenance of warships, whilst on the east coast of Ireland, Haulbowline was begun. The royal dockyard at Haulbowline, situated inside Cork Harbour and officially opened in 1903, was later ceded to the Irish Free State.

The final royal dockyard, that of Rosyth, was not officially established until World War I was at its height. Consideration for the siting of a dockyard in the Firth of Forth had initially been made in 1907, but only a limited amount of progress had been made prior to the declaration of war in 1914. A much expanded works programme was subsequently implemented, with the dockyard being utilized from 1916 onwards.

Abroad, Port Royal, Jamaica, was the earliest royal dockyard, being established during the seventeenth century. Its main role was that of careening ships, having two wharves set aside for this purpose. Heavily damaged by earthquake and fire, this particular yard was abandoned in the early eighteenth century. For the foreign yards, however, their heyday really came during the late nineteenth and early twentieth centuries. In that period considerable expenditure led to the creation of dockyard facilities at Gibraltar, Malta and Simonstown, together with considerable expansion of dockyard facilities at Bermuda. Singapore, was not given dockyard facilities until 1937.

Although Portsmouth immediately springs to mind as the most important of the royal dockyards, this has not always been the case. Throughout the Dutch war period, Chatham was considered to be of much greater importance. The reasons for this were subsequently outlined by Sir William Monson, a high admiral during the reign of King Charles I. According to him:

> Chatham is so safe and secure a port for the ships to ride in that his Majesty's navy may better ride with a hawser at Chatham than with a cable at Portsmouth . . . The nearness from Chatham to London, from whence they may be supplied with all things they stand in need of, for that London is the storehouse of all England. It is necessary therefore that the navy should be kept at Chatham rather than at Portsmouth . . . The water at Chatham flows sufficiently every spring tide to grave the greatest ships. And it is a doubt whether it can be made to heighten so much in Portsmouth as do the like. No wind or weather can endanger the coming home of an anchor in Chatham, and the river affords sufficient space for every ship to ride without annoying one another. As to the contrary, a storm, with a wind from the north-east to the south-south-east, will stretch the cables at Portsmouth; and if any of their anchors come home they cannot avoid boarding one another, to their exceeding great danger and damage, the channel being so narrow.

Later critics, though, rather considered Monson had overstated the case for Chatham. At the time, the country's main opponent was, Holland and the real reason for Chatham's pre-eminence at this time was its proximity to the Dutch coast. Ships could easily be fitted out for combat with the Dutch fleet, whilst providing immediate protection in the event of a threatened attack. In truth, the choice of Chatham or Portsmouth really depended on just who was considered to be the national enemy. During his tour of Great Britain, Daniel Defoe neatly summed it up:

> There is also this note to be put upon the two great arsenals of England, Portsmouth, and Chatham; namely, that they thrive by war, as the war respects their situation (viz.) that when a war with France happens or with Spain, then Portsmouth grows rich, and when a war with Holland, or any of the powers of the north, then Chatham, and Woolwich, and Deptford are in request.

To perform their duties adequately, the royal dockyards needed a great many facilities. As large industrial centres, they were also self-contained units. They were able to manufacture their own cordage, finished sails, anchors, pulley blocks and numerous other items so essential for maintaining the 'wooden walls'. In the nineteenth century they were also to acquire rolling mills, saw mills, paint shops and engine factories. During the early years, the dockyards were of necessity similar in layout. For one thing, the ropery, that area set aside for the manufacture of cordage, required buildings of such extreme length that they had to be placed well away from the central working area. Similarly the mast pond: sometimes called, if somewhat confusingly, a wet-dock, this was where the mast timbers were stored. Held underwater by means of low-level arches, fir timbers might be left to season for twenty or thirty years. Occasionally lime was added to the waters to prevent molluscs or boring worms attaching themselves to the precious timbers. Within the central working area of the yard might be found the timber pound, building slips, the dry-docks and smitheries. Storehouses, accommodation for senior yard officers, the dockyard chapel and offices would be placed around the yard in the most suitable places. Finally, the entire land-side area would be enclosed by a wall, leaving an open waterfront.

Although contemporary accounts of the several yards abound, they are often no more than lists which indicate that the writer had little knowledge about the real purposes of the structures mentioned. Daniel Defoe's description of Chatham, made at the beginning of the eighteenth century, is a decidedly more interesting account and will serve to represent the various other yards during this period:

This being the chief arsenal of the royal navy of Great Britain. The buildings here are indeed like ships themselves, surprisingly large, and in their several kinds beautiful. The warehouses, or rather streets of warehouses, and storehouses for laying up the naval treasure are the largest in dimension, and the most in number, that are anywhere to be seen in the world. The rope-walk for making cables, and the forges for anchors and other iron work, bear a proportion to the rest as also the wet dock for keeping masts, and yards of the greatest size, where they lie sunk in the water to preserve them, the boat yard, the anchor yard; all like the whole, monstrously great and extensive, and are not easily described.

We come next to the stores themselves, for which all this provision is made; and first, to begin with the ships that are laid up there. The sails, the rigging, the ammunition, guns, great and small shot, small arms, swords, cutlasses, half pikes, with all the other furniture belonging to the ships that ride at their moorings in the river Medway. These take up one part of the place, where the furniture of every ship lies in particular warehouses by themselves, and may be taken out on the most hasty occasion without confusion, fire excepted. The powder is generally carried away to particular magazines to avoid disaster. Besides these, there are storehouses for laying up the furniture and stores for ships; but which are not appropriated, or do not belong (as it is expressed by the officers) to any particular ship; but lie ready to be delivered out for the furnishing other ships to be built, or for repairing and supplying the ships already there, as occasion may require.

At this point it is worth saying a little more about the function of a royal dockyard, together with something of the individuals who were employed to build and maintain the nation's warships. Central to the role of building ships were the launchways, as it was upon these that vessels were both built and launched. Of timber construction, they were so designed that completed vessels could be put straight into the water. At first these launchways, or slips, were completely open with no covering whatsoever. At the beginning of the nineteenth century, huge roofs began to be erected, helping to preserve stored timbers and allowing construction to continue in all weathers.

Close to the building slips were the dry-docks. Mostly used for the repair of vessels, larger ships were also built in dry-dock. Nelson's 100-gun *Victory*, for instance, was constructed in the old single dock at Chatham and subsequently floated out. For the repair of vessels it was normal for a ship to be brought in at high tide, with flood gates being closed once the dock had been emptied of water. Not that the first dry-docks were as sophisticated as this; for the most part they were no more than mud embankments. Indeed, it was the soft clay banks found in the Portsmouth area, and along the Thames and Medway, that first attracted the navy. Originally ships were simply hauled on to a convenient beach, cleaned and repaired, then refloated on the next spring tide. Later it became common practice to build up a mud embankment which completely surrounded ships under repair. From this rather primitive design developed the first timber docks, the earliest of these being built at Portsmouth in 1496.

Particularly important during the earlier period of dockyard history were the timber pounds and saw houses. Situated close to the slipways and dry-docks, the timber pounds were frequently too small for the huge quantities of material constantly being purchased. Nor was the situation eased by the haphazard methods adopted in the placement of this timber. Frequently dumped in the nearest available space, it meant that the work-force had to manoeuvre themselves around huge obstacles created with little or no warning. As these timber piles were also unventilated, a large proportion was invariably lost through severe rotting. Eventually, though, in 1772, special seasoning sheds were introduced throughout the royal dockyards, leading to a far more efficient use of timber stocks.

From the timber pounds and seasoning sheds, timber would be taken to the storehouses. These were no more than open-sided buildings enclosing a saw pit. Sawyers would work in pairs, operating a two-man saw. With a piece of timber placed across the pit, and supported by beams, one man would stand in the pit, and another above. As can be imagined, the daily routine was extremely arduous. A normal working day was 6.00am until 6.00pm (with an hour and a half for lunch); the accumulated monotony and an undoubted thirst was broken by each man having an allowance of eight pints of strong beer per day. Drunkenness was not uncommon!

Whilst, of course, all of the royal yards had slipways, dry-docks and timber pounds, only a few had roperies. These were sited at the three most important yards – Portsmouth, Plymouth and Chatham – with these particular dockyards manufacturing sufficient cordage for the other yards. Rope was a particularly important item during the age of sail, with a ship of 74 guns requiring nearly thirty miles. Within the ropery the most important buildings were the rope- and spinning-houses. Sometimes combined under one roof, they were always of an extraordinary length, needing to be as long as the longest piece of rope manufactured. Around these would be clustered a series of smaller buildings which were needed during the earlier stages of the rope-making process.

It was within the rope-house that yarn was spun into finished rope but, as already indicated, this was only the final stage. Hemp arriving from the Baltic during the late summer period was, after a period of storage within the hemp house, transferred to the hatchelling house where it was combed out. This was achieved by drawing wads of hemp across a hatchelling board – wooden blocks pierced with pieces of steel. From the hatchelling house the hemp would eventually be taken to the spinning floor and spun into yarn. Once this task had been accomplished, the yarn was taken to the tarring house prior to storing in the black-yarn house. If there was insufficient time for this last process, untarred yarn would be taken to the white-yarn house instead. Eventually the completed yarn would be transferred to the laying floor of the rope-house for the final spinning into rope.

So far unmentioned were the numerous dockyard cranes, rigging houses, wharves, sail, colour and mould lofts. Whilst most of these need little or no explanation, something need certainly be said of the last group. Regarding the colour loft, it was here that flags used by the Royal Navy were made up. A highly skilled task, all of the work was done by hand, with electric sewing machines eventually being introduced during the twentieth century. In the sail loft, sails were made and repaired, with much of the work undertaken by hand, even today. The sails still produced, however, are only used by small yachts. The mould lofts were often set above the mast houses and upon their floor a full-scale plan of vessels under construction was scribed (or chalked). From these plans templates were later cut.

Of the various groups of workers employed within the royal dockyards, the shipwrights were the most prominent. Not only were more employed than any other group, but they also had the greatest skills. In fact a shipwright could turn his hand to almost anything, and was certainly capable of building and preparing the entire ship. They did not do so simply because work requiring lesser skills was parcelled out to certain other workers, allowing the shipwrights to perform the most difficult tasks. Their work started with the laying of blocks on the slipway, the assembling of the frame and through to the final fitting of planks. Other dockyard workers, such as mastmakers, caulkers, joiners, sailmakers and scavelmen had to set their routine to that of the shipwrights.

The caulkers carried out a trade which was also considered highly skilled. They were responsible for ensuring the water-tightness of any vessels either brought into dry-dock or under construction. Taking oakum, which would be picked from old rope by the young 'oakum boyes', they would roll it into strips for fitting into the seams of the hull. Once the seams had been filled, pitch would then be applied with a pitch mop. The safety of the ship depended upon their skills as just the right amount of oakum had to be used – too little and the vessel would leak and too much would cause the seams to spring.

Amongst the unskilled workers were the scavelmen. They worked closely with the shipwrights, undertaking a variety of non-specialized tasks. They fully maintained the dockyard and were responsible for pumping out dry-docks. Of a lower status were the ordinary labourers, who were responsible for the movement of timber, unloading the hemp ships during the late summer, keeping the yard clean and acting as general messengers and domestic servants. One final group of workers that might be mentioned were the riggers; usually former sailors, they took responsibility for rigging all new vessels whilst regularly renewing all rigging of ships either in-ordinary or about to go to sea. This was naturally a very dangerous job, and led to many accidents over the years.

A particular problem that was confronted by the eighteenth-century dockyards was that of combatting the extensive damage resulting from attacks upon timber-hulled warships by *Teredo navalis*. These slender boring molluscs, most commonly found in tropical waters, would eat their way into the timber hull, soon converting a fine ship into nothing better than matchwood. It was as a result of experiments carried out within the royal dockyards that suitable protection was found, resulting in all warship hulls being eventually sheathed in copper plates. At first the idea did not prove too successful as the plates were initially fixed by means of iron bolts, which only served to generate galvanic corrosion. Eventually, however, a copper-zinc bolt was introduced, and this effectively secured the all-important plates. The coppering of warship hulls, of which much of the early experimental work was conducted at Deptford, resulted in certain other advantages for the Royal Navy. For one thing it produced a certain tactical superiority as British ships, unhindered by weed which accumulated more easily on a timber-bottomed ship, sailed that much better. It is generally felt that this particular dockyard innovation was directly responsible for a victory gained by Admiral Rodney in 1780. Whilst patrolling off Cape St Vincent, his copper-bottomed warships easily overhauled a squadron of Spanish ships whose hulls had not been so treated.

The age of fighting sail, brought to a rather sudden conclusion during the nineteenth century, had also been a time of limited development within the dockyards. Steam power, for instance, had been available for use since the early eighteenth century, but none of the royal dockyards adopted such mechanical advances until the 1790s. At this time steam was restricted to the rope-yards, but was eventually used in the production of pulley blocks, siding or cutting of timber, pumping out the docks and in paint production. Eventually, of course, most aspects of the dockyard were to be mechanised by steam or other sources of power. Rolling mills, huge cranes and various workshops were all steam-powered by the end of the nineteenth century. During the twentieth century, electric and gas power also become common, with electric welding making an entry during the 'twenties.

The late Victorian period saw massive extension works at all of the main dockyards, allowing Chatham, Portsmouth and Plymouth to build ever larger ships. Portsmouth, retaining its pre-eminence, built most classes of battleships, including many of the Dreadnoughts. Indeed, the importance of this particular yard cannot be over-estimated. Whilst numerous construction orders were being placed with a whole host of private yards, the first of most new classes of battleship was constructed at Portsmouth. To this yard, therefore, fell the duty of ironing out any potential problems and paving the way for the private yards. It was a role that the Portsmouth shipwrights carried with great pride.

Today, the three original home yards have changed little since the nineteenth century. All three still have a great number of fine historic buildings, many of which pre-date the Napoleonic Wars. The basic work areas are certainly those established in the reign of Queen Victoria, whilst Chatham still has a working rope-house and colour loft. Portsmouth, on the other hand, can boast HMS *Victory*, an ancient mast pond and numerous storehouses built in the Hanoverian period. Similarly Plymouth, still retaining many of the old storehouses has, as its most interesting feature, the two roperies, both of which measure 1,200ft in length.

Rosyth, of course, does not have quite so much history attached to it. A purely twentieth-century dockyard, it was the home of the Grand Fleet in 1917, carrying out similar work during World War II. As a result, its buildings are much more functional. Portsmouth, Plymouth and Chatham, therefore, are the real historic yards. Aware of this history, the authorities open sections of these yards to the public. Portsmouth's historic enclave is permanently open to visitors, regular tours are arranged at Chatham, whilst a guide exists at Plymouth. A morning or afternoon visiting one of these dockyards is a very worthwhile experience.

2
The Tudor Yards

Portsmouth, known affectionately as 'Pompey', must be considered first of the royal dockyards. It was at the beginning of the twelfth century that this particular area became a centre of maritime activity with a wet-dock being built for the safe harbourage of royal ships. Constructed during the reign of King John, the dock lasted only a few years, but was nevertheless sufficient to proclaim the town a naval yard, if not actually a royal dockyard. After a period of neglect, another monarch turned his attention to Portsmouth. In 1496, Henry VII built a dry-dock, the first to be constructed in England. The dock, built to the north of Portsmouth town on the site of the present No 1 basin, signified the beginning of a true dockyard, and one that has been in constant use since that date.

The Royal Navy, as such, can also date its birth to the reign of Henry VII. Earlier monarchs had found little use for a standing navy, though a few kings had built up small fleets, mainly for transporting troops. For such purposes they usually commandeered a number of trading vessels, rather than purchase or build their own ships. These traders, of course, were not built for war, being extremely small and unable to sail in poor weather. During the later Middle Ages, 'cogs' were most commonly used and often fitted with small wooden platforms, known as castles, upon which archers could gather in an effort to prevent an enemy attack. Sometimes huge sea fights occurred between opposing fleets. On such occasions the tactics employed were little different from those of land warfare. The fight would open with a barrage of arrows in which the English, using the long bow, invariably had superiority over the French, and other enemies, who favoured the crossbow. Eventually one side would feel its archers had done the maximum damage possible and the ships would be grappled for hand-to-hand fighting. Using such tactics, an English fleet commanded by Edward III successfully engaged a French fleet off Sluys in 1340.

According to Froissart, the French chronicler, the English fleet was well ordered, 'the greatest before, well furnished with archers, and ever between two ships of archers he had one ship with men-at-arms'.

King John was an exception: whilst commandeering a great number of small trading vessels for various expeditions to the Continent, he also had a personal fleet of his own. Consisting for the most part of galleys, a faster and more manoeuvrable vessel, it is said that John had some fifty of these warships. A number were permanently based at Portsmouth where, in the year 1212, orders were issued for the enclosing of the dock. In that year the Sheriff of Southampton, then responsible for the small town of Portsmouth, was instructed '. . . to construct a good and strong wall round our dock at Portsmouth without delay so that when winter comes, we may avoid damage to our vessels and their appurtenances'. The actual area of these docks was a series of mud flats, used previously for the beaching of ships in need of cleaning or repair. It was the area now occupied by HMS *Vernon*.

At the time the protective wall was built, a number of storehouses were also erected, and intended for the safe keeping of sails, ropes and anchors. In 1213 a number of items were ordered for Portsmouth, some of which were presumably stored, and included thirty anchors, numerous suits of armour and single-bladed swords known as falchions. Of galleys and other ships, the exact number based at Portsmouth is unknown, but in 1214 a clue is provided when the king sent orders to the Master of the Ships at Portsmouth to 'ready ten of our best Gallies which are at Portsmouth'. Additional instructions required numerous other vessels to have pontoons or castles fitted that they might be immediately ready for the transporting of troops to Angers. Later in that year King John came personally to Portsmouth, from whence he took passage to La Rochelle.

Although the newly enclosed dock was supposed to provide a safe harbour, it had been constructed in a rather exposed position, much subjected to winter gales. On a number of occasions ships were damaged within the walls, whilst a particularly violent gale during the reign of Henry III led to partial destruction of the dock itself. The result was its rather sudden abandonment and the area was subsequently filled. Despite this, certain maritime activities still centred upon Portsmouth. In 1253, for instance, an expedition to Gascony resulted in something approaching a thousand ships being anchored in the local waters. However, unlike King John, Henry III did not choose to maintain a standing navy. He sold off the galleys but retained a few vessels for personal use. These continued to winter at the Portsmouth navy yard with one of them, 'the King's Great Ship', requiring extensive repairs in 1231. On this occasion skilled carpenters were sent from Shoreham, with the vessel presumably beached for the renewal of planking. Such a process would be carried out during a spring tide when the vessel would be run on to a suitable mud bank and then refloated on a high tide. Portsmouth, with its numerous mud banks, provided excellent facilities for these primitive methods of ship repair.

Only a limited number of ships were acquired for royal service during the Middle Ages, and none of these were constructed by ship-wrights directly employed by the crown. Such vessels were invariably built in small merchant yards, or simply purchased abroad. During these early times, towns such as Southampton and Winchelsea commonly built ships for royal use, with the former being perhaps the busier. Indeed, Southampton was very much a rival to Portsmouth in those days; not only was it an area for the construction of ships, but it also had a harbour which was frequently used by the king's own ships and an alternative assembly point for various invasion fleets.

In the year 1415, Henry V mustered a particularly large fleet in the Solent prior to the Agincourt campaign. Of these vessels, twenty-four were actually owned by the king and the largest, the *Holigost*, was built by William Soper, a Southampton shipwright. Completed in 1414 it was a 760-ton carrack which made considerable use of several new innovations. It not only had two masts and fitted forecastles but was armed with three guns. The guns would have been of a very small calibre, designed for firing upon boarding parties rather than at other ships. Another Southampton-built vessel was the *Grace Dieu*, an even larger ship which was completed in 1418. Estimated at some 1,400 tons, it again had two masts and was described as being 176½ft long and 96ft in the beam. Sadly the *Grace Dieu* probably never sailed. Completed late for Henry's initial invasion, she spent many long years laid up in the Hamble, close to Southampton. Clinker-built, she leaked badly, saddening the hearts of the men who had built her. The finest ship yet to have been constructed in the country, she was finally struck by lightning early in 1439, and slowly settled in the mud banks of the river. A number of other royal ships were also laid up in the Hamble during these years, and were eventually sold upon the death of Henry V. Once more an early attempt at building a navy had been destroyed by those somewhat less far-sighted.

And so, at last, to Henry VII, a king who is recognized as a founder member of the Royal Navy. Yet, as such, he did not build vessels specifically for war. Far more concerned with the state of the exchequer, he wished to avoid costly foreign expeditions. Instead, his ships were built for trade, with thoughts of encouraging merchants. Henry VII felt that by building a royal fleet and having some particularly fine vessels, it would encourage the English merchant classes to do likewise. For this reason, Henry's fleet included the *Regent* and *Sovereign*, ships easily comparable with the *Grace Dieu*. Both vessels were of considerable size, with the *Regent* mounting four masts and armed with 225 guns. Extremely small, these weapons were all mounted on the upper decks. At this time no ship could carry heavy cannon owing to the absence of gun-ports which would allow them to be carried on the lower decks.

Having had such large ships built, Henry also found he needed the necessary ancillary services. These ships were too large to be repaired by beaching, and needed a purpose-built dry-dock. As nothing like this existed within the country, it was decided that a royal dock should be built at Portsmouth. Doubtless some consideration was given to Southampton, but the town was probably rejected because of its prospering commercial trade and the need for a separate naval port. At the same time, further use of the Hamble was probably dismissed because of this river's shallowness.

Henry VII seems to have first turned his attention to Portsmouth in 1494 when work was carried out upon the defences of his future harbour. A square tower was erected close to its entrance, complementing the round tower built during the earlier part of the century. About this time a blockhouse was erected on the Gosport side. In the following year, 1495, instructions were issued for work to begin on the dry-dock, with suitable land having already been acquired. Positioned to the north of the town, its exact design is unknown. Certainly it was constructed of timber, with both an inner and outer gate. Upon vessels passing into the dock, the entrance would have been sealed by several hundred tons of clay. Mechanical contrivances such as floating caissons or water-tight gates were quite beyond Tudor engineers and much simpler, if time-consuming, devices were resorted to. Once a ship was berthed and the entrance sealed, the dock itself was emptied by means of an 'injyn' ·· presumably some kind of hand pump.

It was on 25 May 1496 that the completed dock was first used. On

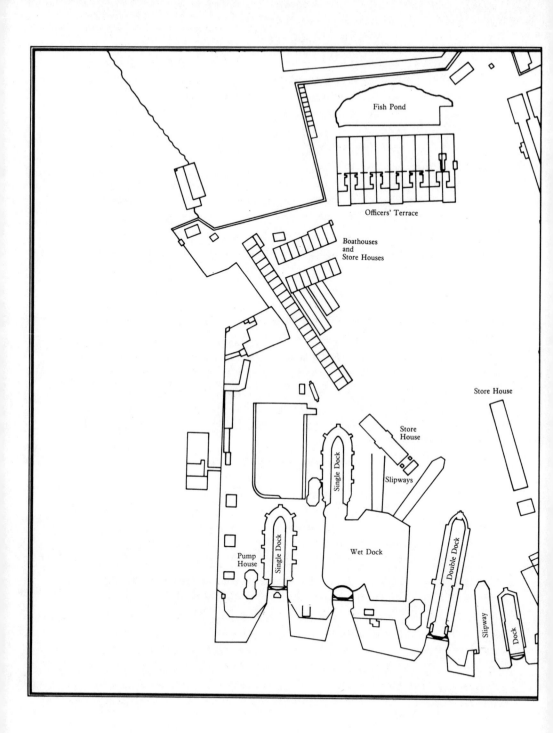

Fish Pond

Officers' Terrace

Boathouses
and
Store Houses

Store House

Store
House

Slipways

Single Dock

Pump
House

Single Dock

Wet Dock

Double Dock

Slipway

Dock

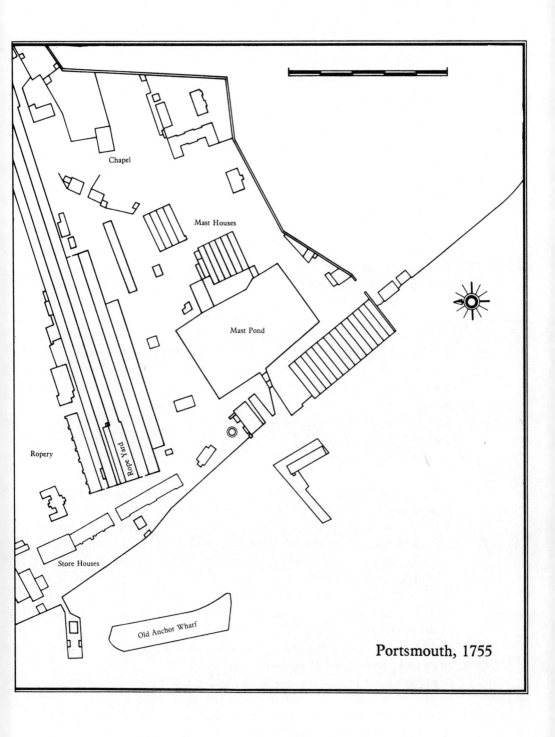

Chapel

Mast Houses

Mast Pond

Ropery

Rope Yard

Store Houses

Old Anchor Wharf

Portsmouth, 1755

that day the *Sovereign* was brought in, but this was no easy task as 140 men, in addition to the ship's crew, had to be specially employed. Furthermore, the process seems to have taken some considerable time with the labour force being employed by both day and night. The accounts further record that the 140 men received, between them, 24/8d together with meals which appear to have consisted of bread, beer and fish. The undocking of the *Sovereign* took place in January of the following year when twenty men were employed for nearly a month. They were needed to dig out the clay and remove huge piles which had been set down at the time of docking. In 1497 the entire process was repeated for the *Regent*.

The reign of Henry VIII heralded a much busier period for Portsmouth dockyard. The new king concentrated a good deal of effort into expanding the navy for, unlike his father, he had numerous military objectives. Furthermore, he was also aware of important changes then coming about in the design of warships. In France, gun-ports had been invented, allowing guns to be carried on the lower decks. A simple innovation, it was to herald revolutionary changes as it allowed much heavier guns to be used at sea. To incorporate gun-ports in his ships, Henry initiated a building programme which was mainly centred upon Portsmouth. Orders were issued for the construction of the *Mary Rose* and *Peter Pomegranate*. Both were designed as warships, the first true English warships, and both were able to mount heavy siege guns previously used only on land. The *Mary Rose*, of 600 tons, was given a total of 78 guns, of which only 28 were the small serpentines, the rest being made up of larger pieces such as the horrifically descriptive 'Murderers' and 'Great Murderers', both huge guns of varying calibre and originally designed for blasting defending walls. The smaller *Peter Pomegranate* was similarly armed, receiving numerous double-serpentines and six 'grete murderers'.

In order to receive their armament, both ships had to be sailed into the Thames where they lay off the Tower of London. This, of course, was an inconvenience. Doubtless Henry felt that a mistake had been made in placing the nation's only dry-dock so far away from the capital: not only were virtually all guns stored in London, but so were large quantities of other materials necessary for the construction of ships. He determined, therefore, to remedy this by establishing two further royal dockyards, both on the Thames.

Even during the reign of Henry VII it had been customary for ships to lay off Erith, with a number of storehouses subsequently hired at

A general view of Deptford dockyard at the end of the seventeenth century

A mid-eighteenth century view of the River Thames anchorage, with Deptford dockyard in the background. Amongst the objects depicted are naval vessels in ordinary (u), a 50-gun ship being rigged (z), dockyard stores (m) and saw houses (q)

Chatham dockyard during the mid-eighteenth century. To the right stands the ropery, with its storehouses, spinning and laying floors. On the four slipways at left are vessels under construction, with additional ships in dry-dock for repairs (*Chatham dockyard*)

Ropeyard workers employed upon the manufacture of cable during the eighteenth century. The equipment in use includes a stake for the support of the rope (V), a top cart (R) and several of the trade tools such as a woolder and a hand winder (X and G) which were both used for winding the rope tighter (*Chatham dockyard*)

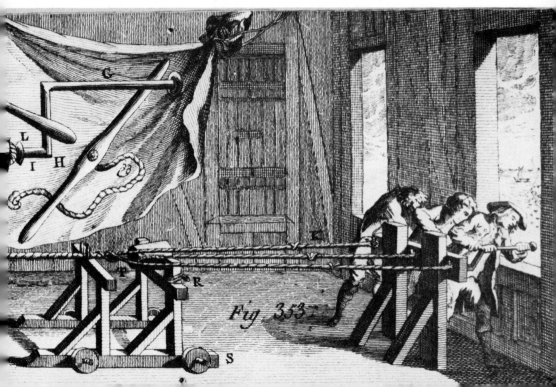

Fig 353.

Sheerness dockyard in 1755. This contemporary engraving shows a 50-gun vessel in ordinary (p), rigging house and sail loft (h), crane (k) and store house (l)

Harwich yard during the eighteenth century. By that date it had ceased to be a royal dockyard, vessels being constructed by private contractors only

Greenwich. Henry VIII, for his part, went somewhat further when, in 1513, preparations began at Woolwich for the construction of a new warship. This was the 1,500-ton *Henry Grâce à Dieu*, destined to be the flagship of Henry's navy. At the time there was no dockyard at Woolwich, or even a tradition of building royal ships. Its advantage lay in the proximity to London where there were skilled shipwrights and numerous merchants able to supply all necessary equipment. Woolwich was not designed as a dockyard from the outset; only the requisite land for constructing new warships was provided. Once work started though, suitable buildings had also to be erected and, before long, Woolwich boasted a permanent collection of storehouses and workshops.

At the time, Woolwich must have been an extremely busy area, for not only was the *Henry Grâce à Dieu* under construction but also a number of galleys. Various kinds of timber, cables, pitch, cork, lanterns, paint and several tons of ballast had all to be transported to Woolwich, whilst the king himself seems to have regularly visited the vessels whilst under construction. For her part, the *Henry Grâce à Dieu* was completed in 1514 and sailed up river to the Tower where her guns were mounted. A large proportion of these weapons were still the small serpentines but she also received two great culverins, one great curtal, a great bombard and several large Spanish and Flemish cannons. Of these various pieces the curtal was a monster gun weighing over 2 tons and firing a 50lb shot over small distances. Culverins, on the other hand, had a longer range as they had a lighter shot of only 18lb. Other features of the *Henry Grâce à Dieu* were her four masts and six decks. As such she was a particularly large vessel and would clearly have impressed the many foreign visitors that Henry VIII took on board. Her bright colours, ornamental woodwork and yellow sails (meant to resemble gold) further added to the display.

Earlier, in 1512, the *Sovereign* had also been brought to Woolwich and taken into dry-dock. This would not have been a permanent dock but a mud embankment. A few months later she was joined by the *Great Barbara*, another of the king's ships, which was taken into a second dry-dock. It is uncertain how long the *Sovereign* remained, or the reason. It is possible that her hull was simply cleaned or, alternatively she may have had gun-ports cut into her sides. Whatever the reason the work was not particularly extensive as she was, once again, back at Woolwich in 1521. Of this second visit a contemporary writer declared:

The *Sovereign*, being of the porterage of eight hundred tons, lyeth in a dock at Woolwich, the same being in such case that she must be new made from the keel upwards.

Perhaps, then, Woolwich had not been planned as a dockyard, but by this date it had clearly become so. Royal ships were not only being built there, but it was also a repair centre with a major anchorage lying close by.

Also during the reign of King Henry VIII there seems to have been some intention of placing a dockyard at Erith, for not only was it an important naval anchorage but it shared with Woolwich the construction of galleys ordered to be built in the year 1512. As such, it can be considered a further royal dockyard, if only for a rather short period. It was never fully developed because the surrounding land was unsuitable and caused essential buildings to subside. As a replacement to Erith, storehouses were built at Deptford, the first being completed in 1513. A basin, or wet-dock, was added a few years later, and was capable of accommodating five vessels. A wet-dock, which usually consisted of an enclosed pond, allowed the fitting out of warships in a much more convenient position since ships could be brought up to a storehouse rather than being anchored in mid-river.

With the rise of the Thames-side yards, Portsmouth lost much of its former importance. The distance of seventy miles from London was proving too great for a nation so heavily dependent upon its rapidly growing capital city. Ships were still sent to Portsmouth, but the proportion was small when compared with previous years. Since Portsmouth was the only yard with a timber-built dry-dock, the *Henry Grâce à Dieu* was brought there in 1523:

... the same day that the King's Ship Royal the *Henry Grâce à Dieu* was had and brought into the dock at Portsmouth of and with gentlemen and yeomen dwelling about the country there which did their diligence and labour there in the helping of the said ship, and also with mariners and other labourers in all to the number by estimation of 1000 persons.' [requoted from W. G. Gates *History of Portsmouth*]

Later, in 1528, the royal accounts note that *Mary Rose, Peter Pomegranate* and a third royal ship, the *John Baptist*, were all careened at the dockyard though, on these occasions, the dry-dock was not used. Instead, mud embankments were thrown up. Possibly the reason was that the dry-dock itself was under repair – it was now some thirty-three years old. In 1536, it is once again recorded in the royal accounts that the *Mary Rose* was again at Portsmouth, this time for a rebuild, when her size was increased from 600 to 700 tons, allowing her to take on more heavy pieces of cannon.

Although perhaps not the sum total of Portsmouth's output in these years, it was nevertheless a long way short of the work being undertaken at both Deptford and Woolwich. But one advantage of Portsmouth which Henry could not ignore was its strategic location: in 1545 the fleet was mustered at Portsmouth in order to defend the country against a projected French invasion aimed at capturing the Isle of Wight. Part of this French plan also involved an attack upon the Spithead anchorage, aiming to tempt Henry's entire fleet into battle. Four French galleasses mounted a surprise raid, the *Henry Grâce à Dieu* being the first English ship into action. There followed a rather protracted battle in which the French were eventually forced to retreat, gaining neither a naval victory nor a foothold on English soil. During the naval engagement, however, one English ship, the *Mary Rose*, was sunk. This was not a result of enemy action but an accident, with water cascading into the lower gun-ports. Only 18in above water, these gun-ports had remained open at a time when the ship was engaged in a complicated turning manoeuvre. Few of the crew survived.

This was to be the last time for a good many years that Portsmouth held a key role in the theatre of naval events. Decline of the dockyard continued in the following decades, accelerated by the establishment of a new anchorage on the River Medway. This occurred around 1547 when a storehouse was first hired for servicing naval vessels anchored in the Medway. Referred to as 'Jillyingham Water', ships tended to anchor close to the small village of Gillingham, with the storehouse being sited in the even tinier village of Chatham. In 1550 it was declared that all royal ships should be 'herborowed' (harboured) in the Medway, with those vessels still at Portsmouth being transferred during August.

With its sheltered deep-water channels, nearness to London and numerous mud banks, the Medway was an ideal anchorage for the Tudor navy. At first only victualling facilities were provided, but in 1570 a mast pond capable of holding seventy-seven masts was dug out, whilst further storehouses, numerous workshops and cranes quickly followed. Despite the growth in facilities, royal ships continued to be careened by the age-old method of drawing ships onto the mud banks. As such, a dry-dock was not to be built at Chatham until 1581, and

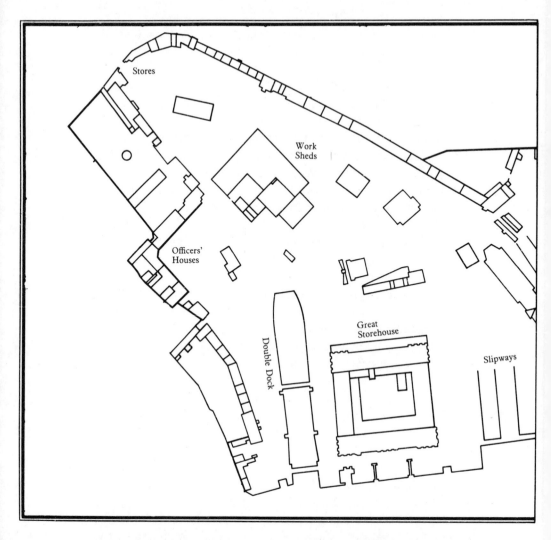

Stores

Work
Sheds

Officers'
Houses

Double Dock

Great
Storehouse

Slipways

then it was only designed to handle galleys rather than the far more numerous sailing ships.

The maintenance of the royal galley fleet was to become a speciality of the new dockyard at Chatham. Galleys, of course, were not particularly common in more northerly waters, but did perform useful work in the towing of dismasted vessels or those trapped by head winds. Few of the royal galleys were built in England – most were captured in battle. Such was the origin of the *Eleanor*, the first of the galleys to use the dry-dock at Chatham. Originally named *Bonavolia*, she was captured from the French during the 1560s, and eventually

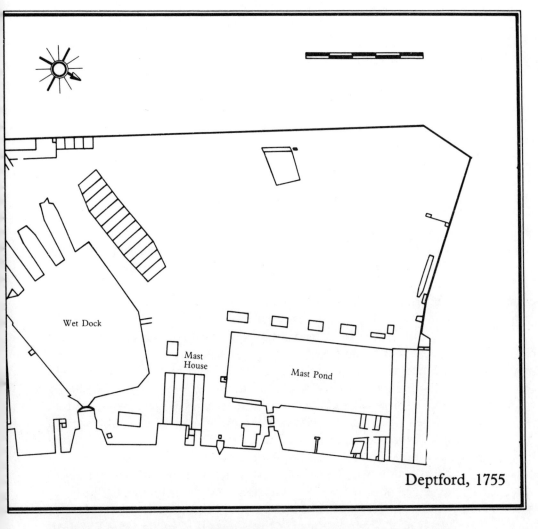

Wet Dock

Mast House

Mast Pond

Deptford, 1755

used for surveying the Thames. As for the dry-dock itself, this was originally built with an earthen entrance. Like the one previously built at Portsmouth it had to be laboriously broken up and then repaired every time a ship moved in or out of the dock. Shortly after, however, flood gates were fitted, showing that some progress was being made in the construction of such docks. The use of Chatham for the anchoring and repair of the royal galley fleet continued into the following century, with work starting in 1605 upon special workshops for the repair of these galleys. Apparently, the royal galleys had suffered much damage from heavy winds in previous years.

Almost from its inception, Chatham became one of the nation's premier dockyards. During the reign of Queen Elizabeth far more money was spent on Chatham than any other yard, a point ably demonstrated by reference to the general accounts. In 1584, a not untypical year, expenditure upon wages and general maintenance were as follows:

	£
Chatham	3,680
Deptford	205
Portsmouth	30
Woolwich	18

Clearly Deptford was Chatham's only rival. Having surpassed Woolwich, Deptford continually undertook construction and repair work on a large portion of royal ships. Amongst the Deptford launchings was that of the *Ark Ralegh*. Later renamed *Ark Royal* she was the first of this illustrious name, serving as Lord Howard's flagship during the Armada campaign. Chatham, on the other hand, launched only the *Sunne*, a small pinnace.

Much effort went into ensuring Deptford's continued efficiency. In 1574 considerable repairs were made to the wet-dock, whilst shortly after it received the advantage of flood gates – previously it had an earthen entrance. In 1588 the dockyard was much expanded when a large expanse of marshland was added. Earlier, on a site close to the dockyard, Francis Drake's famous ship, the *Golden Hind*, was permanently placed on display. Mounted in a special dock, the vessel remained open for public inspection until the reign of Charles II, by which time its timber had become so rotten that it was simply broken up. It should be remembered that Drake was knighted by Elizabeth during a banquet on board the ship at Deptford following his voyage of circumnavigation.

Queen Elizabeth's reign was characterized by long periods of hostility with Spain. The dockyards were at the forefront of this war. Both Chatham and Deptford were extremely well placed for the role of maintaining a royal fleet as any possible invasion threat was bound to centre on the Netherlands where the Spanish had a massive army of occupation. Indeed, the objective of the Armada was not so much direct invasion but rather that of providing a safe passage for troops to reach the shores of Kent. That the project failed was, as much as anything, due to the splendid workmanship of those shipwrights employed at these two dockyards.

It was in the Medway that the main anti-invasion fleet was assembled. Kept in a state of constant readiness, it eventually sailed in April 1588. Proceeding westwards it rendezvoused with a smaller fleet which had been assembled at Plymouth. As yet, no royal dockyard existed at Plymouth but the large natural harbour had long been noted as an ideal site for the assembling of ships.

The defeat of the Spanish Armada came early in the war with Spain, and did not bring an end to the fighting. Indeed, the war was to outlive Queen Elizabeth, placing a great strain upon the dockyards. A number of fleets were assembled for retaliatory strikes, but none met with the brilliant successes to which the Elizabethan seaman had become so accustomed.

During these years both Chatham and Deptford continued to outpace the other yards, with Chatham clearly the superior. In 1590, for instance, it received a particularly grand storehouse, three storeys in height. However, the building was but short lived, being burnt down within three years. Portsmouth and Woolwich, on the other hand, vied for second-place honours. Woolwich, though, clearly had the edge. Since the 1570s it had been equipped with a privately run rope-yard and a timber-built dry-dock. Exactly when the dry-dock was constructed is uncertain, but its completion by the early seventeenth century is confirmed by contemporary observers. Like other docks of the late Elizabethan period, it had the new style flood gates and so did not require the services of numerous labourers to break open the marsh banks. It was this dry-dock which was to bring Woolwich considerable fame during the following century when such vessels as the *Sovereign of the Seas* and the *Prince Royal* were constructed within its walls.

3
The Master Shipwrights

For the royal dockyards, the seventeenth century was the age of the master shipwright. It was a period in which the craft of both designing and building outstanding warships was the province of a few great men. Master shipwrights such as Phineas Pett, Peter Pett and Anthony Deane were the leaders of their profession, responsible for the finest ships of the age. Unlike many of their predecessors, they were armed with scientific knowledge, able to apply the rudiments of geometry and aware of structural principles. Earlier shipwrights had, more often than not, lacked these essentials, being guided by rule of thumb and natural ability.

In England, the master shipwright was something of a new breed. Those great ships of Henry VIII had been designed by Italian shipwrights, some of whom had been brought to Portsmouth and Woolwich for this very purpose. Later, English shipwrights had simply copied Italian workmanship. Some had admittedly gone even further, adding their own designs in an attempt to innovate. Under Queen Elizabeth royal ships had begun to differ substantially from those built in other countries, with a complete rejection of many continental ideas. Some of the ships sent against the Armada were race built, having a much lower freeboard and a greater beam. More manoevrable than Spanish ships, they could carry out sudden attacks whilst quickly escaping danger.

Overall, the royal dockyards were not, at the outset, noted for an ability to produce fine ships. This was, as much as anything, a reflection of their disorganized state. Until well into the sixteenth century the royal yards were without a permanent force of shipwrights. If a new vessel was to be built or a series of extensive repairs undertaken, a requisite number of shipwrights would be quickly engaged. If an emergency existed, such artisans, along with common seamen, would be impressed. For construction of ships such

Launch of the 120-gun *Nelson*, built at Woolwich in 1814. One of the largest vessels ever constructed at that yard, she was later converted to steam (*Greenwich Local History Library*)

Launch of the 70-gun *Boscawen* at Woolwich in April 1844 (*Greenwich Local History Library*)

Accident to the *Perseverance* at Woolwich in February 1855. An iron-built troop-ship, the *Perseverance* toppled over whilst her dry-dock was being pumped out (*Greenwich Local History Library*)

The Clocktower offices at Woolwich depicted shortly before closure (*Greenwich Local History Library*)

as the *Mary Rose* and *Henry Grâce à Dieu*, shipwrights had been brought from as far afield as York, Bodmin, Yarmouth and Hull. Once the given task was complete, the various shipwrights would return to their home ports. Such workmen were not paid a princely sum as wages were deliberately kept to an absolute minimum: during periods of employment shipwrights received between twopence and sixpence a day; sawyers and caulkers twopence to fourpence and labourers twopence to fivepence. In addition the shipwrights were given free board and lodging together with a travel allowance payable when journeying to and from their home port.

The lack of a permanent force of shipwrights employed within the royal dockyards also created further problems for the fleet. Rarely could ships be kept in a full state of repair. Except in times of emergency, such as the years surrounding the Armada campaign, the fleet, moored in the Thames or Medway, was simply allowed to rot. In 1559 for instance, when a full survey was carried out, Queen Elizabeth was informed that of the thirty-two vessels that went to make up the royal fleet, ten were unfit for service.

Henry VIII had not been unaware of this problem. Indeed, he took certain steps which were designed to remedy the situation. He started by appointing some of the more experienced shipwrights to take charge of the dockyards. They were to receive an annual payment in return for which they were to remain permanently available for royal service. The first of these more senior shipwrights was one James Baker, who was appointed on 20 May 1538. At that time he was given a grant of 4d per day (raised to 8d in 1544) as 'wage and fee'. Employed primarily in the Thames-side yards of Deptford and Woolwich, he was responsible for building a good many ships constructed during the later years of King Henry's reign.

As regards the actual title of master shipwright, this was not officially used until 1572. This was when Matthew Baker, son of James Baker, was appointed to the title. Like his father he was given a pension together with an additional wage of one shilling a day. Baker does not appear to have been responsible for any particular dockyard as his duties took him to both Woolwich and Deptford. Probably he worked with a particular group of shipwrights, generally overseeing any work that they carried out. If a new warship was to be constructed, Matthew Baker had to submit designs, visit the royal forests to choose suitable timbers and then supervise all construction work. Later holders of this office, though, were normally appointed to particular dockyards where they were responsible for the day-to-day running. As such, they issued naval stores, organized dockyard security and ensured payment of shipwrights and other artisans.

As the son of James Baker, Matthew would have been taught early in life the craft 'mysteries' which were passed down from father to son. But Matthew Baker was an exceptional craftsman in his own right: it was he, for instance, who laid down the standard methods of measuring a ship's burthen, or tonnage. This was carried out by reference to the number of Bordeaux casks, known as tuns, that a newly built ship could carry in her holds. Amongst those vessels that Baker built was the first *Repulse*, a 700-ton warship launched at Deptford in 1595. Phineas Pett was to serve under Baker for a short time and declared him the 'most famous artist of our time'.

Another of the master shipwrights appointed during the reign of Queen Elizabeth was Peter Pett. For a time he seems to have been responsible for the overall running of Deptford, receiving the coveted title of master shipwright in 1586. The Petts, not surprisingly, had long been engaged in the construction of ships with, it is believed, their own shipyard at Harwich. During the early seventeenth century the Petts were to dominate naval shipbuilding with members of the family holding a variety of senior positions at Woolwich, Deptford and Chatham.

Peter Pett died in 1592 when his eldest son, Phineas, was just beginning to learn the family trade. With this objective in view he took employment as a ship's carpenter on board a privateer. It was upon his return in 1594 that he received instruction from Matthew Baker. In his autobiography Pett was to speak highly of Baker, 'from whose help I must acknowledge I receive my greatest lights'. It is as a result of this autobiography that we know so much of the man. To a certain extent we are even privy to his innermost thoughts, and the recent reprint by the Navy Records Society is well worth acquiring (see Bibliography under Perrin).

In 1599 Phineas Pett became keeper of the plank yard at Chatham and remained in that office for some three years before promotion to assistant master shipwright. In this latter office he was responsible for building a small vessel for the young Prince Henry. Designed on the same lines as the old *Ark Royal*, it was to excite much favourable comment. According to Pett, 'this little ship was in length by the keel 25 foot, and 12 foot in breadth, garnished with painting and carving both within board and without'. Two months in building, it was launched on Tuesday 6 March 1604, 'with a noise of trumpets, drums, and such like ceremonies'.

Having now come to the attention of King James, Pett was soon after appointed a master shipwright at the surprisingly young age of thirty-five. Moving to Woolwich, his first major task was that of supervising the rebuild of the *Victory* and *Ark Royal*. Both were ships that had participated in the Armada campaign and were, by 1606, clearly showing their age. Pett was therefore ordered to completely survey both vessels, remove all outer planking and replace this, together with any rotting parts of the frame. It is also possible that the opportunity was taken to lengthen one or other of the two ships. A rebuild was the most extensive of repairs, with a vessel remaining in dry-dock for a year or more. Once rebuilt, any such vessel was as new; the *Ark Royal*, renamed *Anne Royal*, lasted a further thirty years. Of the *Anne Royal*'s launch in 1608, Pett wrote in his autobiography that 'it was a very blustering day, the wind at south-west, but, thanks to God, with a little difficulty she was launched and brought safely to her moorings'.

Phineas Pett's next task was the construction of the *Prince Royal*. Laid down in the dry-dock at Woolwich in October 1608, she was designed as a prestige ship, and flagship of the navy. Two years in building, she was to meet with a good deal of controversy. Many felt that Pett was the wrong man for the job and, at thirty-eight, was considered too young, having had little experience in building such great ships. Moreover, Pett's design was also criticized. With a beam 10ft longer than any ship previously built, many were uncertain of her sailing qualities, some were critical of the draught and others of its upright hull. Unperturbed, King James allowed building to continue, with a view to the vessel being floated out in September 1610. It was an event which must have caused Phineas Pett considerable embarrassment as she completely failed to move on her original launch day. It is worth considering this event in a little more detail, as Pett, again in his autobiography, gives a good account of just how such large ships were launched at this time:

On Monday morning [September 24], assisted by the help of my brother Simonson and sundry other of my friends, we opened the dock gates and made all things ready against the tide, but the wind blowing very hard at south-west kept out the flood so as it proved a very bad tide . . .
When it grew towards high water and all things ready, and a great close lighter made fast at the ship's stern . . . the Lord Admiral gave me

commandment to heave taught the crabs [small capstans] and screws [bow lines] though I had little hope to launch by reason the wind overblew the tide; yet the ship started and had launched, but that the dock gates pent her in so straight that she stuck fast between them.

Present at this attempted launch was the king, with a great retinue of courtiers. By all accounts he was not particularly amused at Pett's failure, returning to Greenwich 'much grieved'. The young Prince Henry, who was fascinated by ships, chose to remain behind to discuss the problem. He resolved to return that night to witness a second attempt at the launch:

> So soon as the multitude were gone and things quiet, we went presently in hand to make way with the sides of the dock gates, and having great store of scavelmen and other labourers, we made all things ready before any flood came . . .

As good as his word, the prince returned at midnight, just a few hours prior to the next high tide. All was ready, and at 2.00am the ropes were tightened and 'the ship went away without any strain of screws or tackles, till she came clear afloat in the midst of the channel to the great joy and comfort of the Prince's Highness'.

The next part of the ceremony concerned the need to christen the royal ship in a way that would always ensure good luck. There were no bottles of champagne in those days; instead, it was a rather delightful ceremony involving a goblet of wine. The king not being present, Prince Henry was allowed to drink from the goblet before sprinkling any remaining wine on to the deck of the *Prince Royal*. As he did this, he pronounced the name of the vessel, after which there was a fanfare of trumpets. The goblet itself was then thrown over the side of the ship. With the wind howling and waves violently rocking the newly launched ship, it must have been a difficult ceremony to perform. Prince Henry, a sixteen-year-old boy and heir to the throne, probably loved every minute.

Despite the widely felt reservations, the *Prince Royal* did not prove an unsuccessful ship. But her expense was enormous: huge sums were lavished upon decor, with the carvings alone costing £441 0s 4d. Indeed, she was the most decorated ship of her day, sporting a huge coat of arms and a myriad of carvings which were gilt covered on a green background. To the already stated bill for carvings, a further £868 6s 8d was added for painting. As to the vessel herself, she was the navy's first three decker, carried 55 guns and was topped with four masts. A truly huge ship for her day, she was representative of a new age. In the Armada years, the smaller race-built ships had won the battle. Now the emphasis had changed and much larger warships were wanted. The *Prince Royal* was the first of this breed; ranking supreme, she marked a turning point. Hit and run tactics were over; the slogging match was the new order of the day.

Phineas Pett was a very controversial character. There can be little doubt, though, that he was of great intelligence and well deserving of the title of master shipwright. But there was also a dark side. A man of his times, he was not beyond lining his own pocket once the opportunity arose. On a number of occasions he was accused of embezzling government funds, and even reprimanded by the king. That he did not lose his rank or status and was not thrown into the Tower, was due simply to his great professional abilities. The king recognized he was too good a shipwright to be wasted. Whatever his morals, the nation needed him.

In 1608 a special committee was set up to investigate the whole matter of corruption, and considerable attention was given to the dockyards. On that occasion Pett was accused of a great list of misdemeanours and these ranged from the acceptance of bribes to that of misappropriating dockyard timber. Amongst the facts unearthed was that in 1604 he privately built a ship of 160 tons constructed entirely of dockyard timber. Further, her sails and rigging were either 'borrowed out of the store' or purchased at heavily reduced prices. Not content with just building the ship, Pett then appears to have had the audacity to load the ship with guns, ammunition and general stores, all of which belonged to the fleet, and sailed the vessel to Spain where he proceeded to sell the material for a sum of £300. A further charge levelled against Pett concerned the rebuild of the *Anne Royal*. It was stated that the expenses incurred were both 'wasteful and lavish'; apparently Pett charged £800 for a task that should have cost but half.

The evidence against Pett was fairly conclusive. Yet he was never really punished. Instead, he was called before the king and severely reprimanded. It did little good. Within a few years he was again heavily involved in various illicit practices, and before long a second enquiry was instituted. Once more Pett was to find himself subjected to a number of well-substantiated accusations, any one of which would have ended the career of a lesser man. During this second enquiry, conducted in 1618, widespread abuse was found to exist throughout the dockyards, made worse by a high level of inefficiency. Timber stocks were found to be rotting, cordage was invariably bad and extensive quantities of dockyard material were also being sold off for private gain.

Between these two enquiries, Phineas Pett and his fellow shipwrights were given very little work. King James seemed content to run down the navy. In 1607, for instance, the king owned but thirty-seven warships of which a number were said to be 'old and rotten and barely fit for service'. By 1617, the number of royal ships had fallen to twenty-seven. Of these, the Woolwich-built *Prince Royal* was the most outstanding. Chatham had still to build a major warship whilst Deptford was responsible for a rebuild of the *Red Lion*.

But changes were on the way: it was during the reign of King James that a massive plan was instituted for a completely new dockyard to be built at Chatham. Surprisingly, the man in charge of the project was Phineas Pett. As master shipwright at Chatham it was one of his responsibilities, but in view of the disregard he showed for the safety of taxpayers' money, it must have provided him with a great many opportunities to increase his own wealth. Work on the new dockyard started in 1619 and was to continue until 1626. The old yard was now considered inadequate and was to be completely replaced by a new yard slightly further up river. An area of eighty acres was acquired upon which a great number of new buildings, docks and slipways were eventually to be built.

Perhaps the most important feature of the new yard was the addition of a dry-dock. Of this Pett comments in his autobiography:

> The whole year of '18, '19 and part of '20, I attended altogether at Chatham, being employed upon the making of the new dry dock and other businesses under the command of the Commissioners.

When complete, the dock was of sufficient size to accommodate the largest warships of the day for any kind of work that needed to be undertaken. Following its completion a mast dock was added to the area (1619), a sail loft (1620), a rope-house (1621), officers' residences (1622), a second dry-dock (1623) and a graving dock (1624). All this brought a totally new character to the dockyard at Chatham. Previously it had been mainly engaged in the repair and improvement of vessels with only an occasional ship being built there. From the 1630s onwards all this was to change. Increasingly, Chatham became a centre for the construction of many of the largest vessels needed by the

Royal Navy. Of ships to be built at Chatham, perhaps the *Prince* (1670), *Victory* (1765) and *Warrior* (1860) are the most notable but over the years Chatham was to record some 550 launchings – a number which is perhaps only equalled by Portsmouth.

Whilst expansion was in hand at Chatham, little progress was being made at Portsmouth. In 1623 the original dry-dock (the one built during the reign of Henry VII) was filled in, whilst the harbour was considered inappropriate for shipping due to a suspicion that the waters were a breeding ground for the 'worm'. The worm was *Teredo navalis*, a small creature whose ability to severely weaken the structure of any ship has already been mentioned. Unable at the time to combat this menace, the Navy Board carefully avoided any harbours thought to be the home of such creatures. In 1630 Phineas Pett was sent to Portsmouth to investigate the situation, being able to conclude that such rumours were false and 'raised to hinder the keeping of any his Majesty's ships in that harbour'. This last comment was well founded. A number of senior dockyard officials had commercial interests in the continued expansion of Chatham and did not wish to see the growth of an alternative dockyard.

A few years later Pett was given a second opportunity to build a great warship. The request came from Charles I who was determined to make his mark on the maritime world. Approaching Pett during a visit to the royal dockyard at Woolwich, he found the master ship-wright employed in the construction of the *Leopard*, a 34-gun vessel which was to be launched in 1635. The king, 'calling me aside, privately acquainted me with his princely resolution for the building of a great new ship, which he would have me to undertake'. It was on 26 June 1634 that the king made his request, and by October a model of the proposed ship had been submitted for royal approval. To be of 1,500 tons and named *Sovereign of the Seas*, the new vessel was to be the largest of its day. Already Pett had been out into the royal forests to choose suitable timbers. Although these started to arrive early in the new year, they were left to season so work on the new ship was not to begin until 1636.

Woolwich must have been a fascinating place at the time. In January 1636 the keel of the *Sovereign* was laid. Attended by the king and numerous royal courtiers this particular event was turned into a joyous occasion. With the first keel timbers laid, others were added and scarph jointed. Once the necessary length was attained – in the case of the *Sovereign*, this was 126ft – work on the rest of the frame

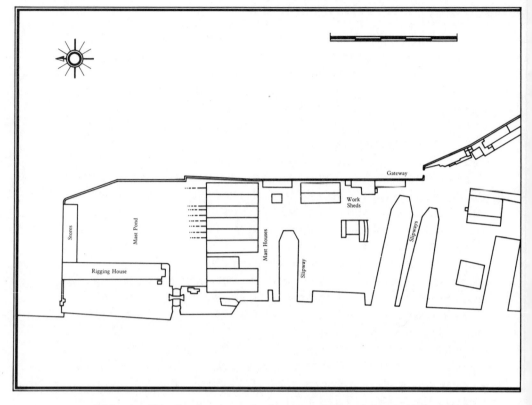

Stores

Mast Pond

Rigging House

Mast Houses

Work Sheds

Slipway

Gateway

Slipways

could begin. The keel was made from specially selected timbers large enough to provide a thickness of 2ft 6in and as great a length as possible. To the keel would be added the stern post and other large timbers which would hold the frame together. A particularly important timber was the keelson, laid over the floor timbers and giving additional strength to the keel. In the case of the *Sovereign of the Seas*, this last timber was said to be of so great a size that twenty-eight oxen and four horses were needed to carry it to the water's edge. Slowly the ship began to gain height; deck beams were added and these, according to one contemporary account, were made from such massive oaks that one tree was able to provide four of the principal beams.

Phineas Pett was present throughout construction, charting the position of every timber, supervising the erection of the frame and ensuring that measurements were correct. It was his task to see that all timbers, planks and other materials were properly seasoned. Sometimes he was joined by the king, and he would show the royal

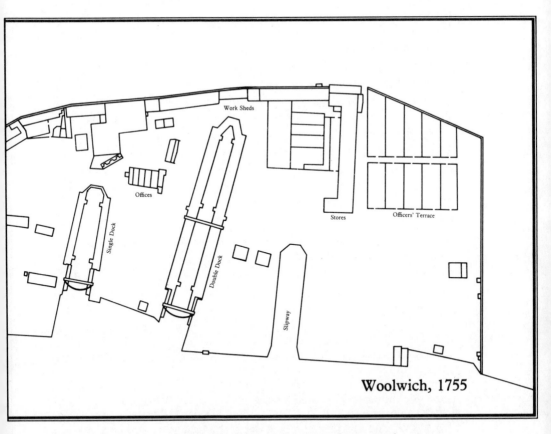

Work Sheds

Offices

Single Dock

Double Dock

Stores

Officers' Terrace

Slipway

Woolwich, 1755

party around the dockyard, demonstrating just how much progress was being made. In 1637 the vessel was ready for launching, an event duly recorded in the autobiography:

> Monday, the 25th of September, was the day peremptorily appointed by his Majesty for launching the great ship; and accordingly all things were prepared in readiness for performing thereof. His Majesty, accompanied with the Queen and all the train of lords and ladies, their attendants, came to Woolwich, for the most part by water, landing at the dock stairs about 12 of the clock . . .

The royal party, though, was to be disappointed. As with the *Prince Royal* some twenty-seven years before, the vessel failed to enter the water due to the poor tide.

A new launching date was set, being timed to coincide with the next spring tide. However, a few nights later, severe westerly winds promised a particularly good tide so Pett resolved upon another midnight launch. With a fast in-coming tide, the ship was actually afloat on a three-quarters flood. This done, a message was dispatched to Greenwich Palace requesting Sir Robert Mansell, the King's Lieutenant, to carry out the naming ceremony. Once launched, the *Sovereign of the Seas* was rigged and then removed from Woolwich to Erith 'by reason there was a greater depth of water to ride in'.

The *Sovereign of the Seas* was considered the greatest ship of her age. That she was launched in 1637 was considered a particularly happy omen, for her computed tonnage was also said to be 1,637. The construction and fitting out of the *Sovereign* swallowed up a massive £65,586. Much of this resulted from ornamentation which characterized every inch of the upper hull. From stem to stern she was covered in carvings of which a massive figurehead depicting King Edgar riding down seven enemy kings was but one small part of the overall decoration. In an account of the ship, published to commemorate her launch, one writer attempted to detail some of these adornments. Even he, though, recognized that the task was beyond him:

> It would be too tedious to insist upon every ornament belonging to this incomparable vessell, yet thus much concerning her Outward appearance; She hath two Galleries of a side, and all most curious carved Worke, and all the sides of the shipp are carved also with Tropies of Artyllerie and Types of honour, as well belonging to Land as Sea, with Symboles, Emblemes, and Impresses apertaining to the Art of Navigation; and thus much in a succinct way.

As a ship, the *Sovereign of the Seas* was to remain afloat until 1696. In her earlier years she saw little or no close action; such a costly ship would have been a liability in battle. For this reason it was not until 1692 that she participated in a major engagement. Only a few years later, though, she was destroyed whilst lying peacefully at her Medway mooring. A cook, having carelessly left a lighted candle in his cabin, was responsible for creating an all-engulfing fire.

Phineas Pett, for his part, also ended his days at Chatham. In 1630 he had been appointed resident commissioner, being the first man to hold this newly created office. As such, he became totally responsible for the running of the dockyard and automatically acquired a position on the all-important Navy Board – the body responsible for dockyards. During his tenure, which lasted until 1647, Pett still got up to some of his old tricks, not the least of which was an illicit sale involving large quantities of naval stores.

In April 1647, Phineas Pett was succeeded in office by his son Peter. Born in 1610, Peter Pett served his apprenticeship at Woolwich where he became a master shipwright. He followed in his father's footsteps for, apart from being a brilliant shipwright, he was not beyond defrauding the government of anything going. As early as 1651, only four years after accepting the new post, numerous accusations were being made about his involvement in 'grand abuses'. Peter Pett, though, was to have an ignominious end. Commissioner of Chatham at the time of the Dutch raid in 1667, he was blamed for the nation's defeat. His neglectfulness, it was said, led to the Medway being unprepared during that fateful year of 1667. Further, Pett was accused of being more concerned about his own property than that belonging to the dockyard. Men who should have been involved in strengthening the yard's defences were engaged in carrying his personal goods to safety. For all this Peter Pett was dismissed from office.

Peter Pett does not appear to have been a popular man and as such was an easy scapegoat for the events of 1667; his dismissal undoubtedly saved a good many other officials from impeachment. Samuel Pepys, in his capacity of secretary to the Navy Board, certainly distrusted the man. In his diary he noted how Peter Pett had removed £300 from one naval charity – the Chatham Chest – merely for supervising the accounts for one year. When it came to the business of the Dutch raid, however, Pepys did recognize that Pett was not solely to blame. Yet afraid for his own position, he joined with many others in publicly criticising the Chatham dockyard commissioner. Evidence from Pepys and others directly resulted in Peter Pett losing office.

Until the period of Peter Pett's demise, the Pett family clearly dominated the three main royal dockyards. Apart from providing resident commissioners for Chatham, other members of the family held key posts at Woolwich and Deptford. At Chatham during the Commonwealth period and the years immediately following, the Petts held three other senior posts. A second Phineas held office as clerk of the cheque, a Joseph Pett was assistant master shipwright and Richard Holbourne, a nephew to the older Phineas, was a master mast-maker. At Woolwich during these years, Christopher Pett was master shipwright whilst a further Peter Pett held this same post at Deptford, being succeeded in 1652 by a third Phineas Pett. This last named was to go some way to reviving family fortunes as, in 1686, he was appointed commissioner of Chatham dockyard.

Over the years, of course, many people became suspicious of the dominance enjoyed by the Pett family within the dockyards. Despite this they remained, until the Dutch raid, an immovable force. Whether king or parliament controlled the dockyards, the Petts survived. Politically the family favoured parliament, with Phineas Pett handing over Chatham dockyard to the parliamentary forces in 1642. Despite this, the family suffered no loss of status during the Restoration, but opposition began to grow. Other shipwrights were encouraged in the hope that the Pett monopoly might be broken. One such shipwright was Anthony Deane who had served an apprentice-ship at Woolwich, being trained by Christopher Pett. Deane was later to be appointed master shipwright at the new Harwich dockyard where he was responsible for a number of fine ships. Considerable ability ensured Deane's rapid promotion: from Harwich he moved to Portsmouth, where he eventually became resident commissioner. Whilst more will be said of Deane later, it should be pointed out that he is most remembered for his *Doctrine of Naval Architecture* which gives a step-by-step outline for the construction of a third-rate sailing ship.

For the dockyards, the Commonwealth was a period of unrestrained progress. War had broken out with the Dutch, and huge sums of money were lavished upon the creation of an efficient fighting fleet. Year after year new ships came off the slipways, with 207 vessels being added during the period 1649–59. A large proportion were captured from the Dutch, though the dockyards of Woolwich, Deptford and Chatham were responsible for thirty-five new launchings. More important, however, was Cromwell's use of Portsmouth: a further nine vessels were built at this yard, with money also being used to construct a new dry-dock, ropery and tar house. It was in the year 1649 that Portsmouth first received a resident commissioner. This was William Willoughby, a roundhead colonel, who died in office. Later his brother Francis succeeded him. Regarding the dry-dock, work upon its construction commenced in 1656, and it was of the type known as a double dock – one able to hold two vessels at the same time. In the case of Portsmouth it could hold two third rates. Such docks were occasionally built as it was a cheap method of accommodating two vessels; on the other hand if work was held up on one vessel, it delayed the departure of the other. Built of timber, Portsmouth's new dock was completed in 1658. Earlier, in 1651, a building slip had been laid down, although the dockyard at Portsmouth had completed its first new vessel one year earlier. This was the *Portsmouth*, a relatively small vessel of 422 tons. The ropery at Portsmouth was added in 1654 when an acre of ground was incorporated with the original area of the dockyard for the purpose.

For Portsmouth the Commonwealth years represented a real change of fortune. After years of continual neglect, the government had been re-awakened to the overwhelming advantages of having a major dockyard along the south coast. For the first few decades though, Portsmouth's growth was slow; the war with the Dutch saw to this. According to the already quoted Monson:

> If Holland or the Eastland become our enemies, then doth Chatham lie most with our advantage to annoy them, if they attempt any part of our North coast, or Norfolk, Suffolk, Essex and Kent, which are places of most peril considering their nearness to the city of London.[1]

For this reason, Portsmouth was not to equal Chatham's importance until the very end of that century. By that time the Dutch could no longer be considered the nation's major enemy, as the aggressive foreign policy of Louis XIV and the formation of the League of Augsburg focused concern upon the French. From that time onwards Portsmouth became the country's premier dockyard, engaged mainly in the repair and refitting of cruisers (see Glossary), although building work was also of considerable importance.

4
Dens of Theft
and Corruption

A truly momentous year, 1660 heralded the nation's return to monarchy. An uncrowned Charles II was ceremoniously brought back from Holland, the two day sea passage being undertaken in the *Royal Charles*. This was a splendid three-decker, which had started life out as the *Naseby*, an 80-gun man-of-war built some five years earlier by Peter Pett at the Woolwich dockyard. Somewhat inappropriately named, she was hurriedly re-christened by the king himself. The figurehead, which depicted a triumphant Oliver Cromwell, was left unaltered at this time. One of the nation's largest ships, she was to bring small credit to the new reign, being captured by the Dutch during their raid on the Medway.

Also on board the *Royal Charles*, and recording every event for posterity, was the diarist Samuel Pepys. A young man of twenty-seven, he was also on the verge of a new career. As secretary to Edward Montagu, the admiral in charge of the king's return, undreamt of opportunities lay ahead. All, of course, was to be recorded in the diaries, which were begun in January of that year and continued unbroken for almost nine years. Using a cryptic shorthand style, the invaluable pages of the diary unfolded a personal view, frequently based on direct experience, of some of the most dramatic events ever to occur in British history. Further, as a member of the Navy Board, many diary entries refer to the dockyards themselves, presenting an unrivalled source for examining progress at this time.

The Navy Board was the body responsible for the running of the dockyards. Originally established under Henry VIII, it was responsible for both the repair and building of all naval warships. It ensured sufficient quantities of cordage, sails and masts, employed the dockyard workers whilst supervising and maintaining all the royal dockyards. At the time Pepys was writing, the board was made up of four principal officers, namely the treasurer, surveyor, comptroller and clerk of the acts. In an attempt to reduce corruption, each was responsible for regulating the duties of the other, although specific tasks also existed. The treasurer, of course, was responsible for finances and, together with the comptroller, witnessed all payments. The surveyor was in charge of stores, with the task of ensuring that the dockyards always had an adequate supply of materials. The final office, that of clerk, was the position held by Samuel Pepys. A senior post, it conveyed responsibility for keeping all records and arranging contracts. In fact, he was really secretary to the board, regularly visiting the dockyards and reporting upon their efficiency. As such he was to extend the nature of his job, showing concern for the quality of supplies whilst unearthing a number of frauds which were practised by both merchants and dockyard officials.

Of the dockyards themselves, these can be grouped into two administrative categories: Deptford and Woolwich, those closest to London, were administered direct from the Navy Board offices in Seething Lane. Each had a master shipwright, but any policy matters, together with day-to-day decisions, was the province of the Navy Office. Because of this, Deptford and Woolwich were regularly visited by the board's four principal officers, while Pepys visited both yards at least once a week. He often made a point of arriving early in the morning, and frequently found those in charge of the dockyards still asleep in their homes.

Portsmouth, Harwich and Chatham, on the other hand, were too far from London for such regular visits so a resident commissioner was appointed at each. In regular correspondence with the London office, they were able to take day-to-day decisions and had a certain autonomy regarding the purchase of materials. These more distant yards, though, were still subject to regular inspections, of which Pepys records a great number. Such visits usually lasted two or three days, the dockyard being thoroughly inspected together with any ships under repair, construction or lying at anchor in the river. One such visit to Chatham, carried out in the summer of 1662, not only reveals Pepys' enthusiasm, but also the dismal inefficiency that existed within the dockyards:

> Up by 4 a-clock in the morning and walked to the Docke, where Commissioner Pett and I took barge and went to the Guardshipps and mustered them, finding them but basly manned. Thence to the Souveraigne, which we find keeped in good order and very clean, which pleased us well; but few of the officers on board. Thence to the Charles, and

were troubled to see her kept so neglectedly by the boatswain Clements, who I always took for a good officer. It is a very brave ship . . . So to the yard and there mustered the whole ordinary, where great disorder by multitude of servants and old decrepit men, which must be remedied: so to all the store houses and viewed the stores of all sort and the hempe; where we find Captain Cockes very bad, and some others.

Apart from the Navy Board, a second administrative body also existed; this was the Admiralty, the governing unit of the navy. In essence the Admiralty was as old as the navy itself, with a group of principal officers being recognized during the reign of Henry VIII. At that time, however, naval policy had really been in the hands of a Lord High Admiral but eventually the Admiralty was to become a properly constituted board, similar to that of the Navy Office. Indeed, during the reign of Charles I such a committee actually existed, to be maintained in a different form by Oliver Cromwell. The Restoration, however, saw the reintroduction of a Lord High Admiral, the office being held by the king's brother, James, Duke of York. Although the Duke of York took considerable interest in naval developments and tried to improve maritime efficiency, his successes were limited due to severe financial constraints.

The link between the Admiralty and the Navy Board is an interesting one. Both worked hand-in-hand with the Admiralty always being recognized as the senior partner. If more ships were needed, or a particular vessel had to be repaired, the Admiralty simply requested the Navy Board to undertake the work. Whilst the Admiralty, in future years, would be in a position to criticize the Navy Board, and sometimes demand, it could never instruct. A ship in the hands of the dockyard was Navy Board property, but once at sea it belonged to the Admiralty.

With a navy that was comparatively small and dockyards of a still limited nature, such an administrative framework should have worked fairly smoothly. That it did not was primarily due to the poor state of naval finances after huge sums had been spent upon the dockyards. When Charles II inherited a £1 million naval debt, savings had to be made. Large numbers were dismissed from within the dockyards, whilst a decline was also witnessed in both the quality of supplies, and the number of times a vessel might be docked for essential repair work. Indeed, one of the tasks given to Pepys was that of overseeing the sale of naval stores in order to pay back certain debts. The method used for these sales is of interest, involving an auction

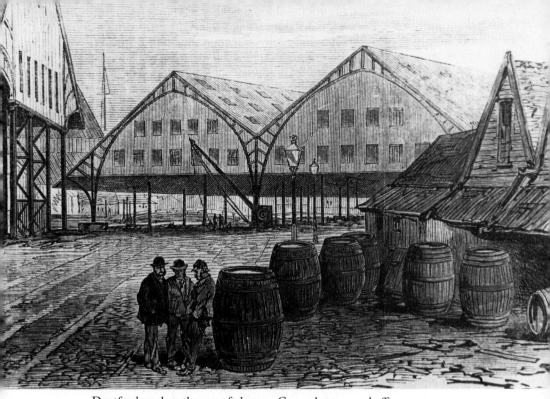

Deptford yard on the eve of closure. General stores and offices

The main dockyard clock at Woolwich. Having survived the yard's closure, it is one of the oldest buildings in the area

JAMES AITKEN.

Alias, John *the* Painter.

James Aitken, an American sympathiser who attempted to destroy Portsmouth
dockyard ropery in 1776

which was conducted with an inch candle. Bidding could only be made while the candle was alight, with auctioned material being sold to the individual who made the final bid prior to the candle burning itself out. During the early years of the Restoration such sales were conducted at Woolwich, Deptford, Portsmouth and Chatham. Of one such auction, conducted at Deptford in February 1661, Pepys commented, '. . . and good sport it was to see how, from a small matter bid at first, they would come to double and treble the price of things.'

It was because of these huge debts that the dockyards undertook only a limited amount of new construction work in these years. Of the vessels built before 1665, only two were larger than yachts, these being second rates laid down in 1661: the *Royal Katherine*, built by Christopher Pett at Woolwich, and the *Royal Oak* which was built at Portsmouth. Pepys, Charles II and the Lord High Admiral were present at the launching of the *Katherine*. As secretary to the Navy Board, Pepys was given responsibility for supplying a silver flagon to be given to Christopher Pett as a commemoration of the launch. Part of the traditional launching ceremony, the size of the flagon varied according to the vessel being launched. On this occasion the silver flagon weighed 66oz and was valued at twenty pieces (about £5 at seventeenth-century prices). Noting the events in his diary Pepys declared:

At Woolwich, I there up to the King and the Duke and they like the plate well. Here I stayed above with them while the ship was launched; which was done with great success, and the King did very much like the ship, saying that she had the best bow that ever he saw.

It was during these years that a number of the older ships were dry-docked to receive extensive repairs, mostly at Chatham. In 1660, for instance, the *Royal Sovereign* (formerly *Sovereign of the Seas*) was brought into that yard for an important refit followed, shortly after, by the *Prince* which was to remain at Chatham for three years, receiving a partial rebuild. Lengthened by 17ft she was eventually to mount 92 guns instead of the 64 that she had been given when launched at Woolwich in 1610. Following the *Prince* into dry-dock came the *Royal Charles*, with the latter re-entering the Medway in October 1664. Not that the repair work on these large three-deckers totally monopolized the dockyards at this time. A number of the lesser rates had also to be dry-docked, whilst ships in-ordinary continued to be maintained. Moreover, in 1661 Woolwich and Deptford yards were busily engaged in preparing a fleet for service in the Mediterranean.

The dockyards at Woolwich and Deptford were able to develop new skills through the construction of several yachts during the first years of the new reign. Built for the personal use of the royal family, they were small but luxurious craft having a shallow draught and rigged with a sprit mainsail. It was during the king's enforced exile in Holland that he gained a passion for such craft, engaging himself in the popular Dutch sport of yacht racing. With the subsequent restoration of the English monarchy, the Dutch government presented him with the *Mary*, a small yacht whose draught was to be copied by Peter Pett. The result of the Dutch influence was the *Katherine*, the first English-built yacht and launched at Deptford in 1661. Rated for 6 guns, she was a nimble little craft and was generally believed to be better than Charles II's Dutch yacht. Not to be outdone, the Lord High Admiral also ordered the building of a yacht. This was the *Anne*, built by Christopher Pett and launched at Woolwich in the same year. In 1662, Woolwich yard built the *Charles*, a further yacht for the use of the king.

It was the lack of finance which also led to the cancellation of numerous schemes designed to improve the efficiency of the yards: at Chatham a projected wet-dock never materialized. At this time only one yard, Deptford, had such facilities to allow ships to be fitted out whatever the state of the tide. It was Peter Pett who proposed the dock, to be sited in St Mary's Creek, a tideway just to the north of Chatham dockyard. The scheme was examined by a number of individuals, including Pepys, but the estimated cost of some £10,000 was considered prohibitive. However, the project was also rejected on more practical grounds as the diary entry for 2 August 1663 indicates:

> Thence to the Docke and by water to view St. Mary Creeke, but do not find it so proper for a wett docke, as we would it, it being uneven ground and hard in the bottom, and no great depth of water in many places.

Pett's concern to increase this type of facility probably stemmed from the recent growth of Portsmouth dockyard; frequently used for the repair and building of ships, it was rapidly becoming Chatham's major rival and Pett saw the need to re-establish the claims of Chatham. If built, the wet-dock would have held twenty-four second rates, and would have removed the need to handle such ships whilst moored in the Medway Estuary. It was, in fact, St Mary's Creek that was chosen during the nineteenth century as the site for three basins (or wet-docks) that are so much a character of the present-day Chatham dock-yard (see Chapter 11).

For Deptford a scheme was also proposed for a much larger wet-dock than the one that already existed there. As designed it would have been sited on land close to the yard and would have been sealed by a great lock. On 16 January 1661, the Duke of York visited the site but seems to have found the land unsuitable. Pepys, for his part, distrusted the very idea of wet-docks, believing that they encouraged the close mooring of ships. In the event of a fire – a rather frequent occurrence within the dockyards – large numbers of ships would be endangered which more than offset the advantage of keeping ships permanently afloat. In January 1663, for example, Pepys had cause to note the large number of ships kept in the wet-dock at Deptford. By this he probably meant eight or nine vessels as this was the approximate capacity.

Another concern of the Navy Board's young secretary was the immense amount of fraud associated with the dockyards. Indeed, they had become notorious for all types of theft and corruption. At every level attempts were constantly being made to swindle the taxpayer. Even members of the Navy Board were not beyond temptation, as Pepys was soon to discover. For his part Pepys was usually considered a fairly honest man; he held an important office and one which could easily have been abused. For instance, hopeful merchants frequently proffered small presents and, although accepted, they were never taken as bribes. As clerk of the acts, Pepys would simply choose the best contract, and should the fortunate contractor reward him, then so much the better. Confiding to his diary on this point Pepys declared, 'Good God to see what a man might were I a knave.'

One particularly profitable contract was that for supplying Baltic timber. The traditional supplier was the appropriately named William Wood, whose timber was always sold at a greatly inflated price. Both William Batten, surveyor of the Navy Board, and Christopher Pett supported the merits of this particular contract as they appeared to receive a small slice of the profits. Pepys, however, did not approve of the situation and enlisted the aid of Anthony Deane, at that time assistant master shipwright under Christopher Pett. Deane proceeded to teach Samuel Pepys a great deal about timber and presented him with a slide rule for measuring quantities. On one occasion Deane even accompanied Pepys to Waltham Forest to make a more careful study of timber supplies. After lengthy research, Pepys felt confident enough to challenge this particular contract. On doing so he was immediately visited by Christopher Pett who tried to persuade Pepys against the rival contract of Sir William Warren:

> There we fell to talk of Warrens other goods, which Pett had said were generally·bad; and falling to this contract again, I did say it was the most cautious and as good contract as has been made here.

Choosing to ignore any advice given to him by Christopher Pett, Pepys subsequently cancelled William Wood's contract, awarding it instead to Warren. In doing so Pepys received a customary gift which, on this occasion, amounted to £50.

It was not only in the matter of timber supplies that Pepys was prepared to go to such great length in checking that the dockyards received value for money. He was constantly occupied in observing the prices of hemp, tar, sail cloth and other materials. It was as a result of this constant vigilance that Sir Richard Ford, supplier of yarn, lost his contract. During a visit to Woolwich, yarn supplied by Sir Richard was examined:

> We found it very bad, and broke sooner then, upon a fair triall, five threads of that against Riga yarn; and also that some of it hath old Stuffe that has been tarred, covered over with new hempe, which is such a cheat as hath not been heard of.

At Deptford in 1663, Pepys uncovered a further example of corruption. Here a senior officer was found to be in league with the flag-makers Young and Whistler; flags of extremely poor quality were constantly being accepted and the officer received a bonus. Pepys immediately introduced a change of supplier which made a saving in the cost of flag material.

Over the years Pepys came to distrust two individuals in particular: Sir William Batten and Peter Pett. Of the two, Batten was the more powerful, being surveyor of the navy and befriended by those in high places. Using his position of trust, Batten was found to be removing large sums of money from the Chatham Chest, a naval charity to which he was treasurer. He allowed himself lavish expenses and created lucrative posts for his many friends, amongst whom was Peter Pett, himself a commissioner at Chatham and partly responsible for the chest; he was found to be equally guilty of awarding himself lavish expenses. In April 1664 Pepys examined the chest accounts and concluded that they show 'what a knave Commissioner Pett hath been all along, and how Sir W. Batten hath gone on in getting good allowances to himself and others out of the poor's money'. By that time a commission had been set up to enquire into the chest accounts and Pepys, as the most active member, was leading the investigation. The eventual outcome, however, was disappointing, with neither Pett nor Batten being punished in any way.

In other areas, too, Pepys found the commissioner of Chatham dockyard wanting. During a visit there in July 1663, Pepys felt forced to remark:

> . . . being myself much dissatisfied, and more than I thought I should have been, with Commissioner Pett, being by what I saw since I came hither, convinced that he is not able to exercise that command in the yard over the officers that he ought to do.

During that year a further visit to Chatham was made and, again, Pepys was most dissatisfied with the prevailing level of discipline. A conversation took place with Commissioner Pett in which he was asked to make a greater effort in correcting the faults of his officers. On this occasion Pepys was accompanied by Sir William Coventry, a commissioner to the Navy Board:

> But being gone thence, Mr Coventry and I did discourse about him [Pett] and conclude that he is not able to do the good in the yard that he might and can and may well do in another – what with his old faults and the relations that he doth to most people that act there.

On 2 August 1663, a further comment concerning Pett appears in the diary, that Pepys was 'troubled to see how backward Commissioner Pett is to tell any faults of the officers and to see nothing in better condition here for his being here than they are in other yards where there is none'. This last reference was a comparison of Chatham yard with those of Woolwich and Deptford.

It was not simply the senior officers, however, who were responsible for defrauding the dockyards; the work-force was constantly engaged in the theft of stores. In their case, though, things seem a little more excusable. Labourers and artisans were rarely paid on time, and consequently always short of money. Even when they were paid, it was usually in the form of tickets which could only be cashed in London. To survive, therefore, naval stores were continually being smuggled out of the yards and into the hands of local receivers. Not that this was a difficult task: few of the dockyards had an adequate boundary wall, whilst no properly constituted security force existed. Indeed, naval stores were not even marked until November 1661 when a royal proclamation was issued stating that, whenever feasible, a broad arrow should be placed on all naval property.

The perquisite of 'chips' was, perhaps, the item which created most problems for the Navy Board. These were the small pieces of timber, sometimes referred to as 'offal' wood, which having been reduced to a length of less than 36in, were useless for dockyard purposes and accordingly yard workers were permitted to remove them. Many workers, however, went somewhat further: either they used the bundles of chips to conceal more expensive items or spent much of the day sawing up good timber for later removal. In May 1662 an order was issued declaring that chips could only be removed once a week, but it was totally ignored.

Another dockyard abuse, and one more likely to be practised by skilled artisans, was that of using dockyard timber and dockyard time to manufacture small trinkets which were later sold. One of the Woolwich shipwrights, for instance, was in the habit of turning the hard lignum vitae timber, more properly used for the manufacture of pulley blocks, into small cups. These were apparently much sought after, the same shipwright actually presenting Samuel Pepys with a sample of his work!

In March 1665 war was again declared. During the Second Anglo-Dutch War the dockyards were to be at the forefront of the fighting as never before. Ill-prepared, badly financed and poorly organised the yards were totally unable to muster an adequate fighting fleet; too many warships needed repair in far too short a time. To help overcome some of these difficulties Harwich dockyard was re-opened, whilst a survey was conducted to find a suitable site for a further dockyard. It was in the first year of Charles II's reign that Harwich yard had been closed as part of the navy's economy measures. Taken over by a private contractor, the yard was actually repossessed in 1664 when Anthony Deane was appointed master shipwright and Captain John Taylor commissioner. Unlike many contemporary figures, both these men were free of scandal, Pepys having been responsible for Deane's appointment. Taylor was also a man of considerable experience, having built a number of second rates at both Woolwich and Chatham yards. During the period of hostilities, Harwich was to prove of some importance, acting as an assembly point for the fleet. Deane, for his part, was soon employed upon the construction of warships, with the *Rupert*, a third rate of 66 guns being launched in 1666. This was the first major vessel built at Harwich and was quickly followed by a number of smaller warships. By 1667, Harwich had been responsible for the launching of two third rates and three sixth rates, making a total of 2,050 tons.

It was Sheerness which was eventually chosen as the site for a new royal dockyard. Close to Chatham, it was intended to act as a forward base, refitting ships that would normally navigate an eight-mile stretch of the River Medway. In August 1665, Pepys accompanied both the Duke of York and King Charles to Sheerness 'where we walked up and down, laying out the ground to be taken in for a yard to lay provision for cleaning and repairing of ships, and a most proper place it is for this purpose'. Planned to help gain victory against the Dutch, the dockyard was nowhere near complete when Admiral van Ghent mounted his devastating attack upon the Medway anchorage in 1667. A fort at Sheerness, still under construction and designed to protect the new dockyard, was totally dismantled prior to the Dutch fleet sailing further into the Medway.

The Dutch raid on the Medway was a serious defeat for the Royal Navy. During the course of the four-day battle, the Dutch captured the *Unity*, a 32-gun warship, and the *Royal Charles*, flagship of 1660. In addition they burnt a further six vessels that were either at anchor in the Medway or being used for the defence of that river. Amongst the ships so destroyed was the *Royal James*, a first rate of 1658 which had been built by Christopher Pett at Woolwich. Also destroyed were the recently built *Royal Oak* and *Loyal London*. The latter, financed by the City of London, had only been launched in June of the previous year, being designed by John Taylor and constructed at Woolwich.

It is likely that the Dutch could well have gone much further in their raid upon the Medway. They came within a very short distance of Chatham dockyard, and might well have destroyed the various docks and timber warehouses. Certainly, if they had chosen to start a fire there was enough combustible material to keep it blazing for several days. That they failed to undertake this course of action was mostly due to the accuracy of those gunners employed at Upnor Castle. This particular structure, which lies almost opposite Chatham dockyard, was built during the reign of Queen Elizabeth to defend the Medway anchorage.

The nation was incensed by the raid; no one could understand how an enemy fleet, suffering only minimal loss, could wreak such damage.

A scapegoat was sought and soon found in Peter Pett, the commissioner at Chatham. He was blamed for every conceivable error and quickly thrown into the Tower of London. In October 1667 he was brought before a committee of the House of Commons to answer various charges. These ranged from negligence to that of refusing to obey orders. Of all the charges the most serious related to the loss of the *Royal Charles*. Apparently he had been given orders to move this ship to a safer anchorage, but had failed to do so. At this enquiry, according to one of Pepys' diary entries:

> Commissioner Pett of all men living did make the weakest defence of himself: nothing to the purpose, not to satisfaction, not certain; but sometimes one thing, and sometimes another, sometimes for himself, and sometimes against him . . .

Orders were, in fact, given to impeach Pett on these various charges, but as Pett would undoubtedly improve his defence and doubtless implicate a good many others, his impeachment was carefully forgotten. His dismissal from office in February 1668 was the only punishment meted out to him. Retiring to the country, he died a broken man in 1672.

The prime reason for the Medway catastrophe was not Pett's incompetence but the severe financial constraints placed upon the navy and its dockyards. In that year of 1667 the fleet had not even put to sea. With no major warships ready to oppose the Dutch, it was small wonder that van Ghent's squadron was successful. But at least something was learnt from these errors: plans were soon adopted for the immediate completion of Sheerness fort and dockyard whilst a new building programme was instituted with the object of replacing all those ships lost in the recent war. (Peace was signed just a few months after the Dutch raid.)

Effort was concentrated upon the building of first rates. These huge three-deckers, it was felt, were worthy of their great expense as they towered over all other warships and presented a massive broadside in battle. The first of these new three-deckers came off the slipways in March 1668 when the *Charles*, sometimes referred to as the *Royal Charles*, was launched at Deptford. Of 96 guns she was constructed by Jonas Shish, master shipwright at that dockyard. As with many previous launchings, Pepys was once again on hand: 'Down by water to Deptford, where the King, Queen and court are to see launched the new ship built by Mr. Shish, called "The Charles". God send her better luck than the former.' Other first rates quickly followed, and these included the *St Michael* (Portsmouth 1669), *London* (the rebuilt *Loyal London*, Deptford 1670); *St Andrew* (Woolwich 1670) and the *Prince* (Chatham 1670). Of the *Prince* it is worth mentioning that she was designed and constructed by Phineas Pett, the third of that name and a further member of the Pett family to become resident commissioner of Chatham yard. At this point mention should be made of three further first rates which were all built at Portsmouth. These are the *Royal James* (1671), the *Royal Charles* (1673) and a second *Royal James* (1675). They were all built by Anthony Deane who had become master shipwright at Portsmouth in 1668 and was to become resident commissioner in 1672. His considerable talents now fully recognized, Deane was considered the leading naval architect of his day. The three first rates built at Portsmouth were all highly regarded, and considered to have great stability. The first of the two *Royal James* was lost during the Third Anglo-Dutch war at the Battle of Solebay – hence the duplication of names.

With a renewal of hostilities between 1672–4, increased expenditure was naturally allowed. By this time Sheerness was in use, tending to take the place of Harwich. Levels of expenditure can best be gauged by reference to the year 1670. In the knowledge that a resumption of hostilities was close at hand, expenditure was higher than normal in that year. Chatham was still considered the most important yard and received £33,674 for the entire year, Portsmouth received £19,704, whilst Deptford and Woolwich received £16,751 between them. These amounts were running costs only and did not allow for any material alterations to the fabric of the yards. It was not until the final months of Charles II's reign that any new projects were to be initiated.

In 1672 Pepys, who now had the complete confidence of the king, was promoted to a senior post in the Admiralty, and was to spend most of his later years seeking to improve the navy. It was his influence which led to the massive shipbuilding programme of 1677, resulting in thirty new warships. Virtually all were built in the royal dockyards, with Portsmouth building 2 third rates and 3 second rates; Woolwich 3 third rates and 2 second rates; Deptford 6 third rates and 2 second rates; Harwich 2 third rates and 2 second rates and Chatham 3 third rates and a first rate. The Chatham-built first rate was the *Britannia*, built by Phineas Pett. She was never one of the most successful ships launched at that yard, being overgunned and top heavy, and had to be radically modified in 1690 to improve stability. This took the form of 'girdling', a process of packing timber planks to the outside of the hull close to the waterline. Parliament granted £600,000 for the building programme. To expedite it, a number of vessels were finished in the continental fashion of launching as soon as a ship could float. This had the advantage of quickly freeing slipways, the ship being finished afloat. The normal dockyard fashion was for completion, except masts, to be undertaken on the building slip itself.

Eventually, some consideration was given to the fabric of the dockyards. During the final years of Charles II's reign, Harwich received a new building slip (1681), Portsmouth a mast house (1685) and Chatham new storehouses and two dry-docks (1685). New building works continued into the next reign with King James, the former Duke of York, sanctioning increased expenditure. New storehouses were built at all the dockyards, whilst Deptford and Chatham received new mast houses. Additionally, the wet-dock at Deptford was extensively repaired (at a cost of £2,430), whilst at Chatham a secure brick wall was constructed to enclose the entire yard. The largest portion went to Portsmouth where twenty new storehouses were erected and a further dry-dock was established, able to accommodate the largest ships of the day.

Overall, though, construction work within the royal dockyards at this time can be considered little more than a cosmetic face lift. All the yards needed considerable expansion whilst most of the storehouses, workshops and docks needed complete renovation. It is unlikely that King James would have been in a position to solve all the problems within the dockyards, but he was never given a chance to try. In 1688 his reign was ended by a bloodless revolution. Replaced by William III, the new king was, if anything, more aware than virtually all his predecessors of the importance of sea power. Consequently, from the very first years of his reign he initiated a high level of expenditure upon the navy and was to be responsible for some of the most radical changes ever witnessed by the dockyards.

5
A Century of Conflict

The 'Glorious Revolution', was a bloodless affair with far reaching consequences. Bringing immediate changes to national foreign policy, it also heralded a new relationship between government and people. Religion, as always, was at the centre, dictating the removal of a Catholic king, and his replacement by a Protestant. The new king, William III, former Duke of Orange, was a declared Francophobe, and already embroiled in a full-scale war with France. England, of course, could not long avoid involvement, especially as the dethroned King James found immediate refuge at the court of his co-religionist, King Louis XIV.

Before proceeding further, it is worth examining in detail the state of the dockyards during that year of 1688. They were to play a vital role in coming events, since the greater part of future hostilities involving English, as opposed to the allied Dutch, forces were fought at sea. Earlier wars against the Dutch had confirmed Chatham in its supremacy, with numerous battle damaged ships invariably directed to that yard. In 1688 Chatham employed a total work-force of 886 men, a figure which equalled all other yards combined. At this time, of course, the Medway still retained its own importance as a naval anchorage, where the nation's greatest warships found refuge. A map of the period indicates sufficient mooring for some fifty vessels made up of 14 first and second rates, 22 third rates and 14 lesser rates. With the constant task of re-fitting such a fleet, Chatham was in a permanent state of activity.

Geographically ill-placed for a war with France, Chatham was to experience a period of decline and the centre of naval activity was to move to Portsmouth. Moreover, the River Medway was silting up, making navigation increasingly difficult. Little of this, however, could be predicted at the time, and writers constantly extolled the immensity of the yard at Chatham, together with the advanced nature of its

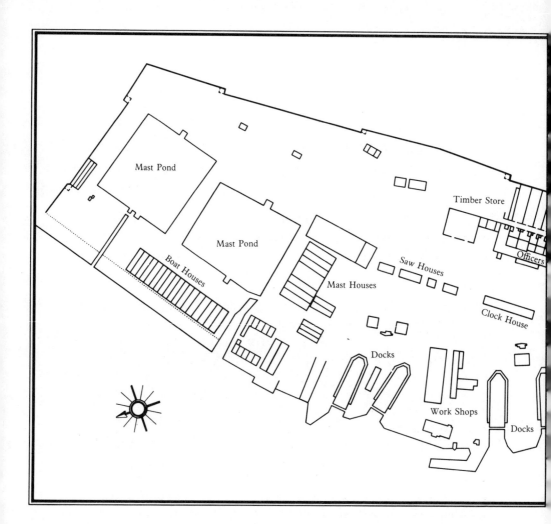

Mast Pond

Mast Pond

Boat Houses

Mast Houses

Saw Houses

Timber Store

Officers

Clock House

Docks

Work Shops

Docks

various dry-docks, slipways and working areas. Indeed, the facilities at Chatham were far in advance of those to be found elsewhere, the yard having a double dock, four single docks, a building slip and facilities for the construction of several further vessels. Those docks at Chatham were amongst the largest in the country, being the only ones capable of accommodating the world's largest vessel, the 100-gun, Chatham-built, *Britannia*. A further important feature of this yard was the ropery that had been erected during the 1620s. Now ageing, it was still well able to provide the needs of this dockyard together with certain other of the eastern yards, having both a separate laying and spinning house, together with numerous attendant stores.

At Chatham, all shipbuilding facilities were conveniently situated

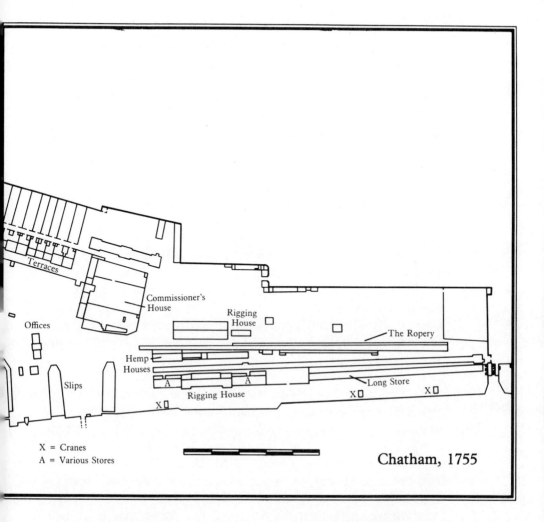

Terraces

Offices

Commissioner's House

Rigging House

The Ropery

Hemp Houses

Slips

A   A

Rigging House

Long Store

X

X

X

X

X = Cranes
A = Various Stores

Chatham, 1755

near the waterfront, a most useful time-saving feature which was a result of the yard's natural shape. In length, the yard measured just under ½ mile, and was further endowed with considerable space for later expansion. Over the years, the Navy Board had pursued a policy of acquiring adjoining marshland which could be added to the yard as and when required. Woolwich, Deptford and Sheerness, on the other hand, could not be expanded so easily as later urban development had encroached upon previously available space.

Set further back from the water frontage at Chatham, and in a much quieter part of the yard, was the officers' terrace, supplying accommodation for the master shipwright, master ropemaker and those of similar standing. The commissioner of the dockyard, for his part, had separate accommodation in a building of much grander style. This was Hill House, standing outside the dockyard, and so used since 1570, although the building itself may have had a much earlier construction date. A brick and timber affair, its occupant in 1688 was Phineas Pett, the last of the family to hold such an esteemed rank at Chatham. A confirmed supporter of King James, he was very quickly dismissed by the new king, being replaced by Sir Edward Gregory. Hill House has already featured in the events recounted, providing accommodation for Samuel Pepys and other Navy Board officers during their frequent visits to Chatham. Chatham yard, with all its buildings and equipment, was valued, in 1688, at £44,940.

Second in importance was the royal dockyard at Portsmouth. Then witnessing a period of expansion, it still had some way to go before it overhauled its larger rival. Standing opposite the French coast, the dockyard was ideally positioned for the new arena of continental warfare. Its large harbour, considered to be one of the most secure, had only recently been given a series of new defensive structures. These, designed by Sir Bernard de Gomme, Chief Engineer to Charles II, included the Gosport Lines to the west and Long Curtain and King's Bastion to the east.

The facilities at Portsmouth yard were somewhat limited, but one double dock and a building slip, and were in need of updating. The dry-dock, for instance, was capable of accommodating the very largest of ships but, being so old, was in the final stages of decay and frequently unavailable. Perhaps the most advanced feature of Portsmouth yard was the ropery. Completed during the reign of Charles II, the rope-house was 1175ft long and considerably underutilized in this period. The yard also had an extensive mast pond, numerous stores and a fine array of workshops. As at Chatham there were a series of terraced houses, residences for the dockyard officers, whilst the commissioner's house was situated near the ropery. The commissioner at Portsmouth also enjoyed the use of a set of stables and a meadow which stood behind the terraced housing. Most of the buildings within the yard dated from the Commonwealth era and Cromwell's plans at reconstructing the navy. In 1688 the value of Portsmouth yard was placed at £35,045.

Two yards which had clearly suffered a severe loss of status were those of Deptford and Woolwich. Having held key positions during Tudor times, they had both been superseded by Chatham. Regularly employing a combined work-force of between 200–300, the resources of Deptford and Woolwich were generally concentrated only upon heavy repair work and in constructing new warships. Both were ideally suited for this type of work as Deptford had three building slips and Woolwich two. Additionally, both yards had double docks whilst Woolwich had a single dock as well. Unlike Portsmouth and Chatham, neither of these yards were called upon to maintain any ships lying in ordinary since the Thames at this point is a freshwater river and so more conducive to corrosion of timber hulls. Newly built ships, therefore, tended to be sent into the Medway for completion.

The most prominent feature of Deptford yard was its wet-dock and adjoining slipway. Little altered since Tudor times, it was constructed of timber and given a value of £2,659. Close by was the mast pond which had been constructed upon reclaimed marshland. As already mentioned, Deptford yard was somewhat hemmed in by the rapidly growing town of Deptford, and small cottages – the residences of numerous dockyard workers – lay within the very shadow of the yard wall. Expansion schemes, therefore, if found desirable would also prove expensive, as was the case with the much smaller yard at Woolwich. In 1688 the two yards of Deptford and Woolwich were given values of £15,760 and £9,669 respectively.

Additional to these four original yards were those of Harwich and Sheerness. Both, at this time, were very small, with Sheerness valued at £5,393. Harwich was the smaller, being without a dry-dock but having, instead, two building slips. Apart from building smaller warships, the only other function performed by Harwich was that of refitting the occasional cruiser. Sheerness, on the other hand, having been built since the Dutch raid, now undertook much of the work that would formerly have gone to Harwich – supplying and refitting vessels of the North Sea fleet and acting as a forward base for the busy dockyard at Chatham. Sheerness boasted a dry-dock, several store-houses, workshops and accommodation for dockyard officers. Close by stood Sheerness fort, providing a most adequate defence, and completely rebuilt following its capture by the Dutch in 1667. Sheerness had not, as yet, been responsible for the building of warships, a situation that was shortly to change. In 1691, the *Sheerness* was launched, a small fifth rate of 32 guns which represented the first in a long line of warships. At that time there was no permanent slip-way, but two launching slips are known to have been added within the space of a few years.

For the dockyard artisan and labourer, Sheerness proved unpopular during the early years; it was associated with illness and bad luck. Situated in the midst of the North Kent marshes, ague (English malaria) was common. Frequently the officers of Sheerness yard were forced to complain that work was much behind because of ill-health. In 1744 this missive was sent to the Navy Board:

> . . . that the labourers are very much reduced by sickness, death etc and have a great deal of work for them . . . we are humbly of the opinion it would be a very great advantage to His Majesty's service that the above mentioned artificers [bricklayers and housecarpenters] and labourers . . . work two tides a day [i.e. three hours extra].

Knowing the area's reputation, few skilled artisans freely chose to work at Sheerness. Those who did were often born there. Hence, in 1774 it was stated that 'the country adjacent to this place is all marshy and has always been reported unhealthy, therefore it has been difficult to procure Artificers and Labourers to reside there and indeed for the greatest part we have, have been bred there.' As well as finding it difficult to acquire a work-force of sufficient size, other problems were also associated with this particular dockyard. For one thing, there was no natural water supply, a situation which continued until the early nineteenth century. Numerous test borings were made, but all proved unsuccessful. Hence most water had to be brought by boat from Chatham. During the early eighteenth century some hundred or more puncheons (large casks), amounting to well over 6,000 gallons, were brought to Sheerness weekly.

At the outset of William's reign a review similar to that outlined above must have been undertaken. Listing the facilities, those responsible for its compilation must have been shocked by the inadequacies revealed. Between them the five major yards could muster dry-docking facilities for only fourteen vessels, a quite insufficient number for a fleet then in excess of one hundred warships. Not that this was the end of the problem: most of the existing dry-docks, together with a large proportion of storehouses and workshops, were in an advanced state of decay and badly in need of immediate replacement. Moreover, the yards themselves were badly sited. The French, with a new naval base at Brest, were well positioned for attacks upon both Channel shipping and the west-coast ports. The Royal Navy, heavily reliant upon the Thames and Medway yards, was at a grave disadvantage. Ships ordered to take up position in the western reaches of the Channel had to tack, often for several days,

Portsmouth dockyard rope-house, which still stands, despite Aitken's almost successful attempt at its destruction. Rope manufacturing itself ceased at Portsmouth during the nineteenth century, and the remaining buildings are used as stores

Launch of the *Waterloo*, a 120-gun first rate built at Chatham in 1833. Soon to be superseded by mechanical power, the *Waterloo* represented the ultimate development of the age of fighting sail (*Chatham Public Library*)

A general view of the Medway anchorage, c1850. One or two vessels are seen lying in ordinary, whilst a covered hulk is seen to the left (*Rochester Public Library*)

Progress upon the nineteenth-century extension to Chatham yard. The massive building located towards the centre was the prison that housed all convicts employed upon building work (*Rochester Public Library*)

against prevailing winds. Further, in the event of battle damage, English ships often had to limp distances far greater than the French. The result was that William III's Admiralty soon determined upon the establishment of a new dockyard to the west, whilst Portsmouth, the nation's most southerly yard, was to be given greatly increased facilities.

The desire for a westerly yard was initially overcome by the use of Kinsale in Ireland. Formerly a supply base, repair facilities at Kinsale were placed under a master shipwright, who proceeded to supervise the cleaning and repair of small warships. The rather limited facilities meant that such work could only be undertaken outside a dry-dock, with ships being heaved over by the application of ropes to the upper masts. With part of the bottom revealed, encrustations were burnt off and damaged timbers replaced.

As the war with France developed, the need for more facilities grew. For this reason, Kinsale was expanded, receiving a commissioner in 1694. Although the most junior of all Navy Board commissioners, his appointment did at least give Kinsale the status of a fully constituted royal dockyard. Apart from the commissioner, there were additional officers to supervise ships in ordinary, payment of the work-force and a master caulker. In 1695 the labour force was recorded as being twenty-eight in number, but rose to sixty-six by the end of the war. However, Kinsale was not destined to be a dockyard of any real size. The Navy Board saw little advantage in having such facilities quite so far from London, with a consequent disruption of any concerted battle plans. Further, Kinsale itself was a difficult harbour to enter, having a bar right across the mouth. Giving a depth of only 16ft at low water, this prevented entry of large ships at any time other than high tide.

As an alternative to Kinsale, it was decided to establish a permanent dockyard somewhere on the west coast of England. As early as 1689 Edmund Dummer, assistant master shipwright at Chatham, was instructed to survey the entire coast line between Dartmouth and Falmouth, subsequently presenting his report in October of that year. His overall conclusion was that Point Froward, at the entrance to the Hamoaze River, Plymouth, would make the best site for such a dockyard. The report came at a timely moment, as the Admiralty had already raised the possibility of a stone dock being built somewhere within the Sound.

Plymouth, of course, was to prove an ideal site for the new dockyard, and had been considered on several previous occasions. Sir

Walter Raleigh had made just such a proposal during the sixteenth century, commenting on the dangers of confining so many warships to the eastern yards. Instead, he felt there were considerable advantages in dividing the fleet between Portsmouth and a new yard 'at the mouth of the River Tamar where it enters the Hamoaze'. During the reign of Queen Elizabeth, Plymouth was frequently used to mount expeditions against the Spanish, with Sir Francis Drake sailing from the Sound in both 1572 and 1587. However, it was not until the Second Dutch War that Plymouth was first given a formalized naval connection, the area in front of Teat's Hill being employed in cleaning and repairing warships. By 1689 Plymouth was also being used as an advanced supply base.

Once Dummer's report had been received, the Admiralty requested the building of a dry-dock, suitable for third rates. The Navy Board eventually settled upon a builder named Robert Waters (sometimes spelt Walters), who agreed to complete the task within fifteen months at a total cost of £10,900. At that point however, the whole scheme was re-examined, with Edmund Dummer carrying out a more detailed survey of the area. This, in turn, led to a proposal for a more ambitious scheme which included a larger dry-dock and an additional wet-dock. Construction work, for which Waters now presented an estimate of £11,008, began in the spring of 1691, with the two docks substantially completed by the end of the following year. A number of additional structures were then begun, and included accommodation for officers, various storehouses and workshops. A particularly important feature was the rope-yard. Set to one side of the dockyard, it included a covered rope-walk measuring 1,056ft. Other buildings known to have been completed by 1698 were a smith's shop with seven fires, a pitch house, stables, saw pits and a main storehouse. The last mentioned was a two-storey, 60ft square building. With additional cellars and a loft, it could hold all the equipment required by two fourth rates.

Perhaps the most interesting feature of the new dockyard was its planning as a single entity. Whereas the other yards developed in a piecemeal fashion, Plymouth was planned and built within a single period of ten years. Other yards, therefore, tended to be cluttered and somewhat untidy whilst Plymouth was logical and programmed; at the very centre was the dry-dock and everything else was in close proximity. Considerable space existed for the storage of timber whilst the sail loft, set to one side, also had ample space which could be used for the drying of sails. Portsmouth, on the other hand, was an example of how *not* to design a dockyard. All the dry-docks were clumped together and situated some distance from the mast pond and other storehouses. Further, the entire yard at Portsmouth was virtually cut in two by the massive ropery which stretched from the landward side to within a short distance of the water frontage. Much time and effort was consequently lost as the work-force circumnavigated this obstacle.

At Plymouth the two docks were the first in this country to be constructed of stone, all earlier docks being built of timber or impacted mud. The wet-dock, 452ft in length, was of sufficient size to accommodate two major warships:

> And as to the use of the Docks themselves they have water enough (By the natural rise of the tide) to Rescue Ships of the first Rate and are soe contrived and fitted with gates and drains and whereby they are capable of affording as good accommodation – (Both of float and Dry work) as any or all the Docks at Portsmouth quantity only excepted . . .[2]

Both docks contained sluice gates, operated by windlasses, so that they could be flooded or emptied according to the state of the tide. This enabled a ship to be brought into the wet-dock at high tide for examination above the water-line. Later, with the dock emptied, an inspection below the water-line could be made, with the vessel entering dry-dock if repairs were found necessary. Providing a great saving of time, it was one further example of Plymouth's efficient design. Elsewhere, a full inspection of a ship's hull could only be undertaken in dry-dock.

Despite the numerous advantages of Plymouth, some criticisms were voiced at this time. Perhaps the most serious concerned the safety of ships when navigating the crooked passage leading to the wet-dock. Such criticisms were strengthened in 1691 when the 70-gun third rate *Harwich* was driven ashore by severe westerly winds. Two years earlier, in December 1689, both the 62-gun *Henrietta* and the 34-gun *Centurion* were also wrecked in the Sound. The Navy Board, for its part, produced a reasoned defence for the siting of its new dockyard:

> These were considerable objections to those who did not properly consider the cause of which was chiefly for want of good pilots for at the same time ships from the third rate upwards seldom or never came to this harbour, and in such cases it is not at all times possible to prevent misfortune there not being anything but may be used to disadvantage either by unskillfulness

or negligence. For experience now tell us that Time and Necessity (those patrons of invention and discovery) have made access into this river very easy by skilful pilots laying buoys, and erecting beacons, and now those great difficulties removed here is as great safety as any other port.[3]

Apart from the new dockyard at Plymouth, considerable money was also expended upon Portsmouth. This was only to be expected: the declaration of hostilities with France naturally led to a large part of the fleet being transferred from the Medway to Portsmouth Harbour. Construction of new docks, therefore, was begun, whilst the old double dock was completely repaired. At first, the new work at Portsmouth was only to have been one new single dock, but this was quickly superseded by a far more ambitious plan. Instead, two wet-docks and two dry-docks were to be constructed to the north of the existing yard upon reclaimed marshland. Work upon this extension seems to have started in 1691, but it was not to be finished for seven years. The contractor, James Fitch, encountered a good many complications brought about by flooding and eventually resorted to constructing a large dam to keep out sea water. Never proving totally satisfactory, much time was wasted in pumping-out operations. Once completed the entire extension was valued at £46,001.

Building work at both Plymouth and Portsmouth was supervised by Edmund Dummer, now holding the position of surveyor and a member of the Navy Board, so it was not surprising that the extension at Portsmouth had many features in common with the new dock at Plymouth. At the core of this extension was 'the Great Basin', a wet-dock capable of accommodating several first rates. As at Plymouth, this wet-dock then gave access to a further dock, known as 'the Great Stone Dock' measuring 190ft in length. A limited rise and fall of the tide at Portsmouth meant that neither dock could be emptied naturally and a complicated system of pumps had to be introduced. An order dated March 1694 indicates that twenty-four individual pumps were necessary, each 11ft in length and having an 8in bore. A second pair of docks, similar to the ones described, was also planned. Only the dry-dock, known as 'the North Dock', was completed, the wet-dock being finished as a reservoir.

Apart from new docks, Portsmouth also witnessed much additional construction work during the first decade of King William's reign. This included storehouses, workshops, a new mast pond with floating boom to secure lighters and a boat pond. The ropery was also enlarged, with a second timber rope-walk, only slightly shorter than the first, added alongside.

The eastern yards, for their part, also featured in this extensive period of dockyard renewal. Deptford, Woolwich and Sheerness all received a number of new storehouses, whilst at Chatham the main addition was a new mast pond. Built upon reclaimed marshland, it contained a series of brick arches designed to keep the masts permanently submerged. Celia Fiennes, who visited Chatham in 1697, commented upon this particular feature: 'I saw severall large shipps building, others refitting; there was in one place a sort of arches like a bridge of brick work, they told me the use of it was to let in the water there and so they put their masts into season.' The total cost of this mast pond, including excavation works, two pairs of gates, wharfing slips and the arches, amounted to £3,180. Next to the mast pond, a new mast house was also constructed, costing a further £872.

With completion of these building works, the functions of the various dockyards were modified. Whilst Portsmouth and Plymouth concentrated upon maintaining a fleet at sea, the bulk of the eastern yards were directed more specifically towards the construction of ships, together with heavy repair work and maintenance of ships in ordinary. Sheerness, because of its greater accessibility, was the exception, continuing its concentration upon refitting and repairing ships of a much diminished North Sea fleet. Only when Sheerness could not cope were the other eastern yards utilized, together with some of the private yards located along the Thames. Harwich, for its part, continued to decline, with a navy officer being placed in charge. Now serving only as an advanced supply base it witnessed only three new launchings during the reign of King William.

Naturally enough, the period 1689 to 1697, being the years of war with France, saw a considerable increase in the work-force employed within the royal dockyards. By the end of the war, over 4,000 labourers and artisans were on the pay-roll, with Chatham and Portsmouth easily the largest. Portsmouth, of course, had witnessed a phenomenal growth rate and, by 1697, was able to boast a work-force in excess of 1,000, and about equal to that of Chatham. Plymouth was also growing, reaching the 500 mark before the end of the century.

Chatham, then, had all but lost its supremacy. In a survey of the dockyards carried out in 1698, Portsmouth was clearly the most important yard. Whilst Chatham was given a rated value of £56,059, Portsmouth's value was £98,430. Only in the area of shipbuilding could Chatham be considered to maintain its original superiority. Between 1691 and 1700 there were as many as thirty-one launchings at Chatham, representing a pace of work well in excess of that at Portsmouth. Not that Portsmouth, as a building yard, should be underrated; several major ships were launched during this period, including the *Russell* and *Shrewsbury*, both 80-gun second rates, together with the *Exeter*, a 60-gun fourth rate.

Other yards employed in the construction of major warships were those of Deptford, Woolwich and Sheerness. At Deptford, second only to Chatham as a building yard, four 80-gun fourth rates were launched between 1691 and 1698.* At Woolwich, apart from a few lesser rates, the most significant launching was the 70-gun *Bedford*. At Sheerness, the appropriately named *Sheerness* of 1691 was followed by the 60-gun *Medway* in 1693. Both vessels, though relatively small, are of some significance, being the earliest launchings at that yard.

With the end of war in 1697, the pace of work did not immediately slacken: numerous warships had to be decommissioned and placed in ordinary, work which was, for the most part, restricted to Portsmouth, Plymouth and the two Medway yards. As each vessel arrived in port, the rigging and sails had to be removed, together with masts and unused stores. Once this had been completed, the vessel would be docked and an underwater survey conducted. At that point repairs, unless of a limited nature, would not be undertaken as the dock could not be spared. Once out of dry-dock, the vessel would be ballasted with gravel and sent down river to a suitable mooring.

Once part of the ordinary, each ship was assigned a small crew whose duty was that of maintenance and the provision of night-time security. Amongst the warrant officers normally appointed to such ships was a carpenter, boatswain, gunner and purser; the carpenter was expected to survey regularly the decks and sides, the boatswain to check smaller items of ship's furniture, the gunner to take charge of artillery, whilst the purser was in charge of provisions. In addition, the Navy Board appointed one senior officer who was responsible for all ships kept in the ordinary. Known as the master attendant, he would occasionally visit every vessel to ensure that junior officers performed their duties adequately.

The war with France, successfully concluded with the Peace of

---

* Although other vessels were built at Deptford in this period, the fourth rates were *Boyne* (launched 1692), *Torbay* (1693), *Cambridge* (1695) and *Ranelagh* (1697).

Ryswick of 1697, was only the first of many similar conflicts. The French, a long-standing enemy, were to become a constant thorn in the side of British expansionism. The following century, with its four major maritime wars, also witnessed a massive growth in naval power. Whereas William boasted a fleet of about one hundred warships, the Royal Navy at the time of Nelson and Napoleon had more than four hundred ships in commission.

Another feature undergoing change concerned the battlefield itself. Fleet actions were no longer to be restricted to the Channel. William had maintained a small fleet in the Mediterranean, but this was neither long-lived nor part of an essential battle plan. Later monarchs were to field huge fleets not only in the Channel and Mediterranean, but also in the South Atlantic, Pacific and Indian oceans. A western fleet was to be created whose maintenance depended on a west country dockyard. As the western fleet grew, so did Plymouth.

The royal dockyards, throughout the eighteenth century, were to be at the very heart of British foreign policy. Constructing such ships as *Victory*, *Ville de Paris* and *Royal George*, they brought the sailing ship to the very pinnacle of perfection. Recognizing their importance, successive governments initiated a series of improvements both to docking facilities and technical needs. The increase in numbers actually employed was remarkable; over the entire century, labourers and artisans within the dockyards more than tripled. As such, the dockyards were easily the largest industrial complexes in the kingdom, responsible for generating numerous additional industries, whose only reason for survival was in servicing the needs of both the royal dockyards and the dockyard towns. Of limited importance throughout the seventeenth century, the royal dockyards were soon to prove indispensable for both the nation's growth and continued survival.

6
A Period of Expansion

The first of the eighteenth-century maritime wars, fought to secure the Spanish throne from French domination, lasted from 1702 until 1713. With the British navy matched against a combined Franco-Spanish fleet, much of the conflict centred on the Mediterranean. At the time, the Royal Navy had no permanent base in this area, making the creation of such facilities a major objective. In the year 1704 a seaborne assault was mounted on Gibraltar, wresting the island rock from its Spanish keepers. Little was then done to improve facilities as, within the space of four years, Minorca was also captured which provided the excellent harbour facilities of Port Mahon, one of the safest anchorages in the Mediterranean. A careening wharf was inherited from the Spanish and quickly utilized, the Navy Board adding a number of storehouses, together with a victualling depot, and careening capstan. This last was a special device set into the wharf and operating tackle applied to the upper masts of a warship about to be heeled for cleaning. Over the years Port Mahon was to prove an ideal base for vessels engaged in observing French activities at Toulon, but it was only to remain in English hands for part of the century, being eventually returned to Spain.

Port Mahon, of course, was not the first of the foreign yards, Port Royal, Jamaica, having been available since the time of the Anglo-Dutch wars of the mid-seventeenth century. Although used as a naval outpost with an officer responsible for overseeing all refits, facilities at Port Royal were limited, and the first of two careening wharves was not established until 1735. The slow development of Port Royal resulted partly from the limited nature of naval operations during the early period, combined with its susceptibility to natural disasters. In 1692 the local settlement was destroyed by earthquake whilst a hurricane in 1712 had a similar effect. Indeed, the Admiralty became so concerned about the safety of Port Royal that it permitted the building of an alternative dockyard on Jamaica, sited at Port Antonio. This particular venture, however, was but short-lived, the new dockyard never becoming a serious rival to that at Port Royal.

The establishment of foreign yards became an increasingly common occurrence because of their importance in helping the Royal Navy to secure free movement for merchant ships in more distant waters. Supervised by the Navy Board, these yards catered for the basic needs of all vessels on a foreign station. Stores such as powder, shot, pitch and tar would be replenished, whilst damaged rigging and masts could be replaced. Fitted with a careening wharf or specially adapted hulk (see Glossary), hulls could be cleaned and new sheathing boards fitted. The work-force employed within these yards was often drawn from the local populace, but caulkers and shipwrights were usually recruited from the home yards. Given a higher rate of pay together with free food and accommodation, such a posting was considered an advantage. Jamaica, however, was the exception, being described by one such worker as 'the Dunghill of the Universe', having a most unhealthy reputation and proving the final resting place of many an aspiring shipwright.

Stores for these yards were usually dispatched from the dockyard at Deptford. This was an obvious form of centralization, encouraged by proximity to the capital. Most shipbuilding materials, but especially masts, spars, tar and turpentine, were obtained through the London merchants and delivered to Deptford yard for redistribution. Because of this particular role, Deptford invariably employed many labourers responsible for the goods' movement and transhipment. Additionally, Deptford yard manufactured a good many anchors, chain pumps and finished sails for foreign yards.

It was in the late spring of 1702 that war with France was declared. For several months the two nations had been making their varied preparations, with the royal dockyards rapidly refitting a great number of ships held in ordinary. The procedure at this point, and one that was to change little throughout the century, was initiated first by the Admiralty, and then by the Navy Board, when specific instructions were given to each of the resident commissioners indicating those ships to be made ready for service. As all vessels in ordinary were without masts, the selected warship would first be towed to a more central mooring so that ballast could be removed. Thus lightened, the vessel would be ready to enter dock at the time of the next spring tide. With most docks having only a limited depth, the additional height provided by a spring tide was essential, being the only way that many of the larger vessels could clear the apron. At Chatham, where there was no wet-dock, ships could only be moved into a dry-dock during a spring tide, but at Portsmouth and Plymouth, ships could be accommodated in a wet-dock at any state of the tide. It should be remembered that Portsmouth had two additional dry-docks and both depended on spring tides.

Once in dry-dock a vessel would receive any minor repairs deemed necessary. The hull would be cleaned, torn or broken planks replaced and seams re-caulked. At the same time, any alterations to the interior of the ship were undertaken. These might result from personal requests by an Admiral, or other high-ranking officer. For example, in 1705 the Earl of Peterborough requested that the *Britannia*, to the command of which he had just been appointed, should have its main cabin and adjoining bedroom 'laid as one' and new gilt rails added.

With such a great demand for docks during the year of 1702, it was important that efficient use be made of all facilities. At that time many vessels spent an excessive amount of time in dock having work completed that could well have been undertaken whilst afloat. This was particularly so with minor alterations to the interior but, additionally, many ships were docked with furniture and stores on board, the removal of such lumber delaying work in hand.

At Chatham and the Thames-side yards, larger vessels would remain docked for a minimum period of two weeks – this being the time between each spring tide. Whilst ensuring a sufficient duration for refitting, it also created an extensive backlog with numerous vessels having to await the next spring tide, even if work had been completed upon the vessel then currently occupying the dry-dock. The situation was made worse at these yards if it was discovered that a newly commissioned ship, thought only to need minimal repairs, needed a much more extensive period in dry-dock, so preventing other ships entering for a month or more. At Portsmouth, where the problem was partially solved by the existence of the wet-dock, it was further suggested that vessels requiring major repairs should be sent to other yards, the reason being that Portsmouth served the major fleet assembly point at Spithead and was therefore more of a naval base than the other yards. The proposal, which was made by the resident commissioner at Portsmouth, Captain Townsend, was dated May 1707 and addressed to the Navy Board:

. . . that for ye future you'll never consigne Ships under great repair, to be done by us, wch Dam up the Docks for so considerable a time whereby we are incapable to answer the Intention of the service in a ffar more preferable manner by keeping them open on emergency as at this juncture happens, and not only so but it is to be observed that generally speaking, Spithead is the Rendezvous of all outward bound ffleets or Squadrons it is also the only place, if either forced by stress of weather or chance of engagement in Channel or Soundings, that you can conveniently come to for succour . . . so that on the whole on wt I have observed, tis absolutely necessary and of great Importance to have always two Docks open . . . no ship during the warr whose repair would take up above two Springs should ever be fitted at this place but sent to other Yards.

Once out of dry-dock a vessel would then have to take on ballast. Usually consisting of washed gravel, it was delivered to the dockyard by local contractors. At Portsmouth, much of the gravel in this period is known to have been extracted from nearby Blockhouse Point, being barged direct to the receiving wharf. Masts would then have to be stepped; weighing in excess of 12 tons, they were installed by using a specially converted dockyard hulk fitted with sheers. The stepping of masts was followed by rigging, an undertaking performed by the dockyard riggers over a period of several days. As the pace of work increased and the need for riggers grew, contract riggers were frequently employed, boosting dockyard capacity for the immediate period of mobilization.

Rigging complete, a commissioning warship was ready to take on the great mass of equipment which combined to make the British man-of-war the most formidable fighting machine of its day. This equipment ranged from various ship-board stores such as water, fresh beef and other foodstuffs through to spare sails, anchors and cannon and shot of which these last were the very purpose of its existence. The routine for loading varied between different yards; at Portsmouth and Plymouth, for instance, the taking on board of stores would be conducted within the harbour, a most desirable practice as both a victualling yard and gun-wharf lay close by. At Chatham, on the other hand, things were more complicated; the difficulties associated with navigating the Medway meant that in an effort to save time, warships were jury rigged and sailed to a further mooring closer to the mouth of the river. Known as 'Black Stakes', this new mooring lay just off the Isle of Grain opposite Sheerness. Here, with ordnance and supplies frequently brought direct from Woolwich and Deptford, the vessel was more immediately ready to journey the small distance to its rendezvous point on the Nore.

Gun-wharves and victualling yards were, of course, essential appendages to the royal dockyards, administered by a sub-section of the Navy Board. The various gun-wharves, which were established to end the necessity of all ships being armed directly from stores held in the Tower of London, were supervised by the Ordnance Board. Woolwich, Chatham, Sheerness, Portsmouth and Plymouth each had a gun-wharf whilst additional supplies were held at Harwich, Hull, Kinsale, Dover, Berwick and Leith. Of the gun-wharves, that at Woolwich was the earliest, with a store established there during the sixteenth century. Enlarged at the time of the Anglo-Dutch wars, it was still small, being no more than half an acre, and much in need of repair. At Portsmouth the Ordnance wharf had been established in 1662 on the Portsea side. Eventually it was replaced during the 1797 to 1814 period by a larger wharf at the north end of the Camber. At Sheerness the gun-wharf was inside the dockyard, whilst at Plymouth the Ordnance Board had acquired the northern end of the yard; it was to move to Mount Wise in 1708 and again to a new site (the present Morice Yard) in 1719. At Chatham the Ordnance Board acquired the site of the original Tudor yard during the mid-seventeenth century, remaining there until its closure in the 1950s. Gun-wharves at all yards were equipped with large storehouses, one of which accommodated the carriages, a shot pound and various smitheries. The wharf itself would be lined with a number of cranes suitable for handling heavy cannon.

The victualling office, administered by the Victualling Commission until replaced by a Board in 1715, had outposts at Deptford, Chatham, Portsmouth and Plymouth, with additional bases as and when required. Initially Tower Hill, London, was the centre of naval victualling but in 1742 a much larger site was established close to Deptford dockyard upon land formerly owned by the diarist John Evelyn. Thereafter it was to be the largest of all the victualling yards, merchants bringing materials which were redistributed to the outposts. Most of the victualling yards had their own stores, cooperage, bakehouse and pickling facilities. Foreign yards tended to be dependent upon an agent who purchased provisions locally. As an institution the Victualling Board possessed a very bad reputation throughout the eighteenth century, often supplying underweight, stale and inedible food. Peas were as hard as lead shot, cheese the consistency of metal whilst bread was invariably full of black maggots and beer tasted like stagnant water.

Once victualled and in receipt of its correct ordnance, the newly commissioned warship would take on a full crew – not an easy task when service in the navy was so unpopular. Frequently the press was resorted to, with a group of seamen under a lieutenant empowered to impress any man without a certificate of protection. Pressed men were first taken to a receiving ship, one of the hulks located close to the dockyard and maintained by that yard. From there they were distributed to various ships awaiting their services. Amongst those men with a protection certificate and so free from impressment, were all members of the dockyard work-force, both labourers and artisans.

The War of Spanish Succession, bringing with it the need to maintain large Channel and Mediterranean fleets, proved particularly busy for all the dockyards. Both Portsmouth and Plymouth, with their unrivalled collection of docks, now bore the brunt of the fitting and refitting work, whilst Chatham, Woolwich and Deptford concentrated far more upon heavy repair work and the building of new ships. During the period 1702 to 1713, Woolwich recorded seventeen new launchings, far more than any other yard, whilst Chatham recorded eleven. For the most part they were the larger warships and included the 70-gun *Resolution* (Woolwich, 1704) and the 90-gun *Sandwich* (Chatham, 1711). Deptford recorded two launchings, but with three docks and a single building slip, it was a yard better suited to repair work.

Concentration upon the war effort and the recent improvement of facilities under William III meant that little was added to the royal dockyards in this period. At Chatham the double dock was lengthened (1703), whilst Medway House, soon to be the residence of the dockyard commissioner, was built. Portsmouth, on the other hand, saw the construction of a brick wall which was designed to encompass the entire yard. Started in June 1711, it replaced a timber palisade which had by then entered into an advanced state of decay. According to a report dated September 1705 the palisades themselves were insufficient to prevent 'embezzlers' forcing an entrance into the dockyard. Further, houses standing close to this fence were often used as hiding places, with dockyard workers passing material through holes in the fence. In July 1710 the paliside was considered to be even more damaged with an estimate of £1,061 given as the cost of a new brick wall. Meanwhile, annual repairs continued. It was in August 1710 that agreement on the building of the new wall was finally reached. At that time it was decided to remove houses built too close to the wall and such land added to the dockyard for the 'better and more compleate building of a wall'. The structure was substantially complete by December 1711 although parts still remained unfinished due to a shortage of bricks. Other dockyards also received new walls during the eighteenth century, the current wall at Chatham dating from 1720 and part of that at Plymouth from 1728.

That Chatham was still an important yard for both construction and heavy repair work has already been noted, with its usefulness as a naval base diminishing throughout the eighteenth century. Situated some 8 miles up river, its inaccessibility was increased by a constant shoaling of the River Medway. In 1702 and again in 1745, projects were undertaken as an attempt to deepen the river, but both proved ineffectual. The problem though was more than just that of navigation: the mooring of ships was also affected, with those of a deep draught having to be given a reduced amount of ballast, a point which was given consideration in a report of 1774:

> The moorings for ships laid up there extend from a little below Rochester bridge, to the lower part of Gillingham Reach, and extend of about four miles, within that space there is only five moorings for ships of 74 guns and upwards where there is water sufficient for them to lay up and swing or float at low water in Spring Tides if they are properly ballasted, but there is for 20 such ships if they are kept at light draught of water but this is very prejudiced to them.[4]

The constant silting of rivers was a perennial problem that faced the various eastern yards, with both Woolwich and Deptford being fellow sufferers. At Deptford, where the problem was particularly severe, it was impossible throughout the eighteenth century to find a mooring of sufficient depth for any large warship whilst at the time of any new launching, the river immediately in front of the slipway had to be specially dredged.

Throughout the War of Spanish Succession Plymouth remained a yard of only limited size. In 1717, for instance, William Sutherland, a contemporary shipwright, was able to state that 'there are six dockyards, four of which I count to be Capital, which are Deptford, Woolwich, Chatham, Portsmouth; Plymouth and Sheerness put together I deem equal with one of the others.' Few would have had reason to disagree. Yet it was a yard clearly destined for better things.

Fully employed throughout that war it was, by the time hostilities ended, boasting a 600-strong work-force. The pressure on its rather limited facilities also generated a renewal programme, leading in April 1714 to the laying of a new apron to the dry-dock and gates to the west dock. Additionally it was decided that the

> mast pond wall to be finished, the walls around the cordage and Deal yards to be built, and both walls around the jetty head which are not above a quarter done. The housecarpenters' work yet to do are the laying floor in the Ropehouse to be new, the beams of the hemphouse which are broken, the sheds in the Lower Storehouse Yards, the Treenail and Board houses must be new built, as must the Great Storehouse and Joyners shop, many piles are wanting at the jetty Head and Point Froward, and many in the mast pond must be new drove being decayed . . .[5]

In 1722 work was begun on a long-expected scheme for the enlargement of Plymouth, which included the acquisition of considerable land to the south of the original yard. Amongst the structures added at that time were a double dock (completed February 1727) and a new building slip (1724). The extension, which was substantially finished by 1730, contained a mast pond, timber pound and eventually another building slip. Bringing the yard to a total of 54 acres as opposed to a previous 40 acres, the entire extension was surrounded by a wall 16ft high and costing £662. By 1739 and the outbreak of a further war, the facilities at Plymouth consisted of the original single dock, the double dock and three building slips. The work-force at that time was 700 and constantly growing.

There was at this time only one real drawback to the yard at Plymouth. The harbour, exposed to those southerly gales that have already been referred to, remained a hazardous proposition. The addition of mooring buoys, frequently used by ships in difficulty, did not solve the problem, with three warships lost during the American war period alone. In 1774 a report on Plymouth admitted:

> . . . that the passage into the harbour is crooked and narrow, and the tide so rapid as to render the getting ships in or out (especially the large ones) very precarious and often dangerous: these circumstances upon urgent occasions might prove fatal, as for instance in the case of our enemys being able to equip and bring a fleet into the Channel before the function of the ships at Plymouth with those at Portsmouth, whereby the former would be cut off from general rendezvous for forming the grand fleet at Spithead: Besides, this port can never be the rendezvous for great fleets in time of war for the want of safe and spacious Roadsteads before the Harbour, the sound being an open and unsafe place for large ships to lay in except in summer . . .[6]

The long years of peace which followed upon the Treaty of Utrecht, signed in April 1713, saw improvements not only to Plymouth yard but also a number of other dockyards. Normally though, such periods witnessed a certain degree of stagnation, but with national foreign policy having devolved into armed diplomacy, the navy was kept at a high level of activity. Indeed conflicts actually occurred with Spain in 1718 and 1727, Gibraltar being besieged in the latter year. Leading up to the war of 1739 there was constant naval activity in the Channel and North Sea areas with additional fleets sent into the Mediterranean and Baltic. Rebuilding work at Chatham resulted in a new ropery (1719), the fine clock tower store (1722) and a sail loft (1734). Deptford received a new dry-dock (1716), allowing three large warships to be accommodated simultaneously. It was also during this period that Deptford was expanded, additional land being acquired in 1725, 1734 and 1744. The spread of housing had created obvious difficulties and the dwellings had to be purchased for later demolition.

Portsmouth continued to be the recipient of most attention, with its work-force reaching a temporary peak of 1,750 during the autumn of 1718. Concerned with refitting the Mediterranean and Channel fleets, the numbers employed rarely fell below 1,000. That Portsmouth continued to expand throughout the eighteenth century resulted partly from its ideal strategic position, a point already noted, and the various inadequacies of the alternative yards. The unhealthy reputation of Sheerness, the dangers of Plymouth harbour and the shoaling of both the Thames and Medway all played their part in encouraging expansion at Portsmouth – the only yard without serious problems. In 1717 new gates were placed at the mouth of the Great Basin, it being found that the earlier ones, having been constructed of timber, were now completely destroyed by the ravages of *Teredo navalis*. To help to overcome this problem, the master shipwright at Portsmouth suggested that the gates be sheathed with copper 'to prevent their being damaged by the worms'. Whether or not this policy was adopted cannot be verified, but use of copper would certainly have prevented worm. The year 1717 also saw the construction of five new terraced houses, known as Long Row, and for the accommodation of the clerk of the cheque, storekeeper, clerk of the store, the first assistant to the master shipwright and the master caulker. All these were senior dockyard officers with the clerk of the cheque keeping the yard muster and pay books, the storekeeper supervising all general stores and the clerk of the store working under

Devonport, south yard basin. Taken in 1901, this photograph is of particular interest as it shows an officer of the Metropolitan Police (Dockyard Division). Then responsible for security within all royal dockyards, this force was replaced in 1934. The building with the Cupola in the distance is the Admiral's House

A further view of the south yard, Devonport, in 1901, showing an area that was to be substantially bombed during World War II. The eighteenth-century terraces can be seen at the rear. Within each of the surviving royal dockyards there exists an internal rail system for the movement of heavy materials. Two box vans may be seen on the right

Interior of No 3 slip, Devonport. Whilst the slipway itself was first established during the mid-eighteenth century, the timber roofing was a product of the early nineteenth century (*Devonport dockyard*)

him. The master caulker, together with the various other trade masters, such as the master shipwright and master ropemaker, supervised various groups of artisans. The type of housing varied little between yards and most terraced accommodation dates to this same period and is of similar design – three storey, brick built with an additional porch frequently added in the nineteenth century.

The long, uneasy and somewhat broken peace eventually ended in 1739. At sea the new period of hostilities took on the prosaic title of Jenkins's Ear, though its continental equivalent was entitled the War of Austrian Succession. For the Royal Navy it was really an extension of previous campaigns, with domination of the Mediterranean quickly asserted. Further activity in the Indian Ocean, using Trincomalee as an advance base, soon achieved supremacy within this area. For the royal dockyards, perhaps the most important move was the creation of a western squadron under Admiral Anson. Aimed at reducing the French Atlantic trading connections, it was a move that brought a considerable growth rate to Plymouth as no other yard was better suited for refitting such squadrons.

Apart from its obvious and rather more direct effect on Plymouth, the War of Jenkins's Ear also prompted the expansion of numerous docks and slips within most of the yards. This was a result of the new establishment introduced in 1745, laying down increased dimensions for the English warship. The first establishment, that of 1677, had been an attempt to standardize design, specifying the size and equipment of all ships in the Royal Navy. Theoretically an excellent idea, it meant that each dockyard had to carry equipment for only a limited number of differing vessels. On the other hand, the scheme had a disadvantage in that it discouraged experimentation, restricting each rate of warship to the dimensions of the current establishment.

The change in 1745 came about as a result of Admiralty pressure. The Navy Board, being responsible for the drawing up of a new establishment, were reluctant to make changes for they would mean dockyards storing much new equipment whilst creating a need for larger docks. However, the war clearly indicated that the size of British warships was inadequate, often proving ineffective in foreign seas. For instance, British third rates were frequently 80-gun three-deckers but 14ft shorter than a French 74-gun two decker. Consequently the British ship tended to ride low in the water, with the bottom gun tier unable to be used on anything other than a very calm day. As the lower tier also mounted the most powerful guns, the shortcomings of such ships can be appreciated all the more readily.

Recognizing the obvious superiority of the French-designed '74', the Admiralty made immediate demands upon the Navy Board for similar vessels. The Navy Board, though, did not take kindly to foreign-designed warships, rejecting suggestions for increased size, believing the current establishment (dated 1719 with unofficial changes since that date) to have adequate dimensions. Eventually, however, a compromise was reached with the Navy Board agreeing to an increase in length of certain ships, but refusing to consider the building of a French-designed 74-gun third rate. The new establishment added 4ft to the 80-gun third rates and 11ft to a first rate of 100 guns.

As already indicated, this necessitated a number of the royal yards receiving enlarged docks and other facilities. At Plymouth, for instance, a new building slip, situated close to the new mast pond, was specifically added for constructing larger ships of the 1745 establishment. In 1749 a further problem was noted when, during a visit of senior naval officers, the master shipwright indicated that the double dock was of insufficient size: '. . . the ships being now so much increased in magnitude, consequently in their Draught of Water, it has become difficult to dock a ship of the third rate upwards in any other than the outer Dock . . .'[7] At Portsmouth, Chatham and Woolwich, the yards responsible for building and repairing first rates, the new establishment also meant an increase in dock sizes with a number of the building slips being lengthened at Portsmouth.

It was not until after the cessation of hostilities that the Admiralty was to receive its much coveted 74s, brought about as a result of changes in Navy Board personnel. The design of the new warship closely followed that of captured French 74s with remarkably few changes being introduced. It was in 1755 that three of these 74-gun third rates, *Dublin*, *Norfolk* and *Shrewsbury*, were first laid down at Deptford. Two-deckers, 165ft in length and a 47ft beam, they were the first of a highly successful class that was soon to dominate the line of battle. The choice of Deptford yard for building these vessels resulted from the yard's proximity to London. Both the Navy Office and Admiralty were in a better position to gauge progress and, as a result, senior shipwrights were frequently transferred to this yard to pioneer new ideas or oversee experimental designs. Another of the experiments pursued at Deptford was the building of the *Brunswick*, a shallow draughted 74. Turning out to be a rather unsuccessful design, it had been hoped that with a draught reduced by some 2ft it might be in a position to overcome problems created by shoaling of the Thames and Medway.

The peace of 1748, signed at Aix-la-Chapelle, was but a short-lived event. It was more of a truce, with war resumed in 1756. Both sides were prepared for this resumption, and the royal dockyards were maintained at a high level of activity. Entering this renewed conflict with over a hundred ships of the line, the war was to end with British mastery of the world's oceans. In the year 1759, for instance, so complete was the list of victories, both on land and sea, that a new first rate, the keel of which was laid at Chatham in July, was given the name *Victory*. Constructed in the old single dock, one of those built under James I but much enlarged, she was to become the nation's most revered warship. Carrying Nelson's flag at Trafalgar, she is permanently dry-docked at Portsmouth and can be freely visited.

For the dockyards, a twelve year peace following the year 1763 was used for the construction of carefully planned extension schemes to both Portsmouth and Plymouth yards. At that time the various eastern yards were ignored, although Sheerness was originally to have received similar treatment. Regarding Sheerness, or 'Sheernasty' as a great many mariners came to call it, a plan was drawn up by Sir Thomas Slade, Navy Board Surveyor, which included new docks, building slips and a series of work sheds. The first phase in this extension scheme was the laying down of chain moorings for the transfer of ships from the Chatham ordinary. It was at this point, however, that a discovery was made leading to the cancellation of the entire project. The Medway at Sheerness was infested with *Teredo navalis*:

> This is only to be accounted for by supposing that the great number of old ships that have been laid there as breakwaters were full of worm from all parts of the world and the constant resort of ships from the Levant to perform quarantine in Stangate Creek. For it is now known that the worm here damages ships almost as much as in the West Indies.[8]

The Portsmouth and Plymouth extensions were the largest construction work since the reign of William. Given a combined estimate of £679,087, both yards were to receive a complete array of new storehouses and work sheds. Of the two, the extension at Plymouth was clearly the more ambitious for it included the North Dock (built 1762), designed to accommodate the very largest of first rates, two new building slips and a double rope-house. At Portsmouth, apart from alterations to existing docks and slipways, new ground was taken up to the north and south-east upon which were placed boat-houses, smitheries, an anchor wharf, sail loft, mast pond, rigging house, a mould loft and various stores, kilns and cranes.

The Seven Years War (1756–63), successful as it was for the British navy, also sowed seeds for a future defeat. Many of the vessels launched in that period, but not the *Victory*, were built of green and unseasoned timber. The war had created such demand for warships that most of the yards completely used up their timber supplies. As soon as timber was brought into a yard, it was being used, an obvious mistake as such timber would inevitably rot, giving warships a foreshortened life.

Despite the timber shortage suffered during the Seven Years War little was done to improve the situation until the early 1770s. By that time, though, a further war was on the horizon and the navy obviously short of seagoing vessels. Those built during the earlier war had simply been placed in ordinary, with the unseasoned timbers simply reducing such vessels to an advanced state of decay. In 1771, for instance, the *Ardent* was given an inspection at Chatham. Built in 1764 it had never been to sea but, by that particular year, needed repairs estimated as at £17,000. In 1773 the following report was made on the *Cornwall*, one of a new class of 74s:

> . . . built in 1761 and which was supposed to want only a small repair (like all the other modern ships) is found to have scarcely a sound piece of timber in her whole frame, her original cost when new was £29,000 and the estimate of her present repair is £23,000, so that in the course of about thirteen years this single ship will have cost the publick no less a sum than £52,000 . . .[9]

For the construction of the English man-of-war, four types of timber were needed – oak, elm, beech and fir. Some of these could be imported, but for oak, the timber used more than any other, there was considered no substitute for that grown in England. Geographically, the Navy Board often went so far as to specify that oak brought into the dockyards should be 'good, sound, Sussex oak'. It was Sussex and the surrounding counties of Hampshire, Kent and Surrey which had the ideal conditions for the growth of *Quercus robur*, the English oak. Apart from the right temperatures, these counties of southern England also had the ideal soils, namely clay or loam. As an alternative to English oak, certain foreign oak, again *Quercus robur*, was occasionally considered. But the manner in which it was transported from central and northern Europe made it more likely to rot. Floated down river, the saturated timber was then loaded into ships for a summer passage in which the steaming wood encouraged the growth of spores.

If the Navy Board had been able to acquire adequate supplies of timber, the English warship would have been built entirely of English oak. As it was, the average 74 still consumed some 3,200 loads of English timber and a further 400 loads of foreign substitutes. A load was the standard measurement of timber destined for the dockyards, one load being the amount of timber which could normally be transported on a wagon drawn by several pairs of horses. According to one estimate 3,200 loads was the approximate equivalent of stripping sixty acres.

Of the various substitutes for English oak, these were most frequently used when either strength was of secondary importance or the quality of the alternative timber supplied was equal to the English oak. Thus foreign oak was invariably used for planking whilst British and American elm was used below the water-line where air was excluded, allowing the elm to remain well preserved. In areas subjected to intermittent exposure to both moisture and air, only oak was adequate. Beech, on the other hand, was employed but infrequently, and then only on the planking below the water-line when insufficient elm was available. The final alternative, fir, was extremely versatile and could be used to construct an entire warship. Its only drawback was a propensity to splinter. Fir frigates built in 1757, and later during the American war of 1812, proved extremely fast but casualties in battle caused by flying splinters were particularly high. So fir, particularly Scottish pine, was restricted to masts and spars.

Although proving a serious problem, the timber shortage proceeded to occupy only a limited amount of Navy Board attention. Certainly nothing constructive was undertaken between the years 1763 and 1771. Matters only changed in the latter year when the Earl of Sandwich, one of the most experienced of all senior ranking naval officers, was appointed First Lord at the Admiralty. Much maligned because of exaggerated recriminations following the loss of the American colonies, Sandwich was most certainly responsible for encouraging a new attitude towards the timber crisis. In his own words, and addressing a parliamentary enquiry at the time, Sandwich declared:

> . . . he came to the management of a fleet that had been exceedingly neglected for some years past, was greatly out of repair, that there was

scarcely any timber in any of the dockyards, and a total despondency at the Navy Office as to the means of procuring it; it being generally understood that the timber of England was exhausted . . .[10]

Sandwich, for his part, did not feel that the situation was beyond improvement. Accordingly, he undertook an investigation which subsequently revealed that at least some of the scarcity 'arose from a combination among the timber growers and timber merchants to keep up the price of the commodity, and from some other inferior causes, particularly the vast and unnecessary profusion of shipbuilding by the East India Company'.[11] Amongst the solutions eventually pioneered was the introduction of a parliamentary bill restraining the East India Company from building so many ships, increasing the agreed orders for foreign timber and refusing to purchase English timber until 'merchants at home thought proper to desist from their combination'. At the same time, attention was also given to how timber delivered into the dockyards might be used to its maximum benefit. A committee was set up and this recommended that all new ships should lay for one year in their frames and that special seasoning sheds be built. Until then, no attention had been given to the proper seasoning of dockyard timber, it being stored in a somewhat haphazard fashion, with timber being directed to the nearest empty space and left there until needed. Improperly ventilated, considerable amounts of this timber began to rot almost as soon as it was delivered and quickly became unsuitable for shipbuilding. All this was frowned upon during an inspection of Chatham which took place in the year 1771:

> Took a view of the timber, plank and thick stuff in the yard, observing all the plank to be laid on the flat and in high piles which is the worst method for seasoning and preserving it; that great part of the rough timber is laid in 2 and 3 tiers high; although there are many vacant spaces in the yard.[12]

At Chatham the new seasoning sheds were completed by June 1772, with those at the other yards quickly following.

Yet the considerable thought and effort that Sandwich directed to the timber problem was insufficient to save the nation from its only major defeat throughout the century. By 1775, the year that America declared independence, the dockyards had been able to achieve little in the repair of those numerous ships that lay rotting in the Thames, Medway, Portsmouth and Plymouth harbours. Nor, due to the earlier timber shortage, were their numbers made up by the building of new ships. In 1775 the Royal Navy, facing a newly invigorated French marine, was at its lowest ebb; not half its ships were anything like ready for combat, and it was not until the latter years of the Napoleonic wars, by which time America had already been lost, that the Royal Navy began to achieve victories which an expectant public constantly demanded.

The lessons of the American war were well learned, however. The further renewal of conflict was preceded by great efforts not only to maintain the fleet in ordinary, but at building new warships to replace the old. Between 1783 and 1790 some thirty-three ships of the line were added, mostly built in the royal dockyards. Additionally, new construction work at Portsmouth, Plymouth and Chatham was undertaken with numbers employed within these yards remaining at a higher level than in previous peace-time years. For this reason, and for no other, the failure of the 1770s was completely reversed during the 1790s. Once again the dockyards had started to produce ships equal to the crews which sailed them. Total victory was on the horizon.

7
The Dockyard Worker: Life in the Eighteenth Century

For the royal dockyards the eighteenth century proved a period of unrestricted expansion, with guaranteed work constantly available. This, combined with a not unreasonable wage, tempted huge numbers into the newly emergent dockyard towns, confident that they too would attain these same advantages. The result was that each of the major dockyards soon fostered its own community which, as often as not, survived within the very shadow of the dockyard wall and clearly separate from the older and more established community. As each year passed, the demands for local housing increased, with small townships rapidly developing into one solid mass of sprawling humanity. In numerous and tightly packed terraced houses, thousands of dockyard workers lived in conditions that would disgrace any modern city.

Around the royal dockyard at Portsmouth, for instance, the community of Portsea was eventually created. Originally part of Portsmouth Common, houses first appeared during the late seventeenth century, with constant growth during the years under review. A thriving community, dockyard shipwrights were clearly respected leaders, being amongst those who approached Portsmouth council seeking land for the erection of St George's church, built in 1754. Of course, not all dockyard workers lived in Portsea, and a great many chose to remain within the walls of Old Portsmouth. At the time the original town of Portsmouth was distinctly overcrowded, described by one contemporary as having a 'great many cross streets and alleys' whilst another reported it as being unclean and 'wretched'. It was doubtless this overcrowding that had led certain dockyard workers to move onto the common with the eventual establishment of Portsea. Other dockyard workers, as is still the case today, found alternative accommodation in Gosport, just the other side of the harbour, and for whom a dockyard ferry was instituted.

At Plymouth, the dockyard with the fastest growth rate during the century, a completely separate community was once again established. In many ways this was hardly surprising for Plymouth town was over two miles from the dockyard and proved most inconvenient for the accommodation of dockyard workers. The new township, originally known as Plymouth Dock, was to be re-christened Devonport in 1824 by which time it had actually exceeded Plymouth in size. According to Daniel Defoe, who visited the Plymouth Dock area in the 1720s, the dockyard had

> brought abundance of trades-people, and workmen to the place, so they began by little and little to build houses on the lands adjacent, till at length there appeared a very handsome street, spacious and large, and as well inhabited, and so many houses are since added, that it has become a considerable town, and must of consequence in time draw abundance of people from Plymouth itself.

Similar developments took place at Chatham where the largest dockyard community was to be found at Brompton, the area closest to the dockyard. It too was a product of the eighteenth century, being totally uninhabited until the 1690s. Four hundred houses had been sited there by 1750, with most of these occupied by dockyard artisans. One small part of Brompton, however, was reserved for dockyard officers, and they acquired for themselves a number of three-storey, red-brick houses which can still be seen in Prospect Row. Separated from the mass of ordinary housing, it represents a clear eighteenth-century class barrier. Apart from Brompton, the Chatham dockyard worker also occupied the town of Chatham itself, whilst numerous others lived in Rochester, Gillingham and even Upnor which is situated on the opposite bank of the Medway. As with Gosport, a ferry seems to have existed at that time. For the dockyard worker who chose to live in Chatham, conditions also were amongst the worst imaginable, with back-to-back housing, limited sanitation and a high mortality rate. According to Edward Hasted, a Kentish topographer who visited the town during the eighteenth century, 'it is like most sea ports, a long narrow, disagreeable, ill built town, the houses in general occupied by those trades adapted to the commerce of shipping and seafaring persons.' Of the Brook, a part of Chatham which lies close to the dockyard itself, Hasted commented:

It consists of a long row of houses, which have of late been greatly increased with streets leading from them up the hill, about the middle of which, at some distance from all others, is a number of houses, built closely together, called Slicket's Hill, so as to form a little town of itself. It is exceeding populous, owing to its numerous connections with the several departments of government, and and the shipping business carried on at it.

Not surprisingly, similar developments on a smaller scale also took place in the other dockyard towns. At Sheerness, the least popular of all the dockyards due to its unhealthy reputation, artisans were originally offered free accommodation on board a collection of hulks moored close in shore. Eventually, however, a proper township emerged, sited a short distance from the main gate and known as 'Blue Town'. This derived from the thick, blue paint which seems to have covered most of the local houses. Purloined from the dockyard, such paint seems to have been the only colour readily available. A short description of the town, again dating to the mid-century period, has been left to us by Edward Hasted. In this passage he also records the origin of the town: 'The numbers of persons necessarily attendant both on the fort and dock-yard, has occasioned the building of a town of several streets in and near it, which is exceedingly populous, many of the buildings being crowded with several families together in one house . . .'

At Woolwich and Deptford the situation was very slightly different, the dockyard worker having become much more integrated. As elsewhere, however, a distinct dockyard community existed, but it was also part of the local township. At Deptford, hundreds of small, timber-built cottages were clustered around the main gate, with King Street, Dog Street and New Street being the most popular residential areas. Frequently housing continued right up to the dockyard wall, whilst numerous alley-ways continued to be created wherever space permitted. Woolwich was much the same, although here housing was kept back from the dockyard wall by the existence of the main London road which ran adjacent to the south wall. During this period, the dockyard at Woolwich also represented the town's westerly boundary with most housing established between the dockyard and the Warren.

Each of the six towns described was totally dominated by its dockyard. A large proportion of the working population was dependent upon the yard for work, whilst many others found employment with contractors, such as those supplying gravel or engaged in the manufacture of additional anchors. But it was clearly those who were employed within the dockyards that reaped the greatest advantage. Unlike the various private firms, the dockyards provided secure, long-term employment. Even during periods of peace the Navy Board was reluctant to dismiss any of its skilled shipwrights, fearing that in the event of an emergency there would be an insufficient work-force capable of rapidly refitting a requisite number of warships.

Apart from a steady wage, the dockyard worker was also eligible for both industrial injury benefits and, from the 1760s onwards, super-annuation. Both were unheard of outside the dockyards and helped to overcome the vicissitudes of a hard world. The superannuation scheme at first covered only shipwrights and caulkers, giving some of those who had served for thirty years or more the possibility of retiring on two-thirds of basic pay. Superannuation was by no means automatic, the numbers being restricted only to the most extreme cases of senility. Later, however, the scheme was extended to include many of the old and infirm working within the yards. Another advantage of dockyard work was the perquisite of 'chips' – the right to remove pieces of wood no more than 3ft in length, and of little use in the construction of ships. Often, however, shipwrights tended to spend part of their time cutting up good pieces of timber so that it measured no more than 3ft and was thus eligible for removal. At Portsmouth in 1705, the Navy Board noted that there was much 'cutting up of useful timber plank etc', subsequently reminding the dockyard commissioner that any man removing chips must be checked in order to ensure it had 'fallen from the ax'. Such exhortations were to be a common feature of eighteenth-century dockyard life, and it was not until the abolition of chips in 1801 that the problem was finally solved. On that occasion shipwrights, house carpenters and joiners (the only workers eligible to the perquisite of chips) were given a cash payment in compensation.

The level of wages paid to the dockyard worker were mainly set in 1691. The result was that during the early years of the eighteenth century, wages could be considered relatively high, but with no further increases forthcoming, the overall value of such payments eventually declined. By the late 1770s, a time when inflation was clearly having an effect, the dockyard worker was more than aware of this devaluation. For instance, the shipwright – the most skilled of all dockyard artisans – received the basic sum of 2/1d per day, an amount frequently below that of an unskilled labourer. Apart from shipwrights, the basic daily rates of pay for other groups of workers are given below. Before examining these it should be remembered that a family of four might require to spend sixpence a week on vegetables, threepence per day on bread whilst rent rarely exceeded £7 a year and could be considerably less.

	s	d
Caulkers	2	1
Joiners	2	1
House carpenters	1	10
Riggers	1	6
Sailmakers	1	10
Labourers	1	1

Senior dockyard officers and clerks were paid an annual salary which was usually well in excess of the wages earned by labourers and artisans. A resident commissioner generally received about £500 together with free accommodation and a generous expense allowance, senior officers about £200 and clerks a minimum of £30.

Not that the matter of dockyard wages ends with an assessment of basic pay – it is merely a starting point. As in so many other forms of employment, overtime work was available whilst the eighteenth century also witnessed the introduction of piece rates. Combined, these two factors could mean a skilled shipwright earning over 12/-d per day and a labourer 4/-d, a sum of money which, of course, was a considerable advancement on the basic rate. But it should be remembered that overtime and piece rates were only available during war, with such high rates of pay being the exception rather than the rule. Also, during these war years the price of provisions at dockyard towns tended to be much higher, with meat and bread particularly affected.

Some workers, however, chose to supplement their daily wage in a dishonest and less acceptable fashion, being engaged in the pilferage of various items of dockyard equipment. Sometimes stolen material was kept for personal use, but was just as frequently sold to the many dealers prepared to trade in illicit material. The true level of theft conducted by the dockyard employee was never accurately assessed but one contemporary felt that the annual loss was somewhere in the region of £½ million.

The theft of yard materials took numerous different forms and was conducted at a variety of levels. The greatest loss, however, resulted from constant pilferage of the smaller and less valuable items since such losses were only rarely detected. Both labourers and artisans frequently concealed items either in bundles of 'chips' or elsewhere about their person. For the most part this kind of activity was completely unorganized but much encouraged by the audacity of dealers who even took up station immediately adjacent to the dockyard gates. In addition more organized thefts were conducted by groups of workers co-operating together; either they would smuggle out a more expensive piece of equipment or return to the yard at night. With extensive waterfronts and a great number of ships lying in ordinary, the various dockyards presented an obvious target for such nocturnal forays.

Within the yard itself, the actual prevention of theft rested with individuals known as warders, rounders and watchmen whilst, on board ships in ordinary, were the appointed ship keepers. Watchmen had first been instituted during the seventeenth century and given responsibility for patrolling the yard during both day and night. In the eighteenth century the basic security force was expanded with tasks being sub-divided so that warders took responsibility for patrolling the yard during daylight hours and watchmen continued this duty at night. At the gates the newly appointed warders were supposed to search each person leaving the yard, but this could never be done with any degree of efficiency. Huge crowds invariably pushed their way out of the dockyards and few were searched. It was quite easy, therefore, to remove dockyard property, a point stressed by Captain E. P. Brenton in his biography of Lord St Vincent and written at the beginning of the following century:

Let the reader fancy . . . 2000 men leaving off work at ½ past 11 o'clock, to make up their bundles of chips. Nor were the chips made in the fair processes of their labour, sufficient to satisfy them; they actually employed themselves in cutting up good and serviceable spars, even under the eye of their officers. But this was not all – these precious bundles contained copper bolts and other valuable articles concealed in them. It is true that these bundles went through a sort of professional examination at the dockyard gates, where a subordinate officer had an iron rod in his hand, with which he occasionally pierced a package here and there; to perform the operation on all would (allowing one minute on each) have occupied upwards of thirty-three hours; and as these were all to be clear of the dockyard and back again to work in the space of one hour, it need hardly be said that the examination was nominal and nothing more.

That theft from within the dockyards was sometimes well organized can be gauged from events at Woolwich in 1784. In that year the Navy Board was informed that during a period of five months large amounts of copper, iron, nails, canvas, locks and bolts, estimated to total £50 in value, had been removed by a few nefarious individuals. Their usual procedure consisted of the careful burying of items and subsequently conveying it 'over the wall where it is low and obscure'. Later the goods were sent into London using a cart 'which comes into town often with fowl baskets'.

For some groups of workers the removal of dockyard equipment was a long-accepted tradition. Such was the case with ropemakers who constantly plundered large amounts of hemp, yarn and finished rope. Usually wrapped around their limbs or other parts of the body, it was relatively easy to smuggle out. In 1801 a search at Chatham revealed that over a quarter of all ropemakers were engaged in such activities. Of this particular incident the dockyard commissioner subsequently submitted his report to the Navy Board:

> . . . made a search this afternoon of the boxes in which they keep their provisions and cloaths, and have discovered small parcels of hemp, some tarred yarns, marked twine and tallow in thirteen Boxes of about 50 or 60, which none of them will own; I have therefore given directions that for the future no boxes shall be kept in the Ropehouses, and each man going out of the yard will be minutely searched.[13]

The usual penalty for those engaged in 'embezzling' dockyard material ranged from whipping, a prison sentence through to transportation. That such penalties failed to deter is almost certainly a result of the low detection rate combined with a total acceptance by the work-force that such acts were a legitimate way of supplementing a regular wage.

So far little has been said about the working day itself. For artisans and labourers a six day working week was the norm with daily hours varying according to the season, the object being to make maximum use of daylight. In winter, therefore, the set hours were 6.0am until 6.0pm whilst in summer the day lasted from sunrise until sunset. Both breakfast and lunch helped to shorten the working day whilst additional breaks were occasionally permitted. Within each dockyard a tap house provided beer, it being unwise to drink water, and such facilities tended to attract the least conscientious. At Portsmouth, in particular, this became a serious problem with the tap house being regularly inspected:

Whereas it has become too common a practice in this Yard for the workmen of all sorts to keep Ill companies in the tapp house drinking and Tippling to the losse of their time and great disservice to their majesty and that ye tapp house is appointed and ordained for to give a pinte of drinke to a man at a time when a dry and that but midling not strong beere which they daily sell here in the tapp house, it being a common practice for ye men to be drunk with it.[14]

As with all pre-industrial enterprises a holiday was a rare event; in the dockyards they were restricted to four annual half days – the king's birthday, coronation day, 29 May and 5 November. On these particular days work was to begin at 6.0am and to be completed at noon. An additional day was allowed whenever a ship was to be launched; officially only those working on the completed vessel were eligible but in practice the entire yard invariably ceased work.

As can be seen, dockyard hours were long and holidays all but non-existent. Overtime also reduced time available and a labourer or artisan might be expected to appear for work on Sundays or well into the night. Yet the pressures of work were considerably less than in a modern-day factory. Supervision was minimal and frequently the one hour lunch break was unofficially extended from 11.30am (it should have been noon) until 3.0pm. Additionally it was not uncommon for a worker to appear at roll call and then secretly leave the yard for the rest of the day. Others took extensive mid-morning breaks, finding an isolated part of the dockyard in order to enjoy a convivial drink or a pipe of tobacco. Smoking, of course, was prohibited with those found 'skulking in corners' forfeiting three days' pay. Even entering the yard with tobacco might lead to a week's loss of earnings. Finally, as an example of changing attitudes, families freely entered the yards and a dockyard worker might well share each meal with both wife and child without actually leaving his work-place.

For most of those employed by the Navy Board, the excessive working hours ensured a daily life totally centred round their work-place. Although movement occasionally occurred between various yards, it was likely that an industrial worker would not only spend his entire apprenticeship confined to one particular yard but also an additional thirty to forty years of his working life. As such, camaraderie was high, with each workman able to recognize the faces of all who worked within the same dockyard. This, quite naturally, led to a desire for co-operation and the eventual establishment of numerous friendly societies and specialist trade organizations to negotiate pay and conditions. The latter, whilst not actually unions, adopted many of the methods currently practised by such organizations.

Amongst the most advanced of dockyard artisans were the shipwrights. They had a strong inclination to develop their resources, eventually establishing a series of co-operative ventures designed to provide essential commodities at much reduced prices. The first seems to have been established in 1758 when Woolwich shipwrights set up a cornmill, those at Deptford a butcher's shop and at Chatham a bakery. In 1796, the Portsmouth shipwrights followed, establishing their own mill which undercut local bakers by 2d on a 6d loaf.

The most significant of all shipwright activities centred upon the industrial dispute. When a difficult situation arose, the shipwrights combined on a temporary basis, prepared to strike until their grievance had been removed. As with modern-day trade unions the strike was only used as a final resort, the petition being the most commonly accepted means of expressing such grievances. If the strike weapon was used, it was not unusual for the shipwrights of several yards to be involved, with a high degree of inter-yard co-operation evident. Not that the shipwrights were the only group of workers capable of taking strike action; both ropemakers and caulkers were also recognized for their militancy.

The eighteenth century probably witnessed some ten to fifteen major dockyard disputes, with a majority involving shipwrights. One of the most bitterly fought of all such disputes concerned the introduction of piece rates in 1775. More commonly referred to as 'task work', piece rates had previously been restricted to the lesser trades with shipwrights continuing to receive the basic daily wage. Whilst it has been noted that piece rates could greatly increase the potential wage, the shipwright was also aware that such work methods would be far more demanding. Indeed, they suspected 'task work' as a Navy Board plot designed to bring about only a small increase of wage for a much greater increase in work.

It was on Wednesday 14 June 1775 that the shipwrights of Portsmouth downed tools, leaving the yard in a 'tumultuous manner' and refusing to return ''til task work was abolished'. Quickly the dispute spread to other yards with the shipwrights at Chatham, Plymouth and Woolwich supporting the strike. Lasting until 21 August, the shipwrights used many of the tactics so frequently adopted by their modern-day counterparts. Demonstrations were held

An indication that dockyard work could be dangerous, this illustration depicts the scene that followed an explosion of the boiler in the hammer-house of Chatham dockyard in September 1866 (*Chatham Public Library*)

Chatham dockyard colour loft, 1902. Female workers are here seen in the manufacture of flags (*Chatham Library*)

Chatham dockyard ropery, 1981. Housed in an eighteenth-century building, it is possible that with the closure of Chatham dockyard, the rope-house will become part of a living museum, with the manufacturing of rope being continued

Dockyard ropery, Devonport, situated in the South Yard. Although partly derelict, plans exist for converting this into an open museum

in many of the dockyard towns, picket lines were invariably established and violence was never far from the surface. Overwhelmed by the justice of their cause, the shipwrights slowly escalated their demands, calling not only for the abolition of 'task work' but also for an increase in basic rates of pay.

For its part the Navy Board remained firm, agreeing only to task work being voluntary but preferring not to see it abolished entirely. Remaining adamant on this particular point they simply sat tight and waited for the strike to collapse. The shipwrights, eventually aware that nothing more was to be offered, agreed to call off the strike. At first none of the shipwrights accepted task work, but eventually a few began to recognize its advantages and joined specially formed task work gangs whose rates of pay clearly exceeded all others in the dockyard. Others, of course, followed and, by the end of the century, it became totally accepted.

Not that all dockyard disputes ended with a Navy Board victory. Some of the strikes that occurred in this period resulted in the reversal of Navy Board policy and the acceptance of work-force demands. Such a situation occurred in 1739 when an attempt was made to abolish the right of chips without giving any form of compensation. Immediately the carpenters and joiners at Woolwich yard went out on strike, being quickly supported by those at Deptford. With a newly declared war about to be fought, the Navy Board was in a very weak situation and quickly re-established the right of such workers to remove chips.

Life, then, for the eighteenth-century dockyard worker was one of slow progress combined with a low standard of living and limited personal freedoms. The nineteenth century failed to bring about any further improvements, and the real value of basic wages continued to decline. In addition the spectre of widespread unemployment now emerged, created by a long period of peace following the collapse of Napoleonic France. Even worse, perhaps, was the arrival of steam power and iron shipbuilding. Whereas the shipwright had once been a craftsman, able to control the pace of his work and performing everything by hand, he was now confronted by huge sheets of ready cut metal that, as often as not, required little more than welding. At such times the noise and dirt must have been quite unbearable. As such, material improvements did not emerge until the present century, being the result of constant working-class pressure over a long period.

8
A Fiery Interlude

On the evening of Saturday 7 December 1776, just a few hours after darkness had fallen, the numerous inhabitants of the Portsmouth Common area suddenly found their peace shattered by a continuous tolling of the dockyard bell. Those employed within the dockyard, and for the most part they were still at work, immediately realized its significance: it was the pre-arranged signal indicating a fire within the dockyard. From all quarters men rushed to the scene; some grabbed the leather buckets strategically placed around the yard, others took axes whilst numerous shipwrights began to manhandle some of the fire pumps brought to the yard after a fire a few years earlier.

Panic was evident. The blaze, clearly visible over a great distance, was located within the ropery. Flames had quickly spread the entire length of the rope-house, with considerable amounts of hemp and tar adding to the conflagration. Urgently the men set to work, aware that the entire dockyard was in danger; even the town itself was far from safe. Informed citizens feared the worst. They were the ones who knew that close to the dockyard wall there were stored some two thousand barrels of gunpowder, whilst tied to a nearby quay was a fully loaded ammunition ship. Things looked bad.

Amongst the first to arrive at the scene of the fire was Commissioner Gambier, the man in charge of Portsmouth dockyard, and soon to submit a full report to the Navy Board. At 7.0pm he rapidly penned his first impressions, dispatching the letter by express rider. Clearly shocked, he intimated the fire to have been burning a full hour, with the entire rope-house partially destroyed: '. . . the fire is amazingly violent and quick that 'twas impossible to save that Building.' In fact the fire had started some several hours earlier, but the smoke had not been seen until 5.15pm. It was at that time the alarm bells had been rung, whilst the fire itself quickly spread along the roof of the main rope-house building. For his part, Commissioner Gambier continued to monitor the situation, being able to supply those various officers at the Navy Board with a further missive at around 10.15 that evening:

> Since my last we have continued our utmost endeavours to stop the further progress of the fire; which I have the pleasure to say is totally confined to the Ropehouse, that the remainder or embers of it may burn some time, such precaution has been used that I see no reason to apprehend any further progress of the fire, or any loss to the Crown than the Ropehouse, and the greatest part of the Princess Amelia and Deal Castle's rigging.

Better news indeed, but the crisis was far from over. The whole dockyard was really no better than one huge fire trap, with numerous tightly packed buildings sited within a few yards of the ropery. At any time sparks could set one of these alight, whilst the tar house stood in particular danger. Attached to the rope-house by an overhead spout, it had only been saved when a group of shipwrights managed to cut this link. Nevertheless, packed with inflammable materials, it had constantly to be watched and hosed throughout the night.

The following morning, a Sunday, the rope-house was still burning. Clearly, though, the fire had been successfully isolated, allowing a large proportion of the work-force to concentrate upon its final extinction. It was not, however, until the afternoon that Gambier was able to inform his London colleagues that only a few pieces of smouldering timbers remained. A total disaster had seemingly been averted.

It was not until the Monday that a full investigation was begun. Numerous officers and dockyard labourers were interviewed, whilst watchmen and turnkeys were all asked if they had seen anything suspicious. Amongst those questioned was one Richard Faithful, turnkey to the rope-house and the man responsible for sounding the alarm. Justly proud of this deed, he nevertheless concealed information that eventually led to his dismissal. On the day before the fire he had come across a stranger who had become locked inside the hemp house which stood only a short distance from where the fire had started. Instead of reporting the matter to the nearest officer, he had released the man, accepting his reason for being there as that of curiosity.

Of the interviews conducted with ropemakers, Gambier discovered that they had been employed on the laying of cables, and had made four of 21in diameter each. These had been subsequently coiled and removed to the storehouse by about 2.0pm. All the men had then left the ropery, with various houseboys being left to sweep up and let the window shutters down. Thereafter the ropery had been deserted, with Richard Faithful responsible for checking each of the three rope-house floors at about 5.0pm. It was then that he detected smoke emanating from the south-east corner of the building where some hemp had been left for future use.

The dockyard authorities initially accepted the whole matter as some kind of accident. Plans were put in hand to rebuild the rope-house, whilst numerous workmen were to be temporarily transferred to Woolwich, Chatham and Plymouth to help these yards increase their rope output. The first real clue as to a possible cause did not emerge until at least a week had elapsed. This was when a certain Mrs Boxall, keeper of a local boarding house, informed Admiralty officials of an incident that had occurred a few days before the outbreak of fire. Apparently one of her lodgers, whom she named as James Hill and a painter by trade, had spent much of his time in creating small fires. On one occasion she became so alarmed by the smell of smoke and turpentine that she abruptly entered his room where she found a canister which contained various powder substances, a tinder box, matches and one or two other 'combustible' items. All this so alarmed her that she asked Hill to leave immediately.

Mrs Boxall also gave a description of the man, declaring him to be of about 5ft 7in in height, having sandy coloured 'loose' hair and of about twenty-six years of age. Clearly though, at this point, the dockyard authorities had no reason to suppose the complicity of James Hill but, to coin a modern phrase, they did circulate his description so that he might be eliminated from their enquiries.

The activities of James Hill were, however, to prove rather more incriminating than the evidence given so far by Mrs Boxall. With the description circulated, two dockyard artisans came forward, namely William Weston and William Abraham, who both reported seeing such a man within the dockyard itself. Even worse, though, was a report of a man fitting that same description who, on the very afternoon of the fire, took a ferry to Gosport and demanded of the boatman 'to make haste'.

Increasingly, the evidence was beginning to point towards that of deliberate arson. Nichols, deputy surveyor of Portsmouth Yard, was subsequently dispatched to every painters' shop in Portsmouth, Common and Gosport, seeking out any further information concerning James Hill. A few seemed to know of him, and Nichols soon discovered that he was an itinerant journeyman in search of daily employment. Nobody, though, could indicate his present where-abouts.

Meanwhile, the man's description had been circulated more widely, with a Captain King of Titchfield reporting that he had employed Hill to repaint his house sometime in January or February 1776. Captain King gave a more detailed description of the man being sought: 'a macaroni* painter, his hair clubbed a well cocked hat, and appeared, for his occupation above the common degree and with respect to his person that he was a thin man with light hair about 25 or 26 years of age.' King also indicated the man to be an American, a fact which clearly disconcerted the authorities, believing that he could well be set on the destruction of other royal dockyards, a point which was not far from the truth.

In fact James Hill, whose real name was James Aitken but frequently referred to as 'Jack the Painter', was an American sympathizer. Of Scottish parentage, he had emigrated to the colonies some years previously. An enemy of England, he had determined on his own plan to help the colonists in their recently declared struggle, returning to Great Britain sometime in 1775. Travelling the countryside he had visited each dockyard in turn, ascertaining vital information as to their layout and security. Indeed, he found entry into the dockyards remarkably easy, and was frequently to be found in earnest conversation with those employed by the Navy Board. It was while examining the Portsmouth yard that he had accepted the job of repainting Captain King's house. At that stage, Aitken, Hill or 'Jack the Painter' was privately financed and somewhat low on funds.

Eventually, the would-be incendiarist took passage to France where he gained the support and financial aid of various American colonists, including a certain Silas Deane. It was apparently during his visit to France that he was promised a commission in the American service should his endeavours prove successful. By November 1776 he was back in England.

Preparations now went ahead fast and furious. Landing at Dover he proceeded directly to Canterbury where a tinsmith made certain canisters, chimney-like in shape, to a specification produced by Aitken. An essential part of the plan, these were later to be filled with brimstone matches and small pieces of hemp. Once fired, the device

* The 'macaroni' reference in Captain King's description denoted Aitken to have continental tastes in clothing. The word's usage is similar to that of the nursery rhyme 'Yankee Doodle'.

would burn slowly and so provide time for escape. Fairly ingenious, they did not work with a high degree of efficiency, being inclined to extinguish themselves prior to their igniting a carefully laid trail of turpentine and gunpowder. It was an attempt to make these canisters work more effectively that had led to James Aitken's removal from the lodgings of Mrs Boxall at Portsmouth. Also purchased at Canterbury were other essential materials such as turpentine and matches.

Surprisingly Aitken did not choose Chatham or Sheerness as his first target, but travelled instead to Plymouth. Late one November evening, he attempted to gain access to the yard, choosing to clamber over the outer wall. Immediately detected by one of the night watchmen he beat a hasty retreat, determining instead upon Portsmouth yard.

Taking up lodgings with Mrs Boxall, he made several visits to Portsmouth yard, finding entry through the various gates a particularly easy process. On 6 December, he gained entry into both rope- and hemp-houses, sprinkling turpentine and gunpowder over anything which he considered combustible. Reporting upon events that were made public after the trial of James Aitken, the *Hampshire Chronicle* of 17 March 1776 referred to the moment that the incendiarist discovered the door of the hemp house to be locked:

> . . . upon which he pulled off his shoes, and got up into the loft, hoping to get out that way, but found it impracticable. He then returned below, and hearing a person at one of the doors, he cried Halloo! and was asked what he did there? He replied that he went in from motives of curiosity; and was locked in; upon which he was released.

It was on the Saturday that Aitken was forced to leave his lodgings, but already the plan was near fruition. During that morning he arranged accommodation in two of the timber-built houses sited close to the dockyard, both of which he intended to fire. The idea behind this was that the dockyard fire pumps would already be in use by the time of the rope-house fire. During the afternoon he was once again inside the dockyard, renewing his labours there. Eventually, following difficulties with getting his matches to light he started a small fire in both the rope-house and south hemp-house, the latter quickly burning itself out.

The details of his escape – for he left Portsmouth immediately and failed to start fires in the two lodging houses – was also reported after the trial:

He overtook a market woman in her cart as he was running along the road, when he got into the cart and begged the woman to drive fast, wanting to get by the centinels who are posted four miles round Portsmouth. The woman drove pretty briskly; but at Kingston had occasion to stop to buy a pair of pattens; he begged she would not, she replied she must, but would not stay. When she stopped what she bought came to a shilling, sixpence of which he threw down, and a little beyond Kingston he jumped out of the cart and made the best of his way to London. After going some way he turned round and saw the flames of the rope house which appeared as if the element itself was on fire. He walked all night, and two dogs barking at him, he fired a pistol at one and he believes killed or wounded it.

Arriving in London, Aitken attempted to make contact with those sympathetic to the American cause. As might be expected they refused to have anything to do with him, realizing that should he be captured at any time, their own arrests would be certain. From London Aitken travelled to Bristol where, on 19 January, he fired a series of warehouses.

For the dockyard authorities at Portsmouth, the link between Aitken and the fire was eventually finalized during the third week of January. It was then that the tin canister, abandoned in the south hemp-house, was discovered lying amongst some dunnage (see Glossary). The canister apparently contained a composition of tar, oil and matches with paper and bits of rope fibre round the outside; matches, apparently dipped in brimstone and partially burned, were also found. As the tin box was later discovered to be identical to that witnessed by Mrs Boxall, the evidence became conclusive. A description of the tin, said to be 10in long and $3\frac{3}{4} \times 2\frac{1}{4}$in, was advertised, it being hoped that the manufacturer would come forward.

For a time it seemed that James Aitken would go unpunished. Certainly the trail had long since grown cold, with nobody having seen him since that afternoon in December. Then came the report of a disastrous warehouse fire in Quay Lane, Bristol. A circulated description of a man seen in the area bore a remarkable similarity to James Hill, whilst a lodging-house keeper also mentioned a 'tin machine', later described as being 'somewhat like such as moles candles are made in with a cover with holes somewhat like a nutmeg grater'.

The search for James Aitken was renewed with even greater vigour. Once again his description was circulated whilst the dockyards were ordered to prevent entry of any stranger. Finally, on 29 January, the search looked as if it might have reached a successful conclusion:

Commissioner Gambier received a note informing him that a man
much resembling James Hill had been detained in the village gaol at
Odiham near Basingstoke. As so often happens in criminal matters,
the man was arrested not for suspected arson but a totally different
crime – that of house-breaking. According to the information that
Gambier received, 'the said man answers to the description in every
respect, I found on him a loaded pistol, a viol bottle of spirits of
turpentine a bundle of matches dipped in brimstone and a box of
exceeding fine timber made of silk.' With much hope in his heart,
Gambier immediately dispatched both Abraham and Weston, the two
dockyard employees who had seen Aitken in the yard, to Odiham.

Under watch by the entire nation, for all newspapers were reporting
events in great detail, the two artisans identified the man as one they
had seen within the dockyard. Also arriving in the Hampshire village
of Odiham were two of Sir John Fielding's Bow Street Runners. They
were part of a new special constabulary created to patrol the London
area, but the urgency of suspected arson within a dockyard had led the
Admiralty to seek their help.

From the village gaol at Odiham, Aitken was taken direct to London
where he was examined in the presence of Lord Sandwich, other high
ranking members of the Admiralty and Sir John Fielding himself. One
or two key witnesses were brought forward who had little difficulty in
recognizing the supposed culprit. Throughout Aitken proclaimed his
innocence, but few impediments to an immediate trial were seen so it
was scheduled for the next Winchester assize.

The trial of James Aitken, alias Hill, began early on the morning of
Thursday 6 March and lasted for much of the day. A host of witnesses
were called, including a Canterbury tinsmith who had made one of the
original canisters, Elizabeth Gentle from whom matches had been
purchased on the day before the fire, Thomas Mason who had seen
Aitken at Bristol and Mary Bishop who had sold him turpentine. Once
again Mrs Boxall told her story, whilst Weston, Abraham and several
other dockyard employees all identified Aitken. Amongst the most
damning of evidence was production of the tin canister found in the
south rope-house, immediately recognized by the Canterbury
tinsmith, and a French passport found amongst the possessions of
James Aitken at the time of his arrest.

With so much evidence against him, Aitken's only defence was that
of mistaken identity. He used this to the best of his ability but the jury
remained unconvinced. Unanimously, and in less than a minute, they

pronounced him guilty. The judge, clearly in accord with the verdict, passed the only sentence available – death by hanging. A public affair, James Aitken breathed his last within sight of the dockyard, being brought to Portsmouth Hard where the sentence was carried out on 10 March. According to the *Hampshire Chronicle*, whose correspondent was on the scene:

> He appeared to be very penitent, but had no clergyman with him, which gave many people reason to believe he was Roman Catholic. He harangued the populace for a long time, acknowledging the heinousness of his crime, and the justness of his sentence, concluding with saying he had been wicked, but he hoped, through the merits of Christ to be forgiven. He then spent a long time in prayer, in which he seemed very earnest, particularly for the welfare of his Majesty, his dying prayer being that he might overcome his enemies. The signal being given the executioner drew him up, and he was launched into eternity.
>
> After hanging the usual time, his body was lowered down, put into irons, and afterwards carried over to Blockhouse Point, where he was hung on a new erected gibbet, pursuance to his sentence.

The fire that James Aitken started was neither the first such fire at Portsmouth nor would it be the last. Over the years all the royal dockyards were subjected to a great number of fires, some beginning accidentally and other showing definite signs of arson. Both the Admiralty and Navy Board were aware of the dangers and a large number of precautions existed. Smoking was not permitted under any circumstances, strangers were banned from the dockyards whilst a thorough search was supposed to be conducted each evening with officers responsible for ensuring that all fires were completely extinguished. During the night both rounders and watchmen were supposed to keep a special watch for any sign of fire, particularly during the warm summer months. Theoretically this should have been sufficient to reduce the incidence of fire, but unfortunately carelessness combined with laziness and ignorance of such standing orders led to the free admission of strangers and the improper extinguishing of workshop fires.

The procedure, in the event of a fire was clearly laid down. Whoever detected the fire was to warn the entire dockyard by ringing the bell. If the incident occurred at night, all those who heard the bell were supposed to enter by the main gate and offer what help they could. Meanwhile the various 'rounders', the men responsible for nightly patrols, would start rolling casks of water to wherever the fire might be, whilst watchmen would conduct the engines.

These engines were really no more than small pumping devices of a type frequently on display in numerous town museums. Mostly built of oak, they had a cistern, two single-acting pumps, wheels and drag handles. A number of these would be stationed in the engine house – a building located towards the centre of most yards – with the key held by the officer of the guard. As to the number available, these varied according to the size of the yard; Chatham at the end of the eighteenth century for instance, was able to boast eighteen large and twelve small engines. At Portsmouth towards the end of the eighteenth century the most powerful pump could discharge 180 gallons per minute and throw it a distance of some 50yd. Other fire-fighting equipment to be found within the royal yards included numerous leather buckets and 'fire poles with hooks ladders etc'.

As already indicated the most dangerous area within a dockyard was clearly the ropery where a great deal of inflammable material was stored, the tar-house being an exceptional point of risk. At Portsmouth alone there were three great rope-house fires between 1760–76. The last, that caused by James Aitken, has already been considered, but the other two are of equal interest.

The original rope-house at Portsmouth, erected during the previous century and constructed of timber, was substantially unchanged by the time of the first disastrous fire which occurred on 3 July 1760. Breaking out just after midnight, the fire raged well into the afternoon. Starting in the rope-house itself, it quickly spread to the long storehouse and two of the hemp-houses. In an attempt at isolation from the rest of the yard, many other buildings were partially demolished in order to create fire breaks. As to the cause of the fire Richard Hughes, then commissioner at Portsmouth, quickly gave the Navy Board a full description:

> The night had been excessively tempestuous with great flashes of lightning one of which at 11 o'clock had almost blinded the watchman at his post and another about ten minutes before the flame appeared had passed him like a ball of fire in line of direction towards the place where it broke out; in which apartment as there was a considerable quantity of dry flax and hemp I imagine it took fire and was the occasion of this accident.

The numerous buildings damaged during this particular fire were substantially repaired. A wartime situation prevailing, little time could be spared for their replacement, with many of the timber-constructed buildings continuing in use.

For the various dockyards, the tar-house provided a major fire hazard. This building contained the large tar kettle through which the untarred white yarn was slowly drawn before its transference to the black-yarn house. Throughout the working day, tar had to be kept at boiling point; the chimney was supposedly swept twice a week. Often neglected for months on end, the unswept tar-house chimneys frequently caught fire, endangering nearby buildings. At Portsmouth tar heaters were frequently 'mulcted', or fined, as a result of their failure to ensure adequate sweepings. An additional tar-house fire hazard was the failure on the part of these same tar heaters to properly extinguish their fires.

It was on 27 July 1770, that Portsmouth's second great fire occurred, causing considerably more damage than the first. Discovered at 4.30am it seems to have started on the laying house floor and quickly spread. Consuming three hundred barrels of tar, pitch and turpentine, flames quickly spread to a newly completed hemp-house as well as the house carpenters' shop and a mast-house. In all, damage on this occasion was estimated at around £150,000.

Whereas the first of the rope-house fires had resulted in the Navy Board adopting a policy of repair, such notions were firmly rejected in 1770 when, with damage far more extensive, a completely new double rope-house was designed, built primarily of brick. Numerous other buildings in the area of the ropery were also replaced, mostly in brick. It was this newly completed rope-house which became the subject of James Aitken's attack in 1776. That this particular fire was restricted only to the rope-house was due in no small measure to the policy of rebuilding in brick and so clearing a great number of the highly vulnerable timber structures which were usually to be found in such close proximity. As to the rope-house itself on the occasion of the third fire, its brick shell mostly survived, and this was fully utilized in a rebuilding phase which began just a few months later.

Returning to the second of the dockyard fires, that of 1770, considerable suspicion also existed that this too was the result of deliberate sabotage. Found close to the scene of the fire were eleven musket cartridges, all of which had been carefully concealed. A subsequent report was sent to the Navy Board: 'Very presumptive suspicions that the Fire could not happen by Accident, arises from the circumstances of the musquet cartridges.' These suspicions were confirmed just a few days later when a 'Gallipot' filled with brimstone and covered with oakum was also found. A £1,000 reward was offered for apprehension of the person or persons responsible.

For a time the Navy Board was on the verge of near panic as, within a few days of the Portsmouth fire being reported, they were also informed of a fire having occurred at Plymouth yard on exactly the same date. Although much less spectacular – the reported incident being no more than a few smouldering bags of newly delivered charcoal – the coincidence of dates could not be overlooked. As it happens, however, the date of the Plymouth fire had been incorrectly transcribed, with it really having occurred on 24 July. Moreover, there could be no doubt that this particular affair was an accident.

Throughout the years no dockyard was safe from the ravages of fire. At Plymouth a somewhat more disastrous fire took place in July 1761, breaking out in five separate places. Possibly a further example of arson, it caused damage estimated at £49,800. Other fires at Plymouth occurred in 1799 when the dockyard church was destroyed, and in 1812 when many of the rope-yard buildings were gutted. A new ropery was built in 1814 and a new church in 1817.

Undoubtedly the most spectacular fire in a royal dockyard took place at Deptford during the previous century, in the summer of 1667, and led many people to believe it was the first sign of a Dutch landing. According to a diary entry of John Evelyn:

> June 17, 1667. This night, about 2 a clock, some chipps and combustible matter prepared for some fireships, taking flame, in Deptford yard, made such a blaze, and caused such an uproar in the town, it being given out that the Dutch fleet had come up.

Other large fires occurred at Deptford in 1738 and 1793. The yards of Woolwich and Sheerness seem to have suffered fewer fires although in 1739 there was a particularly serious fire at Sheerness, later attributed to the sale of spirits within the yard. The most serious Woolwich fire was almost certainly one that occurred in 1799 which totally destroyed the *Grampus*, a 50-gun fourth rate then moored in a mid-river position. Burnt right down to the lower decks, fire-fighting parties had been unable to reach the vessel due to a strong head wind.

During the latter years of the nineteenth century, fire still remained a major hazard but its ravages were greatly reduced. The introduction of more effective fire-fighting equipment, increasing use of brick and more rigorous security checks all played a part in reducing the frequency of fires. Surprisingly though, strangers were still in a position to enter the various yards, and it was not until the first few years of the present century that this anomaly was attended to.

9
Technical Innovations

The extensive dockyard improvement scheme, initiated during the early 1760s was, with additions, part of a continuous rebuilding programme lasting until 1805. Portsmouth gained numerous storehouses, further residential accommodation together with improvements and additions to the various docks and slips. Construction of three major storehouses, the North (1763), Middle (1776) and South (1782), came during the earliest building phase, with all three structures currently surviving in the form of the dockyard museum and bookshop complex. Originally the Middle Storehouse (now designated No 10 storehouse) had a fine clock tower which was used to indicate official dockyard time, but it was destroyed in 1941. Other stores were built in this period to the west of the wet-dock.

The new residential accommodation, consisting of a small group of unpretentious terraced houses in Short Row, was substantially the same as that located elsewhere. Completed in 1787 they then accommodated the yard surgeon, master ropemaker, clerk of the ropeyard and the boatswain. An interesting point is their association with Thomas Telford who, as Admiralty Clerk of the Works, was responsible for their construction. Also built at around this time was a much grander house, purpose-built for the dockyard commissioner. The original house, built in 1665, was no longer considered suited to the needs of a commissioner in the nation's largest dockyard. In constructing the new house the original dockyard chapel, dating from 1707, was demolished and the present day chapel, St Anne's, erected on a new site (1785).

Other buildings which date from this era and which for the most part still remain, are the South Office Block (1786), the North Office Block (1791) and rope-house with attendant buildings. When originally planned, the new ropery was to have been constructed on marshland then being reclaimed to the north of the yard. The series of

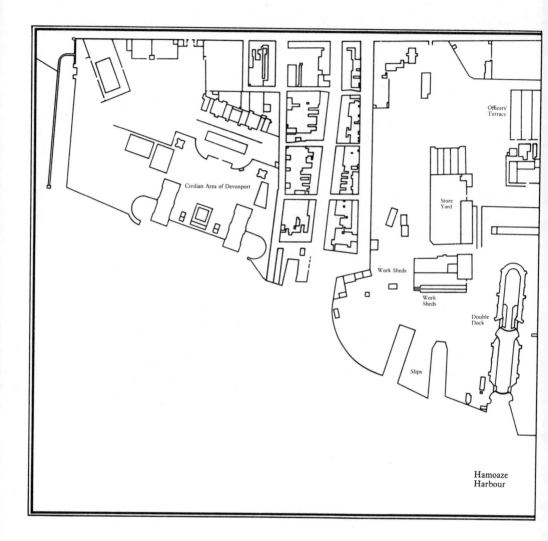

Officers' Terrace

Civilian Area of Devonport

Store Yard

Work Sheds

Work Sheds

Double Dock

Slips

Hamoaze Harbour

disastrous fires brought a sudden change to the plan, making it necessary to build a new rope-house before this land became available. Subsequently the new ropery of 1771 was built on the site of the older rope-house and continued to straddle the entire yard. The rope-house still remains, used as a storehouse since the manufacture of rope ceased in the nineteenth century.

The most important feature of any naval dockyard, particularly if it is engaged in refit work, will be the docks themselves. Of these, Portsmouth required an abnormally high number, allowing this particular yard to maintain and refit the various battle fleets

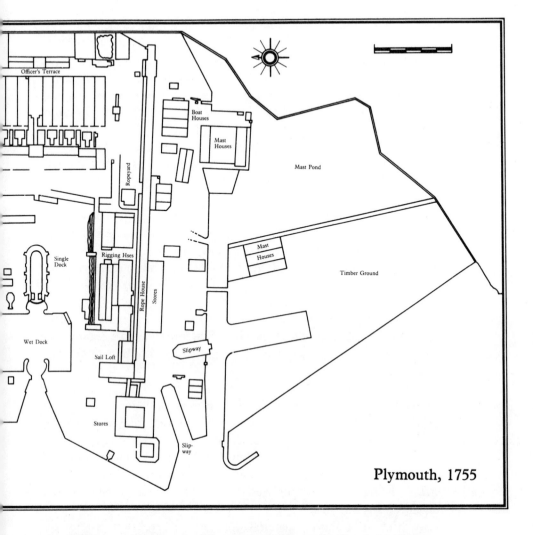

Plymouth, 1755

Officer's Terrace

Boat Houses

Mast Houses

Mast Pond

Ropeyard

Rigging Hses

Single Dock

Mast Houses

Timber Ground

Rope House

Stores

Wet Dock

Sail Loft

Slipway

Stores

Slip-way

assembling at Spithead. The later phase of the improvement programme, recognizing this need, was responsible for adding three new single docks and so increasing the number of docks available to six, of which one was a double dock. During this same period the seventeenth-century wet-dock was enlarged, allowing seven vessels to be fitted concurrently.

Plymouth also saw the original improvement plan extended, with the New North Dock of 1789 being completed to a much larger specification than the one envisaged some years earlier. Including this new dock, therefore, the number of dry-docks at Plymouth was brought to a total of four. One of these, the double dock which was able to accommodate two vessels, was also deepened by 20in in 1773 to allow greater flexibility. The increased size of the New North Dock, so the story goes, was dictated by the launch of a French first rate, the *Commerce de Marseilles*. A 120-gun monster, she was larger than any British ship and would not have entered any existing dock. Boasting that one day she would be captured, the Navy Board permitted Plymouth's new dock to be given the necessary dimensions to accommodate the French vessel. As it happens, desire became fact when, in 1793, this particular warship was captured at Toulon and duly entered the New North Dock.

The new ropery at Plymouth was substantially complete by the year 1771. Constructed of stone, it had been transferred to a new site close to the south-east boundary wall. Away from the centre of the dockyard, it was allowed much more room to develop and ceased being a hindrance to the rest of the yard. Replete with separate laying and spinning houses, both of which were 1,200ft long, Plymouth yard had a much greater capacity for the manufacture of rope than any other yard. Other structures within the area of the ropery, and all completed in stone, were a tar-house, two black- and white-yarn houses and two hemp-houses.

Work continued at Plymouth throughout the 1770s, with further storehouses, a mast house and new wharves all being constructed. Between 1771 and 1775 three slipways were added, one of which was of limited size designed for constructing frigates. All of these greatly increased the yard's capacity for the building and launching of new warships. The dockyard's boundary wall, extended so that it might enclose the ropery, was completed in 1773 whilst a new mast pond was finished two years later.

Much of the building material used in this extension programme came from Marble Hill, a large natural incline existing within the southern boundary of the dockyard. Supplying both lime and stone, it was an obvious way of removing an unnecessary object which would otherwise have prevented fulfilment of the original plans. Part of Marble Hill does, however, remain as a memorial to King George III who visited the yard in 1789; so impressed was he by the view gained from the remaining mound that he declared it his wish that no more of the hill should be removed. In 1822 a small pavilion was placed upon the mound to commemorate this earlier visit. The view, from what is nowadays known as 'King's Hill', is still as impressive. Located in an

Interior of Devonport rope-house, depicted in 1901 at a time when cable was still being manufactured

Aerial view of Portsmouth Harbour, c1925, showing part of the dockyard. Clearly visible is the historic enclave with HMS *Victory* berthed in No 2 dock (*Portsmouth Central Library*)

Main Gate, Portsmouth dockyard, c1900 (*Portsmouth Central Library*)

Main Gate, Portsmouth dockyard. Part of the dockyard wall, which dates to 1712, may be seen

extreme corner of the rope-yard, quiet and untroubled by the busy modern yard, it provides an ideal haven in what will one day, perhaps, become an historic enclave fully open to the public.

As to the relative merits of Portsmouth and Plymouth, these were fully recorded during a joint Navy Board and Admiralty visitation, or inspection, made to Plymouth yard during the summer of 1771:

> . . . it will be granted that this harbour has many advantages over that at Portsmouth, such as the depth of water for laying up more large ships; its situation being a readier outlet into the ocean, therefore for cruising squadrons it is without doubt the best port; but the crookedness and the intricacy of the entrance of the harbour render the getting ships in and out the more precarious, and for the want of a spacious roadstead it can never be a principal rendezvous for great fleets in time of war the Sound not being a safe place for ships to lie in except summer and then only for an inconsiderable number because of the small space of clear ground. In case of any disaster of grand battle at sea, the whole works here would be exposed to a sudden attack, the place not capable of being so secured and defended as Portsmouth is. Portsmouth is more central and happily situated for facilitating a junction of our ships from eastward and westward with a spacious and safe road for the rendezvous of the whole fleet . . .[15]

By comparison with Portsmouth and Plymouth, the other four home yards were virtually ignored by the improvement programme. Chatham, third largest royal dockyard and much in need of renewal, had received no large-scale building or rebuilding work for over fifty years apart from a few slipways and other minor structures. In noting this fact, the already quoted survey presented to the king in 1774 stated that '. . . those [buildings] now there have been very good when first built but as this was the yard that has had no considerable building in it, such as remain of those that were first built are in a very decay'd state and must by degrees, as money can be spared from other services, be pulled down and rebuilt.'[16] As might well be expected, a considerable amount of the money allocated to Chatham in this period was spent on simple repair work. The visitation of 1771 reported that the west wall of the long storehouse was much in decay, that the number one dock was in need of repair and that the north wall of the dockyard was much deteriorated.

In 1772 Chatham had been allowed two additional slips, bringing the total to six, but nothing had been done to improve the four dry-docks, some of which had remained substantially unchanged since the beginning of the century. In fact it was not until 1785 that thought was finally given to improving the situation. Following an official visit many buildings were condemned whilst numerous others were considered to be in need of repair. Work was immediately started upon replacing the long storehouse whilst plans were also finalized for rebuilding the ropery. A strict order of work was established by which buildings were only removed if they did not interfere with the continued manufacture of cordage within the ropery. In a letter from the Navy Board dated 5 April 1787, it was stated that work should begin at the south end of the ropery, the present spinning house should be taken down immediately and the spinning of rope continued in the laying house. The new ropery was to have a double rope-house built to the same design as that already existing at Portsmouth. Substantially completed by December 1790 the new rope-house was over 1,100ft long, divided into one hundred bays with two separate sections for the accommodation of both laying and spinning floors. Of brick construction, it had a lead roof. In 1786 the main storehouse had been completed, followed by new rigging, yarn, tarring and hemp houses.

Deptford, now clearly fourth in size, continued to specialize in ship-building. A yard with considerable problems, a few of these were noted in that same report of 1774:

> is useful for building both large and small ships there being a sufficient flow of water for launching them although not a sufficient depth at low water to lay the large ships on float, therefore after such are launched not a sufficient depth at low water to lay the large ships on float, therefore after such are launched they are moved at the first opportunity that offers for sailing them down the river to be laid up at other ports . . .[17]

To facilitate this role of shipbuilding new land was acquired from the victualling office and a mast pond built. Additionally three slips, all built between 1765 and 1775, were added to bring the total number of slipways to six. Little was done to improve the dry-docks, facilities remaining much the same as when William was on the throne.

One important task undertaken at Deptford was the refitting of vessels used by Captain James Cook during his three voyages of discovery. Between 1768 and 1776 the *Endeavour, Resolution* and *Discovery* were all provided with increased accommodation and the facilities required by vessels engaged in scientific research. Unfortunately the last refit, that of 1776, was carried out under wartime conditions and proved somewhat shoddy. On that occasion the *Discovery*, a former Whitby collier, was badly sparred and caulked.

Throughout the subsequent voyage problems were evident, reflecting badly on the supposedly skilled artisans of that yard.

It was perhaps the yards of Woolwich and Sheerness which benefited least from improvements during the latter quarter of the eighteenth century. At neither yard was a great deal of work undertaken, facilities at Woolwich only being updated. To this end some £40,000 was spent in the years 1791 to 1793. Having two docks and four slips, the report of 1774 declared of Woolwich:

> The conveniencys and inconveniencys belonging to this yard are much the same as those at Deptford, except the inconveniences of getting large ships down river after they are launched is not as great as at Deptford. This yard is much smaller than Deptford and will not contain a proper quantity of timber suitable to the works that otherways might be carried on for building and repairs of ships.[18]

Despite the high level of expenditure upon both Portsmouth and Plymouth and the later improvements to Chatham, Woolwich and Deptford, the royal dockyards became the subject of growing criticism. Much of this was directed towards the ineffective use of facilities and lack of centralized planning. This should have been cured by the improvement programme itself, but docks and slips continued to be inconveniently sited with little thought given to the future. Storehouses remained inadequate in size, older buildings were left in a state of decay and there were too few workshops. With huge sums having been spent on three new roperies, the cordage needs of the navy should have been solved once and for all but, as soon as war broke out in 1793, the royal dockyards again found themselves in difficulty, calling upon private ropemakers to make up the deficit. Anyone visiting the yards in this period would have found them badly designed; ill-planned structures cluttered up the central working areas, making the task of shipbuilding and repair an unnecessarily protracted affair.

Part of the problem lay with the Navy Board, an archaic body consisting of many elderly individuals who rarely gave a thought to retirement. Crucial to dockyard planning was the surveyor, always a former shipwright, but totally lacking in scientific knowledge or civil building techniques. Sir Jacob Ackworth, who held office during the mid-century period, was a case in point: having first entered dockyard service in 1682, he much preferred the practices of a previous century and bitterly opposed new ideas. Constantly acting as a brake to progress, he failed to provide the kind of leadership that could have resulted in more efficient and better organized dockyards.

Perhaps the Board's greatest failure was the lack of attention given to technical progress and new sources of power such as steam. Even relatively straightforward advances such as the use of covered slipways, long used in the East India Company yards, were not adopted until the second decade of the nineteenth century. What advances were made must have been partly the result of an Admiralty decision to create the office of Inspector-General, the holder of which was responsible for considering all matters relating to the improvement of shipbuilding and repair within the royal yards.

The first and only holder of the newly created post, appointed in 1796, was Samuel Bentham, a former shipwright apprentice of Woolwich dockyard. An innovator of the first order, Bentham was a man totally suited to the new post, having devoted a great deal of his early life to acquiring scientific knowledge. Born into a rich and influential family (his brother was the noted writer Jeremy Bentham), he had been able to spend the year following the completion of his apprenticeship in visiting the other royal yards. In 1780 he journeyed to the Continent, taking in both Holland and Russia to expand his knowledge of maritime construction work. His stay in Russia was prolonged by his employment in their military service. Returning to England in 1791, he immediately came to the attention of the Admiralty. At that time various proposals were made for his permanent employment within the dockyard service but none offered him sufficient independence. Eventually the office of Inspector-General of Naval Works was created, a post which Bentham immediately accepted, using it as a means of introducing steam-powered machinery into the dockyards.

Visiting each of the yards in turn, Bentham proceeded to make numerous suggestions for improvement. Many of these, however, were opposed by a Navy Board highly suspicious of the new Admiralty appointment. Because of this situation, many of Bentham's ideas could only be introduced years after their conception. Such was the case in 1797 when he suggested the erection of a copper furnace. Rejected at the time, it was not until October 1803 that such machinery found its way into Portsmouth – a needless delay of six years.

It was to Portsmouth that Bentham directed most of his attention, being responsible for the enlargement of the wet-dock together with additional dry-docks. His first objective, however, was that of introducing steam-powered machinery, the first of which was put into operation in March 1799. Powering the main pumps of the reservoir, it was soon followed by a steam-powered wood mill, metal mill, millwrights' shop and the much celebrated block-making machinery.

There can be little doubt that the Portsmouth block-making machine was Bentham's greatest success in his plans for restructuring the royal dockyards. Designed by Marc Isambard Brunel and built by the distinguished engineer Henry Maudslay, it represented the merging of several strands that were eventually to place the dockyards on the road to full mechanisation. The block, a simple encased pulley, was used extensively throughout the rigging of British warships as a means of providing simple mechanical power. A third rate, for instance, might require about 900 such pulleys, while the royal dockyards as a whole consumed 100,000 a year. Normally hand-produced and frequently in short supply, pulley blocks consisted of several component parts which could be machine made in a much more efficient manner. In 1801 Samuel Bentham was approached by Brunel who had already conceived a rough design layout in which each component part would be mass produced.

As might be expected, Bentham was impressed by the prospect of greatly reduced costs and an end to the problem of the blocks being in short supply. The Navy Board was eventually convinced of the proposal's feasibility, and the block mill and machinery were built and installed between 1802 and 1806. Accommodating forty-five machines and initially powered by a 12hp steam engine, the mill was soon producing more than the annual requirement.

Over the years many of the steam-powered machines that had been introduced at Portsmouth were adopted in some of the other dockyards. Chatham, for instance, to meet an increasing demand received a block-making mill of its own, whilst a complex saw mill was also put into operation. This particular facility combined an underground canal and an overhead rail system to transport timber to and from the mill. Again designed by Marc Isambard Brunel, it was sited close to the timber pounds with the underground canal feeding timber directly into the saw house via a steam-powered crane and the overhead railway responsible for the removal of finished planks. The entire complex was powered by a Maudslay-built beam engine with steam provided by two boilers. A similar mill was established at Woolwich a few years later.

For the royal dockyards, the introduction of steam power was only one of the great improvements associated with this period of development. Of equal importance was the introduction of the covered building slip. For centuries ships had been built in the open with both shipwrights and vessels exposed to every kind of weather. Often it led to ships rotting whilst still in frame, and the work of shipbuilding was considerably slowed by adverse weather. The idea of covering the slips was pioneered in sixteenth-century Venice and eventually adopted by the Navy Board upon submission of plans by Samuel Bentham. The earliest yards to receive covered slips were Chatham (1811) and Plymouth (1816).

Another of the advances made in this period, but not attributable to Bentham, was the construction of a breakwater at Plymouth. Resulting from Admiralty concern over the dangers associated with entering the Sound, they commissioned a survey into the best means of protecting this stretch of water. Doubtless their concern was prompted not only by a steady loss of ships but also the time lost through the western fleet frequently having to take refuge at Torbay. As Torquay was incapable of supplying back-up facilities, many ships had to be transferred to Plymouth for work that could have been undertaken whilst sheltering from the heavy seas. The survey was carried out in 1806 by the engineers John Rennie and Joseph Widbey.[19] Taking only five weeks to complete their investigations, they strongly recommended a free-standing solid breakwater sited close to the entrance of the Sound. Alternatives, such as a pier protruding from Penlee Point, were rejected because of fears of silting.

It was not until June 1811 that sanction was finally given to the building of a breakwater with a length of 3,000ft at an estimated cost of £1,055,200. The building materials were to be rough stone blocks, some of them weighing 10 tons, and rubble to fill the gaps. Work on the breakwater began in August 1812 and was not to be completed until 1841. In the first year of operation some 43,789 tons of material were sunk, and the first signs of the breakwater appeared above water in 1814. As work progressed, continual improvements in the safety of the harbour could be detected, with vessels frequently sheltering close to the artificial barrier.

In the light of John Rennie's great experience as an engineer, it is interesting to consider observations he made on the various royal yards in 1807. These were prompted by a commission of enquiry that had been set up to examine defects in all naval establishments. Rennie was singularly unimpressed; he considered Plymouth to be the most suited, noting the spacious harbour, general lack of silting and the navigational hazards that would eventually be overcome by the breakwater. Portsmouth, on the other hand, was more heavily criticized for, at that stage, the harbour was showing definite signs of silting, whilst he considered the dockyard to lack adequate space for the various buildings and machine shops being built.

Perhaps the most startling of his observations concerned the dockyards of Woolwich and Deptford, both of which he recommended for closure. Too far up river, they suffered from a lack of space and were constantly subjected to silting and so could not be used effectively. Commenting on Woolwich, but later using a similar argument for Deptford, he informed the committee that 'the enormous expense of removing the constant accumulation of mud in front of the dockyard and the confined and defective arrangement of the dockyard itself, were ample reasons for it being condemned as unfit for the construction and repair of great ships.'[20] To replace the two yards, Rennie suggested the founding of a new dockyard at Northfleet, down river but still on the Kentish side of the Thames and not far from Gravesend. With the purchase of sufficient land, it would prove an ideal site for a dockyard, designed at the very outset for building, constructing and refitting the largest of the nation's warships. Included in the new Northfleet dockyard would be two large wet-docks, eight dry-docks and eight building slips:

> Ships will be launched immediately from these docks and slips into the great wet dock, without communicating with the river, and all vessels in ordinary may be moored on its north side, where there will be room enough to moor 70 sail of the line; or, if fewer ships of the line, a proportionate number of frigates and smaller vessels, without impeding or interfering with the works carrying on upon the south side.[21]

In the event, the committee accepted the proposed scheme, recommending implementation in its entirety. The government went as far as acquiring the necessary land but unfortunately the pressures and expense of the war made and scheme impracticable and the project was cancelled with the return of peace.

At Chatham, Rennie was just as radical in approach. Noting the restrictions of space and the shallow state of the Medway, he proposed the addition of massive wet-docks formed out of the Chatham and Limehouse Reaches of the Medway. This would have provided considerable additional space for both dry-docks and slipways, whilst the entrance of the proposed wet-dock, being situated near Gillingham, would go some way to alleviating the hazards of navigating the various twists and turns between Chatham and Sheerness. None of this, however, was constructed, again due to the expense involved.

John Rennie, as indicated, was highly critical of dockyard design and layout. In examining each of the dockyards he had suggested some very radical alternatives to the piecemeal improvement programmes that were more usually adopted. He was aware, as were most critics, that essentially the design of the six main yards had been determined during the sixteenth and seventeenth centuries. To impose upon this the needs of the nineteenth century was insane. Doubtless the Navy Board and Admiralty were aware of this, but the necessary advances that Rennie indicated were beyond their limited finances. A confident wartime Admiralty promised itself new dockyards upon the return of peace, but with its arrival in 1815 government concern with the yards diminished. The sound proposals of John Rennie were quietly forgotten. Indeed, some thirty years later, when the Crimea was being fought and the ships themselves undergoing change, the dockyards remained unaltered. A chance to solve Britain's shipbuilding and repair difficulties had, once again, been passed over.

10
War and Peace

The maritime conflict of 1793 to 1815, a period beloved by numerous writers of fiction, was a long drawn out affair and one that was to establish British naval supremacy on a global basis. Throughout, British warships were stationed world-wide, with major fleet actions occurring in the Channel, Atlantic, Baltic and Mediterranean. The royal dockyards, hard pushed to maintain a navy which had reached epic proportions, had a greatly increased work-force that was employed by both daylight and candlelight. No opportunities were missed in a constant programme of building, refitting, and repairing the nation's warships. It was a situation not to be witnessed again until our own century when, once again, invasion was threatened.

For the dockyard towns the Napoleonic Wars represented a boom period with regular work and high wages available. Between 1792 and 1801 there was a 50 per cent rise in the number of artisans and labourers employed, with both Portsmouth and Plymouth exceeding the three thousand total. These, of course, were the two busiest yards, continuing as naval bases and responsible for assembling the Channel and Western fleets respectively. From these two yards were prepared most of those vessels involved in such sea fights as the Glorious First of June (1794), Camperdown (1797), Nile (1798), Copenhagen (1801) and Trafalgar (1805).

Heavy repair and new construction work continued to be the province of the eastern yards, with Chatham, Deptford and Woolwich responsible for a great number of launchings. In this particular area Chatham still reigned supreme with just over thirty new launchings, amounting to 33,212 tons, during the French war period. At Woolwich there were twenty-five new launchings (22,063 tons) and at Deptford eighteen (22,229 tons). Most of these new vessels were third rates, frigates and sloops but several first rates were also constructed. Amongst these larger warships were the *Ville de Paris* (Chatham,

1795), *Queen Charlotte* (Deptford, 1810) and *Nelson* (Woolwich, 1814). Additionally Chatham undertook a major rebuild of the *Victory*.

The six established royal dockyards were in no position to undertake all the demands placed upon them, a situation which led to a number of merchant yards being contracted to build and repair smaller warships. Numerous brigs, sloops, frigates and third-rate 74s were built under contract, launchings taking place not only in the Thames and Medway, where the bulk of the private yards were to be found, but also in such diverse locations as Topsham, Harwich, Bristol and Buckler's Hard. For its part, the Navy Board preferred vessels to be built under direct government supervision, always suspecting the quality of merchant-built warships. For this reason a number of additional building yards were established where the Navy Board appointed its own officers. Amongst such yards, and each under the authority of a master shipwright, were those of Falmouth (1805), Milford (1810–13) and North Yarmouth (1807–14). Of these yards, that at Milford Haven is worth considering in more detail, as its establishment was directly responsible for a more permanent royal dockyard that was eventually founded close to Pembroke.

Following a recommendation made by Lord Nelson, land was first rented at Milford in the year 1800. At that time two French builders, Louis Barrallier and his son Louis Charles Barrallier, were placed in charge. Royalist sympathizers, they were appointed to teach local shipwrights the art of building ships to the more advanced French designs. Administratively the yard was not officially established until 1810, but it was building warships prior to that date. First of the Milford ships was the *Lavinia*, an 18-gun sloop launched in April 1804. Others quickly followed and included the 74-gun *Milford* of 1809. Commenting on all this in 1808, a visitor to the yard noted:

Just below the terrace on the south shore lies the dockyard, under the direction of Mr Louis Barrallier, a foreigner whose models and skill in shipbuilding are highly spoken of and approved. He has been appointed to superintend the building of three King's ships after his models. The 'Nautilus' and 'Lavinia' already built there and launched, have proved the best of their class, and the 'Milford' of 74 guns, now building and to be launched in the spring of 1809, will no doubt confirm the policy of keeping such a permanent institution in Milford Haven, and by that means securing a nursery of native artificers under an experienced naval architect, with all the advantages of the King's stores, and the best models to follow.

Since Milford was proving an increasingly successful venture, the Admiralty determined upon purchasing the land currently being used and decided upon a permanent establishment. At first negotiations went ahead without any problems until, with the death of one owner, the inheritor demanded a much larger sum of money. The result was the Admiralty purchasing alternative land on the opposite bank of the Haven at Pater. This was the future Pembroke dockyard. Work at Milford did not cease immediately as the *Rochefort*, a 74-gun third rate, was still under construction. Launched in April 1814 the yard at Milford was abandoned soon after.

With the global nature of the Napoleonic Wars, it was to be expected that the number of foreign yards would increase. Few, however, could provide anything more than careening facilities, as the building of dry-docks in foreign climes was not undertaken until the late nineteenth century. Amongst the more important foreign bases at this time were those of Antigua, Bermuda, Bombay, Gibraltar, Halifax, Jamaica and Port Mahon.* Of these, Antigua and Bermuda were relative newcomers, their importance accentuated by the loss of the American colonies. English Harbour, Antigua, was first used at the beginning of the eighteenth century and could then provide no more than an open beach. Improved facilities were developed throughout the century, with much being added during the 1770s and '80s. By the Napoleonic era English Harbour boasted stores, a boat-house, sail loft, capstan house, careening pit, saw house, copper stores and a house for the resident commissioner. Bermuda, established even later, was first used as a naval base in 1795. With rather limited facilities at that time, plans for a more extensive yard were enacted in 1809 when land was specifically purchased in the form of Ireland Island to the east of Bermuda. Amongst the earliest structures to be completed were storehouses, careening capstans, a boat shed and various residences.

The final conflict with France, ending in 1815, heralded a long period of unbroken peace. Theoretically, with renewed continental trade, it should have brought prosperity. This, however, was not to

---

* To this list might be added Toulon (captured and temporarily used in 1793), Corsica and Elba (1795 to 1797). In each case the Navy Board appointed a certain Mr Goderich as acting master shipwright to these captured foreign yards. In 1800 Malta was also acquired with Royal Navy warships using Grand Harbour, Valetta. Malta, though, was to become of much greater importance later in the century.

be. National unemployment was high and returning soldiers had difficulty in finding new jobs. For the dockyard towns life was particularly harsh. With a local economy geared to the needs of war, Chatham, Sheerness, Plymouth and Portsmouth all witnessed mass unemployment. Salvation, which could only come with war, or the threat of war, was not to arrive for a full three and a half decades. Meanwhile a period of unabated misery was unleashed.

Throughout the Napoleonic period the dockyard worker had been allowed extensive overtime. Often he worked a seven-day week, with an additional two to three hours allowed most evenings. Take home pay naturally increased, the amounts earned often being four times above normal. None of this continued; overtime disappeared and with the cessation of hostilities there followed an eventual reduction in the basic working week. Instead of being employed for six days (the basic working week) a five and a half day week was introduced and even this was eventually reduced to a mere five days. Income, of course, was reduced accordingly.

It was, however, the unemployed who suffered most. Huge lay-offs were witnessed at the older dockyards, with only Pembroke continuing to expand. The result was that in 1816 a number of the Portsmouth and Plymouth shipwrights moved to Pembroke, being the only means of securing work. The new dock town at Pembroke mushroomed with those entering the town sometimes being forced to occupy rooms before the floors had even been laid. Those who came to Pembroke under such circumstances frequently rented a suitable site and built their own accommodation. Short of money, the resulting cottages were of a rather squalid nature – those in Bush Street, for example, were derisively termed Pigs' Parade. According to one writer who was referring to this rapidly built housing, 'a man could put his arm through the chimney and open the front door'.

As a royal dockyard Pembroke was officially established in October 1815, being placed under the immediate control of a master shipwright whose wage was set at £600 per year. At that time the yard encompassed 87 acres upon which a few timber workshops had been erected, whilst a frigate, the *Lapwing*, had been run ashore to provide office accommodation. With no proper covered slipways two vessels then under construction, the *Valorious* and *Ariadne*, were being built in the open. Both 28-gun frigates they were to be launched in February 1816. Enclosing the entire dockyard was a paling fence serving only as a demarcation marker, being low enough to jump.

Work was in hand for the improvement of the dockyard, with contractors employed upon building a more substantial brick wall, further stores and covered slipways. A sketch of the dockyard, completed in 1817, clearly shows such a slipway, with its design very similar to those already constructed at Plymouth and Chatham. The first vessel built under the new covering was the *Racer*, a small cutter launched in April 1818. More building slips, a dry-dock and a chapel were to follow during the 1830s. By that time the dockyard had been officially designated Pembroke, its former title of Pater Yard all but forgotten. The nearby community had also taken on the new name, being known as Pembroke Dock.

The considerable expenditure upon Pembroke meant less being available for the more established yards. Nevertheless, some new works were put in hand, whilst a number of older buildings were repaired. Chatham, for instance, received a new dry-dock, built by convicts, whilst most yards saw additional covered slips introduced. At Sheerness on the other hand, a more ambitious scheme was approved, with much of the dockyard redesigned and numerous modern features introduced.

Reference should be made to a number of iron-framed buildings which were being constructed in the yards. Amongst the earliest of these was the Portsmouth pay office of 1798, an undistinguished building that was to be the forerunner of greater things. Fine examples of such buildings and still to be seen at Portsmouth are the Old Fire Station (1843), No 6 Boathouse (1843) and the No 3 Ship Shop (1846) and at Sheerness the Boathouse (1859). This last is a four-storey, iron-framed building some 200ft in length and is one of the earliest multi-storey, iron-framed buildings in existence. Other examples of iron-framed buildings are to be found at Chatham and Plymouth but those built at Woolwich, such as the steam-hammer house and forge of 1818, have been demolished. Certain of the covered slips, particularly those built at Chatham from 1846 onwards, are also of iron construction.

Plans were first put in hand for the modernization of Sheerness yard as early as 1813 when John Rennie was commissioned to oversee new construction work. During the French wars period, Sheerness had proved a particularly useful dockyard, its limited resources coming under great pressure. Admittedly thoughts had turned to consideration of its closure, since it was exposed and ships anchored off Sheerness were frequently subjected to damage. As an alternative site for a dockyard, the Isle of Grain had been advocated by several

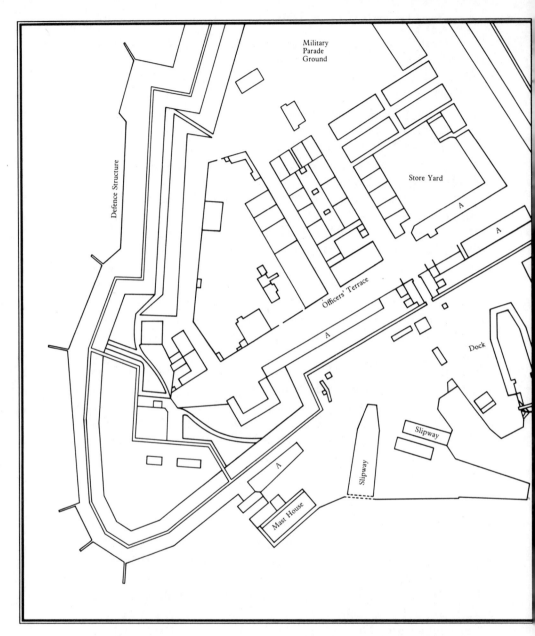

Military
Parade
Ground

Defence Structure

Store Yard

A

A

Officers' Terrace

A

Dock

Slipway

Slipway

A

Mast House

experts amongst whom were Samuel Bentham. Lying on the opposite shore of the Medway and in the lee of prevailing winds, Grain had the added advantage of allowing unrestricted development. The wartime emergency precluded the adoption of such a scheme, and later economies killed it altogether.

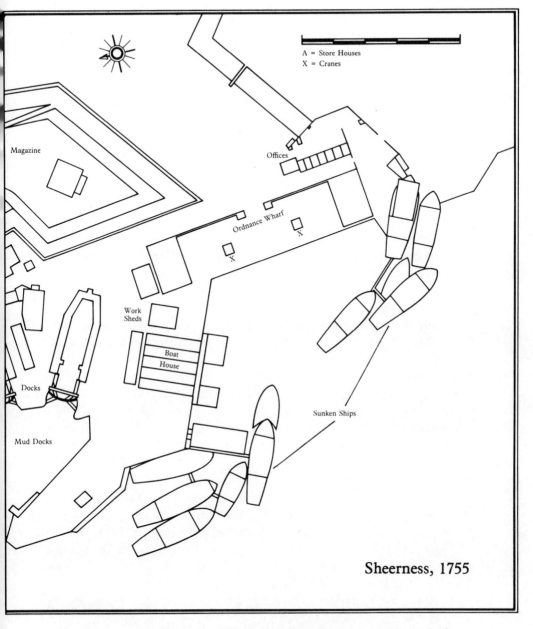

But Sheerness was in need of modernization; few improvements had been made since the early eighteenth century, whilst the entire yard was in a state of disrepair. Rennie's improvement scheme – virtually an entire rebuilding of the yard – was originally supposed to include a wet-dock and five stone dry-docks, but the number of dry-docks was reduced to three. Additionally a sea wall, mast pond and locks were constructed. With the work completed by September 1823 at a total cost of £2,586,083, the complex was opened by the Duke of Clarence, the future King William IV, at a special ceremony.

Administrative changes in the bodies governing the royal dockyards were overdue by the early nineteenth century. In 1832 the Navy Board was abolished whilst in 1834 a special dockyard police force was created. The Navy Board, responsible for administering the dockyards, had become an amorphous body renowned for its inefficiencies. Also responsible for stores, hospitals and barracks, the Board seemed incapable of running even one of these institutions satisfactorily. The result was that the Admiralty, following an Act of Parliament, took direct responsibility for the various areas of administration, including the dockyards. Four naval lords (the future sea lords) were given combined responsibilities for both the fleet and the dockyards with a direct link to each yard via specially appointed naval superintendents; it was they who replaced the resident commissioners, being drawn from naval officers not lower than the rank of captain.

The other administrative change referred to, the creation of a dockyard police force, was a short-lived affair. Replacing the rounders, porters and watchmen that had been created at the time of Samuel Pepys, they themselves were replaced in 1860. At this time the Metropolitan Police (Dockyard Division) was formed and they continued to serve until 1934. The Royal Marine Police was then formed, followed in 1949 by the Admiralty Constabulary. Dockyards are currently in the hands of the Ministry of Defence Police, a body which replaced the Admiralty Constabulary in 1960.

It was during the first few years of Queen Victoria's reign that the name of Devonport was officially instituted. The local township of Plymouth Dock first adopted the name Devonport in 1824, but the dockyard itself retained the earlier name. Eventually, in 1843 at the time of a visit made by Queen Victoria, the name of Devonport was also transferred to the dockyard.

At the same time as the administrative changes, the royal dockyards were having to adapt to technical changes resulting from the use of steam power at sea. In 1822 the wooden paddle steamer *Comet* was launched at Deptford, being the first such vessel built in any of the government dockyards. Subsequently used as a harbour tug, she was only 150ft long and powered by a side-lever engine capable of producing 80hp, fitted by Maudslay, Sons & Field whose works were at

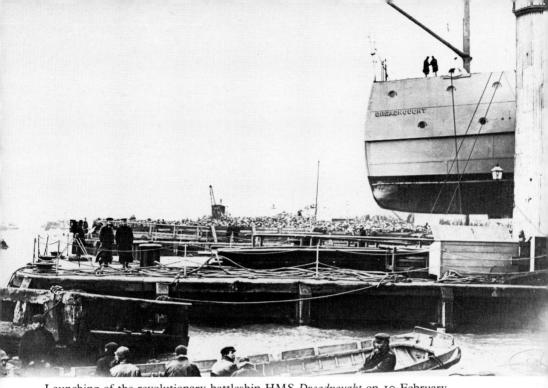

Launching of the revolutionary battleship HMS *Dreadnought* on 10 February 1906. Within a few years, war at sea had been totally transformed (*Prescott Frost Collection, Portsmouth Central Library*)

Portsmouth dockyard, c1900. A carefully posed photograph which shows members of the Metropolitan Police (Dockyard Division) in their secondary fire-fighting role. Behind them is the cast-iron water tower, built in 1843, which originally supported a massive water tank used mainly for fire-fighting purposes

Rosyth under construction. With the Forth Railway Bridge clearly visible in the distance, work is in hand upon the tidal basin (*Dunfermline Central Library*)

Visit of King George V to Rosyth dockyard in 1916 (*Dunfermline Central Library*)

Lambeth. The royal dockyards then had neither the capacity nor the expertise to undertake such work so the manufacture and fitting of engines had to be left to the private sector. Following the launch of the *Comet* came the *Lightning* of 1823, a further Deptford-built paddle steamer. Fitted with three guns, she had the honour of being the first steam warship in the Royal Navy to go into action, being used against Barbary Coast pirates.

A limited number of other steam-powered warships followed, construction being initially limited to the two Thames-side yards. A growth in demand led to other yards sharing in their construction with paddle sloops being launched in 1832 at Chatham, Plymouth and Sheerness.* As with so many other steamships of this period, these sloops were of a hybrid design, being fitted with sail. For its part, the Admiralty did not wish to build too many steam-powered warships, recognizing the vulnerability of huge paddle wheels which also restricted the number of guns that could be mounted. It was only when the paddle was replaced by the screw that such disadvantages were overcome.

In 1832 the dockyard at Deptford was temporarily closed. Long recognized as an ill-suited yard for repairing vessels, it had been engaged of late in the construction of very small warships. Its proximity to the Maudslay works at Lambeth had boosted its usefulness for a short period, but its key role in the building of steam vessels was soon acquired by Woolwich. The site of the former dockyard was not abandoned for, in 1833, the area was utilized as a centre for the breaking up of old warships. In 1844 the entire dockyard was reopened and again used for building warships. First of the vessels to be launched at Deptford during this time of resuscitation was the *Worcester*, a 50-gun man-of-war that had remained on the stocks since the 1830s. Deptford was finally closed in 1869.

It was not until the 1840s that the royal dockyards started to develop a work-force skilled in the manufacture and repair of steam engines. At first all such machinery had been installed and repaired by the manufacturers but in 1843 all this was to change with the completion and opening of the Woolwich Steam Factory. Part of Woolwich dockyard, it was a 7-acre extension which included all the

---

* The names of the 1832 paddle sloops, and in each case representing the first steam launchings at each yard named, were: *Phoenix* (Chatham), *Salamander* (Sheerness) and *Rhadamanthus* (Plymouth). First Woolwich-built steamer was the *Echo* (1827) whilst at Portsmouth it was the *Hermes* (1835)

paraphernalia required for the maintenance of large ship engines. Included was a vertical-cylinder boring mill, a triple iron shed and the steam engine factory itself. New dry-docks, a wet-dock, building slips and mast house were also added whilst the years immediately following saw the enlargement of the older dry-docks. The contractors for the extension were Messrs Grissel and Peto who were paid £80,000. For Woolwich town it acted as a great boost for the local economy as the steam factory was soon employing a thousand men and boys.

Before long, and resulting from a rapid increase in the use of steam, the Woolwich Steam Factory was strained beyond its comparatively meagre limits. Furthermore the siting of Woolwich yard, so far up river, meant that it was not particularly well suited to the task of maintaining the larger vessels which were being driven by steam power. All this resulted in a government announcement of 1843 that three additional steam centres would be created – at Plymouth, Portsmouth and Malta.

Undoubtedly the largest of these new centres was Portsmouth. Some 20 acres in extent, it was built to the north of the seventeenth-century wet-dock upon land specially taken over. At the centre of the new extension was a 900ft × 400ft wet-dock, known as the Great Steam Basin, whilst to one side were built three dry-docks. Other important structures were the No 2 Ship Shop (1847–9), used for the building and repair of vessels, the No 3 Ship Shop (1845–6), in which engines were constructed and the No 1 Smithery (1852). The Great Steam Basin was opened by Queen Victoria in May 1848.

At Devonport the new steam yard had also to be built as an extension, with a 7-acre site being acquired near Keyham Point. A detached area it had to be linked to the main dockyard by a 900yd tunnel. Construction of the Keyham Yard began in 1844 when the world's first steam-powered pile driver, designed by James Nasmyth, began work on a coffer dam. Able to deliver blows at the rate of eighty per minute, this 4-ton steam hammer was soon driving huge piles to the required depth in only 4½ minutes compared with more than 12 hours working by the old method. Upon its opening in 1853, the new steam yard at Keyham included two basins, three docks, foundries, machine shops, offices and the factory building itself.

The steam yard at Malta was a much smaller affair, consisting of little more than one dry-dock (1848) and the requisite number of storehouses and machine shops. Malta had little history as a naval dockyard, being in Admiralty hands only since the beginning of the century, yet its strategic value was to be increasingly recognized throughout the following decades. Steam-powered warships were in constant use by the mid-nineteenth century in the Mediterranean where improved facilities had long been overdue. The dockyard at Malta was eventually to have five dry-docks and was even being earmarked for the construction of ships in the 1880s when a slipway was added and work began on a frigate, the *Melita*. The experiment proved unsuccessful as building time was twice that of a sloop constructed in one of the home yards.

In the 1850s a further technical advance had to be taken into account by the royal dockyards when the advantages of iron construction became more apparent. Since 1842 the 70-ton *Rocket*, a commercially built iron paddle steamer had been in use at Woolwich dockyard but the Admiralty remained unconvinced as to the advantages of such material for warships. Even as late as 1851 the Admiralty had proved to itself that such material was useless: tests were undertaken at Portsmouth in which a dockyard-produced target, built to represent part of an iron frigate, had been fired upon. So weakened had the material become that any ship so attacked would have been in danger of sinking. Similar tests upon timber-built ships were not carried out, however.

The conclusions of 1851 had to be completely reassessed in the light of the Crimean War and the defeats constantly suffered by timber warships when under shell fire. At first, however, little was done; the Admiralty simply preferred to cling to the familiar. But when, towards the end of the 1850s, a warmongering French government sanctioned the building of an ironclad battleship, the British Admiralty had to follow. The outcome was that in May 1859 the Thames Ironworks at Blackwall was instructed to build an iron-framed and armoured battleship. Subsequently named *Warrior* she was the nation's first modern warship.*

The first armoured battleship built at a royal dockyard was the *Achilles*, launched at Chatham in 1863. Vessels such as the *Achilles* have to be regarded as largely experimental; the royal yards had no experience of ironclads and their potential was being assessed by the

---

* A point worth noting about the *Warrior* is her continued survival into the twentieth century. For many years she was retained at Pembroke dockyard, but is currently being restored at Hartlepool. It is possible that she might later be brought either to Portsmouth or Chatham for permanent display.

Admiralty. The yards had come under a great deal of criticism; it was frequently claimed that the private yards were more advanced and better able to handle such work. Indeed, a powerful lobby supported and financed by merchant contractors suggested that all royal yards should be closed and their work undertaken by the private sector.

As might be expected, the period during which the *Achilles* was built was extremely hectic; a great amount of new machinery was introduced into Chatham yard, including a Nasmyth steam hammer, specialised bending, cutting and drilling equipment whilst No 1 dock was lengthened and transformed into a giant covered workshop. It was here that the metal plates were assembled and then transferred to the *Achilles* which was under construction in No 2 dock.

At the time of her completion the *Achilles* was one of the largest warships in the world. She had a total length of 380ft and displaced some 9,820 tons. This may not sound much in this day and age but sufficient to say that the *Achilles* dwarfed the *Victory* and every other ship ever built in the royal dockyards. Like so many other vessels built at this time the *Achilles* was a hybrid, having steam engines below and rigging above. Replete with canvas sufficient to cover a total area of 50,000 sq ft she also had 750 tons of coal in her bunkers. With thirty miles of rigging cordage she also carried a 12½-ton screw propeller. Because of the great amount of deck clutter produced by three masts and two funnels, her considerable array of guns were mounted on the broadside pattern. It was not until masts and rigging could be totally dispensed with that central turrets were introduced to the upper decks.

Despite her hybrid appearance the building of the *Achilles* signified a watershed. Before the *Achilles* the royal yards had built nothing but ships of timber. Within a few years all was to be changed. The government dockyards, accepting this new challenge and proving themselves capable of competing with the private yards, were transformed. A new era had begun.

11
The New Era

The launch of the *Achilles* was an event accompanied by relief within all the dockyard towns; too many people had been suggesting that the royal dockyards were entirely out of date and would be unable to construct one of the new ironclads. All, however, were proved wrong by events at Chatham: not only was the *Achilles* completed within three and a half years of being laid down – a time span not dissimilar from the private yards – but she was also an advance upon previously built ironclads, being armoured both on the water-line and above. Moreover, her construction was just as sound as the ironclads built at private yards, with her building costs remaining well below the extravagant sums that had been predicted by those opposed to the continued existence of the royal dockyards.

As well as being a vindication of the royal dockyards as a whole, the building of the *Achilles* also marked a turning point for government-employed shipwrights. Previously their skills had been directed entirely towards the construction of timber-built warships with only a limited knowledge of the use of iron. Now things had to change; they had either to learn new skills or be replaced. In the private yards, where shipwrights had refused to accept change, a new kind of worker had emerged in the form of the boilermaker and ironsmith. Superseding the commercially employed shipwright, they now handled a high proportion of all shipbuilding outside the royal yards. A similar situation looked as if it was about to occur at Chatham when the *Achilles* was laid down, with large numbers of ironworkers being admitted into the dockyards. In February 1861 Lord Paget, Secretary to the Admiralty, announced a drastic cut-back in dockyard shipwrights, their numbers being replaced by those skilled in the building of iron ships.

At Chatham during the 'tooling up' period, there were immediate fears of mass redundancy. For shipwrights the future looked bleak, with many receiving formal notice of dismissal. Some, however, were designated for retraining, but the majority saw poverty as the only future. Then, in July 1862, events took a sudden and dramatic turn. The ironsmiths, in a burst of trade solidarity, refused to train any more shipwrights, calling upon the Admiralty to employ only those who had served a full ironsmith's apprenticeship. Surprised, if not a little put out, the dockyard authorities refused to accommodate such demands. This, of course, might have been the end of the matter but, as it happens, the ironsmiths forced the issue by calling a lightning strike and picketing the main gate. Doubtless they felt secure in the belief that work on the *Achilles* could not be continued without them – a miscalculation that was to have considerable repercussions. Within the dockyard, members of a small rival union to the one calling the strike had remained at work and were now used by the Admiralty in a rapid retraining programme. Two hundred odd shipwrights were transferred to the *Achilles* whilst many previously dismissed were re-engaged. The result was that numerous shipwrights became competent ironsmiths and were soon training their own apprentices. The *Achilles*, completed by shipwrights, was a victory for a threatened trade and, because of these events at Chatham, shipwrights still predominate in each of the royal dockyards.

Although the *Achilles* was the first iron-hulled battleship to be built in any of the royal dockyards, its launch was actually preceded by that of four iron cased but timber-hulled warships. These were the *Prince Consort* (launched Pembroke, June 1862), *Caledonia* (Woolwich, October 1862), *Royal Oak* (Chatham, September 1862) and *Ocean* (Devonport, March 1863). A further five ironclads of a similar type followed the launching of the *Achilles*, these being the *Royal Alfred* (Portsmouth, October 1864), *Zealous* (Pembroke, March 1864), *Repulse* (Woolwich, October 1866). *Favorite* (Deptford, July 1864) and *Royal Sovereign* (Portsmouth, 1864). Ordered during the 1860s, these vessels had been originally designed as traditional timber-built fighting vessels of a type commonly constructed within the royal dockyards. In 1861, with the French already building ironclads, it was decided to convert a number of ships then under construction or nearing completion. The first of these, the *Prince Consort*, was originally laid down at the Pembroke yard in August 1860, being then designated a 90-gun second rate. Only partially complete by May 1861, she was ordered to be given iron plates over the timber hull. To accommodate the increased weight her two gun decks were cut down to one, so reducing the number of guns to thirty-three. A further measure concerned an increase in the length of the hull, compensating for the loss of the upper gun deck. This was done through the simple expediency of cutting her in two, pulling the sections apart and placing a new frame in the middle. Care had to be taken that the newly inserted portion was of sufficient strength to support the engines. As first of the timber-framed ironclads, the *Prince Consort* met with a few construction problems of which one concerned coppering. This, of course, created an electrical reaction with subsequent corrosion. A Muntz-type metal was eventually substituted.

The other iron-cased vessels were similarly converted, with each an improvement on predecessors. Whereas, for instance, the *Prince Consort* received plates of 4½in, combined with sixteen 7in and four 8in guns, the *Repulse* received 6in plates, together with twelve of the much more powerful 8in guns, and the much later *Prince Alfred* ten 9in guns. The *Royal Sovereign*, one of the last of this series, was different again in that she received circular open-top armoured turrets (as opposed to the more common broadside pattern), whilst all her rigging was removed, leaving her dependent entirely upon steam.

The conversion of these timber-hulled vessels was, of course, no more than a stop-gap measure designed to overcome a temporary fear that the French might soon be in a position to dominate the oceans with their own ironclads. Naturally emphasis was placed on the construction of purpose-built iron-hulled warships, with a number being launched in the royal dockyards. Chatham remained supreme in this field, launching the *Bellerophon* (April 1865), *Hercules* (February 1868) and *Monarch* (May 1868). Of the other royal yards, the armoured corvettes *Pallas* and *Penelope* were launched at Woolwich (March 1868) and Pembroke (June 1867) respectively. In March 1870 the *Iron Duke*, protected by 6in and 8in iron plates, was launched at Pembroke followed by the *Devastation* at Portsmouth in July 1871. This last was a further example of a turreted ship for she, like the *Royal Sovereign*, had all masts and sails removed and massive 35-ton, 12in muzzle loaders placed on deck. Extensively armoured throughout, the thickness of some of her plates measured 14in.

The changeover to the building of iron warships meant many alterations to the royal dockyards. Not only was much new equipment added but, with vessels frequently a great deal longer than their timber counterparts, many of the already existing dry-docks and slipways had to be extended. At Chatham the revolution in shipbuilding actually coincided with a previously agreed extension scheme, whilst at Portsmouth a new extension was begun in 1867. Woolwich and Deptford yards, on the other hand, were closed as a result of the newly introduced shipbuilding material.

Work on the Chatham dockyard extension programme was started in 1862, being designed to both expand and modernize the existing facilities. It was the most complete renewal programme ever carried out at Chatham, with 380 acres added to the existing site of 97 acres. Much of the new work was concentrated on St Mary's Island, a newly reclaimed piece of marshland which had been specially purchased. Included in the new construction work were three basins, large numbers of machine-shops and four dry-docks. Total expenditure amounted to £3 million, with building work essentially complete by 1885. The basins, built along the line of St Mary's creek, were the first wet-docks ever built at Chatham, each designed for a specialized role. The largest was a 28-acre refitting basin whilst the other two, both of 21 acres, were for repairing and fitting out. Leading off the repairing basin were the four dry-docks, each a uniform 469½ft. Also constructed were a factory building, a pumping station and hydraulic capstan. Much of the work was undertaken by convict labour, housed in an immense prison built on St Mary's Island. Before this, convicts used in dockyard work had been housed in numerous rotting hulks moored in the Medway. Amongst the prisoners brought to Chatham were Irish Fenians convicted of plotting explosions within the central London area.

At Portsmouth, where the extension was built on newly acquired land to the north, the total size of the yard was increased from 116 to 300 acres. Proposed during the year 1864 and finally agreed in 1867, the extension included a refitting basin (14 acres), rigging basin (17 acres) and a repairing basin (22 acres). As at Chatham a number of dry-docks, eventually totalling four, led out of the repairing basin, with the final two being added in 1896. Varying in length, the smallest of these docks was 456ft long and the largest 564ft. During construction of the final pair it is said that 1,100 men were employed. The extension as a whole was opened in 1876 and then included numerous workshops, steam-powered machines, brass foundries, an electrical shop, specialized equipment for handling iron plates and a pair of steam-operated sheer legs that were capable of lifting 160 tons. At the time these sheers were considered most impressive as they could be extended 40ft over the vast repairing basin. Large numbers of convicts were constantly employed in digging out foundations and similar unskilled tasks. In common with Chatham a public works prison was built. Much of the displaced soil was removed to Whale Island to create a much larger island of 1½ miles in circumference. This then became a naval gunnery school, being christened HMS *Excellent*. Previously the gunnery section had been housed in a series of hulks.

The closure of the Woolwich and Deptford yards really emerged out of a government scheme, announced in July 1864, to concentrate on fewer shipbuilding centres. It was suggested that Devonport and certain of the overseas yards should be expanded, while Pembroke, Woolwich and Deptford would be closed. Discussions went ahead, but it was soon clear that Pembroke was undertaking such important shipbuilding works that closure was out of the question. The closures of Deptford and Woolwich were announced in March 1868 and January 1869 respectively. Both yards were closed in late 1869.

It is difficult to envisage the crisis which enveloped the townships surrounding the two doomed dockyards. Whilst many were promised alternative employment at both Chatham and Portsmouth, 563 were dismissed in the subsequent run-down period. Most of those offered alternative dockyard work had to leave an area within which they had acquired long and deep associations. Families were split up and houses had to be sold at rock bottom prices. In the end some 1,235 were transferred to other dockyards, mostly Chatham, and another 249 were given early pensions. A final group received assistance in emigrating to one of the colonies. A mass of equipment was also transferred to Chatham, further helping this yard to take over all work previously handled by the Woolwich steam yard.

The mid-Victorian period, then, witnessed a great many changes within the royal dockyards. Throughout the emphasis was on efficiency and economy, with a greater acceptance of innovation. Portsmouth, of course, remained the premier yard with a work force that had reached 7,615 by 1890. Much of the yard, and particularly those parts established during the eighteenth century, had been converted to an alternative use. Dominating part of this new area, for instance, was Anchor Lane, the site where huge anchors, in long lines and regular order, were assembled like an invading army that had been drawn from the novels of H. G. Wells. Buildings, too, were converted. The great rope-house, once the target for James Aitken's incendiarist attack, was disestablished in 1868 and converted to storage.

Work at Portsmouth was still diversified, embracing shipbuilding, repair and maintenance whilst successfully mastering new techniques. Whilst the first Portsmouth ironclad had not been launched until 1869, this singularly late start was followed by a rapid succession of new and improved designs. It was at Portsmouth that the first of any new class was to be laid down, a fact signalled by the launch of the *Inflexible* in 1876. A forerunner of future big-gun ships the *Inflexible* was armed with four huge 16in guns that were located in two armoured turrets which weighed 750 tons each. Other important lead ships launched at Portsmouth were the *Royal Sovereign* (1891), *Majestic* (1895), *Canopus* (1897), *Formidable* (1898) and *London* (1899).

The second most important royal dockyard during this mid-Victorian period was that of Chatham. Temporarily at least it had regained much of its earlier prestige with the building and pioneering of the early ironclad designs. With the extension complete, numbers employed were well in excess of rival Devonport, a total figure of 5,670 being recorded at Chatham during the year 1890. Sharing with Portsmouth a large proportion of all new construction work, Chatham was launching an average of two new warships a year. Largest of these vessels were the *Venerable* and *Irresistible*, both 15,000 tons, although many of the Chatham launchings were an array of smaller vessels such as the new torpedo gunboats and cruiser types. Yet Chatham was soon to be facing serious problems. The large-scale extension scheme was a product of the 1860s and few envisaged the massive size that future warships, such as the Dreadnoughts and super Dreadnoughts, would reach. Eventually facilities at Chatham became too restricted for these larger battleships, and Chatham was soon relegated to the handling of a smaller class of vessel.

In the year 1890 the combined work force for the Devonport and Keyham yards was 5,206. Suffering from a loss of status, Devonport was no longer building the very largest of battleships. Between 1870 and 1890 the main concentration of work was upon the building of gunboats. In 1890, however, the 7,350-ton cruiser *Edgar* was launched at Devonport being, at that time, the largest possible ship that could be launched within the yard. At her launching the *Edgar* had a clearance space of only a few inches, and it was evident that much work had to be undertaken if such drawbacks were to be overcome.

It was during the 1890s that work started upon the improvement of the two West Country yards. Within the older Devonport section (nowadays known as the south yard) both slipways and dry-docks were improved, whilst Keyham (the present-day north yard), witnessed a general extension programme. Of particular importance to Devonport was the construction of a new slip, replacing the old mast pond which had been filled in, and suitable for the building of battleships. Extending some 750ft it brought new work to the yard: the first battleship built at Devonport was the 12,950-ton *Ocean,* laid down on 15 February 1897. Sixteen and a half months on the slipway, she was not completed until February 1900, being much delayed by the non-delivery of materials. Other vessels built at this time were the ram cruisers *Arrogant* (1895) and *Furious* (1896), together with the battleships *Implacable* (1898) and *Prince Edward* (1902). All were built on the new slipway. Other changes to Devonport were the building of the No 3 dock on the site of the old Union Dock, whilst an old graving dock was replaced by a new jetty and sheer legs. A new drawing office, mould loft and the No 4 machine shop also date from this era.

It was in 1899 that construction work began on a northward extension to Keyham yard. Estimated to cost £4 million the scheme included two tidal basins and two dry-docks, bringing shipyard facilities in this area to a total of 246 acres. For nearly seven years the excavation, reclamation and construction work was carried on at a quite incredible pace, the official opening ceremony being conducted in February 1907. By then two basins, one of 10 acres and the other of 34, together with two dry-docks had been completed. These last measured 650ft and 790ft in length. An additional two locks had also been constructed. The extension, though, was still not completed; a number of workshops and a cantilever crane were not finished until 1910.

Following the Devonport and Keyham yards, Pembroke was probably next in importance. Employing a work force of 2,092 in 1890, it differed from the other yards in that it concentrated entirely upon the building of ships. Encompassing an 80-acre area it was a remarkably modern yard, having all the facilities necessary for launching the very largest of vessels. Amongst the more notable ships built at Pembroke were the *Repulse* (1892) and *Hannibal* (1896) both of which were advanced battleships displacing in excess of 14,000 tons. Pembroke possessed thirteen building slips but only one dry-dock where launched vessels were taken for completion. The general facilities are best conveyed by a description of the yard that was first published in 1875:

Workshops necessarily abound here: there are joiners', millwrights', blacksmiths', plumbers', coppersmiths', coopers', wheelwrights', painters', pattern-makers, and armour plating shops. But among the many we have enumerated, perhaps that of the blacksmiths will attract the greatest attention. Here are about 200 busy hands, all dimly seen working amid heated air, smoke, and the glare of the numerous glowing fires of its forges; and on all sides is heard the din, clang and clash of hammers and machinery forging and manufacturing the various kinds of heavy iron work now so requisite in the present advanced state of shipbuilding. Here, also, are three immense steam hammers, beneath whose ponderous heads ponderous masses of red hot iron are continually becoming subject to their will. Adjoining is the Galvanizing Shop, where the process of galvanizing all the small iron work, in order to prevent it rusting, is going on.

At the west side of the yard are the steam saw mills, worked by the aid of very powerful machinery; the sawing room is well worthy of a visit. To the south of these where the open space is chiefly used for the stacking of wood, is a large square basin, known as the 'pickling pond', in which the elm and pine timber is kept, to prevent it decaying before being taken into use.

Near the docks lie numberless armour plates, varying in thickness from two to fourteen inches, destined to cover the sides of those powerful ships of war, which are being constructed in the neighbouring sheds; the machinery for boring these plates for the rivets, and for shaving and shaping them to the turns of the ship's sides also exists here.

Sheerness, smallest of the older established home yards, now concentrated upon repair and maintenance, having only one building slip. With a work-force that had never exceeded two thousand, the yard had changed very little since 1823. As a dockyard it was heavily dependent upon Chatham and tended to be used as an advanced base for those vessels entering and leaving Chatham. Numerous ships, therefore, anchored at Sheerness both for compass adjustment and the taking on of coal and ammunition. An interesting description of the yard appeared in the November 1901 edition of *The Army and Navy Illustrated*:

At the present time the establishment possesses three docks entered from the steam basin, and two from the lower camber, as well as one important building slip adjoining to the latter. The dockyard basin is 521-ft. long, and has an extreme breadth of a little over 300-ft., and upon its margin are the great mast sheers and boiler sheers, as well as a powerful crane. The largest of the docks is No. 3, with a length of 286-ft. 8-in. No. 1 dock is only a few inches less, but No. 2 dock, which is housed in, does not exceed 224-ft. Two of these docks have been increased in length by about 25-ft. since they were first constructed, and the Admiralty some years ago entertained the idea of still further enlargement, in order that second class cruisers, or even larger vessels, might be docked but for various reasons which do not seem to be well known, but which were doubtless concerned with considerations of high policy, the idea seems to have been abandoned. Docks Nos. 4 and 5, which are entered from the lower camber, are smaller than the others, and are adapted for sloops and gun boats only. All the docks at Sheerness are of the best workmanship, and in their character leave little to desire, although the officers of the yard may well wish they were adapted for larger work. It must, however, be remembered that Sheerness and Chatham are in a very real sense sister establishments, each being complementary to the other, and that what Sheerness cannot do can be undertaken with ease at the larger yard. . . .

One further home yard has yet to be mentioned – Haulbowline, situated on an island in Cork Harbour. Not to become fully operational until 1894, building of this dockyard began during the 1860s. At that time a good deal of land had been reclaimed adjacent to Haulbowline Island preparatory to the building of docking facilities. It was within the man-made extension to the island that a 9-acre wet-dock was constructed with a 417ft dry-dock leading out of the south-east side. Much of this work was carried out by convict labour brought from the nearby prison on Spike Island. Haulbowline was never to be a particularly large dockyard, employing a total of 619 men in 1903. Strategically placed, Haulbowline was designed to provide fleet maintenance facilities and its one dock, amongst the largest in the country, was able to accommodate the very largest of naval warships.

Of the foreign naval yards, Malta was clearly the most important; it was here that the Mediterranean fleet was based, with maintenance, docking and coaling facilities available. In 1871 a second dry-dock had been opened and other improvements made, whilst in 1889 the entrance to Grand Harbour was given a torpedo-proof breakwater. The Mediterranean, of course, was a particularly important centre of naval activity during these years, the navy being used to keep a watchful eye upon rapidly changing events in France, Italy and the Balkan countries. The opening of the Suez Canal in 1869 brought even greater prominence to the area, leading to the creation of further dockyard facilities on the island of Gibraltar. In 1890 the decision was taken to modernize the harbour and restructure the dockyard, work beginning in 1895. At that time three dry-docks, coaling facilities, cranes and workshops were added. The dockyard at Gibraltar, however, was not particularly well placed, being sited to the west of the island within range of Spanish artillery fire. For this reason an eastern dockyard, sheltered by the tremendous height of the rock itself, was proposed. A £20 million scheme, nothing came of the idea.

The dockyard at Antigua, little changed since the days of Nelson, was rarely used and was abandoned in 1899. Bermuda, on the other hand, was built up during this period and by the later years of Queen Victoria's reign included a large number of working sheds and stores. In 1869 a floating dock, the largest in the world, was taken to Bermuda, but remained in use for only a few years, being damaged by hurricanes in 1878. A second floating dry-dock arrived in 1906, a few years after work had started on a new extension at the yard.

As a world-wide policing force the Royal Navy had a great number of bases throughout the world which provided a variety of facilities. For the most part, however, these bases, such as Singapore, Madeira, St Vincent and Weihaiwei, were little more than coaling yards.

The preceding account of the royal dockyards takes the story to the very beginning of the twentieth century. The Victorian years, with their rapid progress, had virtually changed the yards out of all recognition. Most had certainly grown in size, with the home yards employing, during the year 1900, a total work-force of 32,353. This represented a total increase of 35 per cent since the year 1800. Admittedly Woolwich and Deptford had been closed, but Chatham's extension had provided adequate compensation whilst Keyham and Portsmouth had also grown.

In many respects, a similar pattern of events was to recur in the twentieth century. Whilst none of the dockyards were to receive major extension programmes, some were closed and others given increased facilities to compensate. The docks and slipways were to receive most attention for, whilst the nineteenth century had provided adequate land for future buildings, nobody had predicted a continued growth in the size of warships. Beginning with the Dreadnoughts and super Dreadnoughts, the royal yards had to be constantly updated to cope. In this respect, Portsmouth and Devonport became the real beneficiaries with Chatham, unable to handle such vessels, beginning to concentrate on submarines. Pembroke was eventually closed during the inter-war period whilst a new yard was established at Rosyth.

12
The Dreadnoughts

On Monday 12 February 1906, at around noon, the revolutionary new battleship, HMS *Dreadnought*, was launched into the cold waters of Portsmouth Harbour, an event that was to change naval warfare completely. The Dreadnought, first of the all big-gun ships, was soon to be the most powerful vessel afloat, being better armed and faster than any comparable warship. Ten 12in guns meant that the Dreadnought could successfully engage at a greater distance than any rival, whilst recently developed Parson turbine engines, allowing a maximum speed of 21 knots, gave her the ability to outrun any potential opponent. Even her armouring was superior: whilst most battleships possessed 7in plating, the *Dreadnought* had 11in.

The *Dreadnought* suddenly made obsolete all battleships in service and under construction. *Hibernia*, for instance, a battleship launched at Devonport only eight months earlier was such an example; possessing only four of the extremely powerful 12in guns, plating of just 9in and a maximum speed of 19 knots, the *Hibernia* was clearly inferior. Additionally it should be noted that the *Hibernia* was 1,000 tons lighter and was 35ft shorter than *Dreadnought*. Apart from having only triple-expansion engines and lighter armouring, the main reason for the *Hibernia*'s obsolescence was nothing less than a lack of fire power – she was not an all big-gun ship, having a mixed armament which included the smaller 9.2in and 6in guns. As a result, a much closer range was required which effectively meant that a vessel such as *Hibernia* might well be a useless heap of scrap metal long before her guns could be effectively engaged in conflict with a vessel such as the *Dreadnought*.

Returning to that memorable day in February 1906, it is worth considering the all-important event in a little more detail. *The Times*, in common with so many other newspapers, had a correspondent present: 'The crowds were enormous, and the space in which they congregated was so vast as to preclude the making of any trustworthy estimate of their size in arithmetical terms.' A launch of any new vessel from a royal dockyard has always been a fairly grandiose affair, and that of the *Dreadnought* was no exception. Apart from specially invited guests and many of the dockyard workers themselves, the general public also attended, many of whom arrived by special train from London. Most important of all, however, was the presence of the king himself. Brought to the dockyard by the royal yacht *Victoria and Albert*, he was there to conduct the launching, an event noticed by the entire nation.

Celebrations overall, however, were a little restrained due to the recent death of the King of Denmark, a distant relative of Edward VII. Normally the launch of a new battleship would have been marked by a display of flags, bunting and specially erected arches, but these were felt inappropriate for a king in mourning. Nevertheless *The Times* felt it was an opportunity to wax lyrical:

> . . . the ceremony itself, while it was very simple, was so impressive and so beautiful as to be quite independent of any artificial enhancement. There are few acts more poetical than that of launching a great ship, few spectacles more moving and more thrilling than that of the vessel in which so many hopes are centred gliding with swanlike grace into the water which is henceforth to be her element.

With the royal yacht moored within the harbour, the king could be easily transferred to the dockyard. At approximately 11.15 am, he was brought to the south railway jetty where he boarded a specially prepared train that included a small saloon carriage. Troops guarded the train's route but no music was played out of respect for the king's recent bereavement. At the slipway itself, final preparations for the launch were in hand. A number of shipwrights were employed underneath the vessel, and their labours could be clearly heard throughout much of the unusually silent yard. Indeed, they supplied virtually the only music heard on that occasion, with some of their number singing and humming such tunes as 'Rule Britannia!', 'Swanee River' and the occasional hymn. Again, *The Times* reported:

> Every now and then their enthusiasm finds expression in resounding cheers, which give the note of the all pervading feeling. The knocking away of the blocks on which the vessel rests continues without cessation. These must be removed before she can start on her passage down the ways on the bidding of the King, and the process of hammering at them is watched with deep interest by thousands of spectators on either side of the ship.

A further view of Rosyth, showing the tidal basin which was originally completed in 1913. Designed for the accommodation of destroyers and submarines, this is the earliest part of the dockyards. Dredged soil was used as a foundation for many of the buildings within the yard (*Rosyth dockyard*)

A general view of the Rosyth dockyard syncro-lift complex. The 425-ton mine-sweeper *Cuxton* is being lifted prior to her transfer to the undercover refitting sheds (*Rosyth dockyard*)

Once the king had arrived upon the launch platform close to the bows of the ship, the naming ceremony could begin. The ship was blessed with a psalm, a prayer and a hymn. Below the last few blocks were removed:

> The eagerly awaited moment had by this time arrived, the last blocks had been removed, and nothing now remained to be done but for the king to cut the cord which restrained the vessel. His Majesty ascended the dais in front of the bows, and taking in his hands the flower hidden bottle of wine . . . he dashed it against the ship. The force of the blow was insufficient to break the bottle, cushioned as it was by its bouquet of flowers. A second attempt, however, was successful, and all that remained was to cut the cord.

A special mallet and chisel was handed to the king and used to cut a ceremonial cord that proceeded to move a series of weights which in turn removed the dog shores from underneath the vessel. With nothing holding her in place *Dreadnought* moved forward, bringing shouts of glee from the assembled masses. Within a few minutes the vessel had been fully launched, tugging at the restraining ropes that prevented her moving more than a short distance from the end of the slipway. The naval revolution had begun.

As a fighting ship HMS *Dreadnought* could not only boast her great speed and a remarkable fire power but also a record building time. Laid down in October 1905, launched in February 1906 and completed during the autumn of that same year, few building yards could achieve such a rapid pace. Indeed, most battleships were rarely completed in under three years, with much of the completion time being occupied in a long wait for the requisite guns. In the case of the *Dreadnought* a number of corners were ruthlessly cut. Guns originally earmarked for two pre-Dreadnoughts still under construction were transferred to Portsmouth for the first all big-gun ship. It is during completion time that engines and boilers are also shipped, masts stepped and cabins finished. Again, all this was carried out in remarkably quick time, with a greater number of workmen employed than was generally the case.

As for the completed *Dreadnought*, trials began sometime towards the end of 1906. Steaming to the Mediterranean and then on to Trinidad, the *Dreadnought* completed an exhausting 7,000 mile round trip with only minimal problems. Thereafter she joined the main battle fleet and was to remain in service until 1918, although she saw remarkably little action, not even being present at Jutland. In 1915, however, she did ram and sink a U-boat whilst her almost continuous presence at sea did much to weaken the resolve of the German High Seas Fleet. Eventually, after being transferred to the Reserve at Rosyth, *Dreadnought* was sold prior to being broken up in 1923.

Other Dreadnoughts naturally followed: between 1907 and 1914 a total of twenty-six Dreadnoughts were built for the Royal Navy, exactly half constructed at Portsmouth and Devonport with the rest emanating from the private yards. The first of the Devonport Dreadnoughts was the *Temeraire*, an 18,800-ton giant that not only had a main armament of ten 12in guns, but also a total of sixteen 4in guns. Laid down in January 1907, she was launched in August of the same year, joining the first battle squadron in May 1909. Like *Dreadnought*, the *Temeraire* saw service throughout the war years, being present at Jutland before transferring to the Mediterranean in 1918.

Although Dreadnoughts were built at both Portsmouth and Devonport, and in about equal numbers, the former yard was clearly of greater importance. It was at Portsmouth that the first of each new class of Dreadnought was laid down, and any problems were solved there. Devonport and the private yards took their lead from Portsmouth, while the level of expertise was always greatest there. Apart from the *Dreadnought* herself, Portsmouth also launched the following name class Dreadnought battleships during the pre-war years: *Bellerophon* (1907), *St Vincent* (1908), *Neptune* (1909), *Orion* (1910), *King George V* (1911), *Iron Duke* (1912) and *Queen Elizabeth* (1913). The *Royal Sovereign*, last of the Portsmouth Dreadnoughts was launched in April 1915. Of 25,750 tons and armed with eight 15in guns, the last Dreadnought was one of the largest vessels ever built at Portsmouth being exceeded only by the 27,500-ton *Queen Elizabeth* already referred to.

At Devonport the largest of the pre-war Dreadnoughts, and also the largest vessel ever built at the dockyard, was the *Warspite*. A sister ship to the Portsmouth-built *Queen Elizabeth*, she was also of 27,500 tons and armed with eight 15in guns and fourteen 6in guns. Laid down in October 1912 she was launched in November 1913, eventually serving the Royal Navy in two world wars. *Warspite* saw action at Jutland in 1916, at Narvik in 1940 followed by Matapan in 1941 and the invasion of Sicily in 1943. Other Dreadnoughts built at Devonport were *Collingwood* (1908), *Centurion* (1911), *Marlborough* (1912) and *Royal Oak* (1914). This last was the same *Royal Oak* sunk at Scapa Flow in October 1939. A further Dreadnought, the *Resistance*, was to have been built at Devonport but was cancelled in August 1914.

To facilitate the building and maintenance of such large warships, both Devonport and Portsmouth underwent major alterations. At Devonport most of the facilities required were incorporated in the new extension scheme that had been started during the previous century. Additionally though, the No 2 slip was converted into a dry-dock and a new shallow dock was built. In 1913 work began on a turbine shop, the purpose of which was to repair and maintain the massive units responsible for powering the new class of battleships. At Portsmouth a number of dry-docks and building slips were extended. The largest dry-dock at this yard was No 14, originally completed in 1896; situated to the south of the repairing basin, it was considerably lengthened. The result was that this particular dry-dock could accommodate the very largest of vessels afloat, and celebrated its reopening in November 1914 with the docking of the pre-Dreadnought battleship *Hindustan*. This was followed in January 1915 by the 26,350-ton battle cruiser *Queen Mary*. Portsmouth, during this same period, also saw the construction of new stores, workshops, two 10-ton travelling cranes and a 250-ton crane. Work also began on demolishing the old rigging and sail lofts, buildings that were clearly of no value to a steam-powered navy.

Amongst the other yards Chatham, for one, had successfully developed a new specialism which replaced its previous role of constructing major warships. Since 1908 Chatham yard had been concentrating on submarines, launching in August of that year the C17. Built on the No 7 slip this particular vessel was surrounded by a veil of secrecy which at one time gave rise to thoughts of a possible launching at midnight. According to one of the local papers, the *Chatham News*:

The so called moonlight launch of a submarine from the slipway at Chatham yard caused quite a commotion in the London press, which appeared to have overlooked the fact that submarines were being built at this port. As for secrecy this has been strictly observed at all the launches of submarines from the slips of private firms, whereas at Chatham, the workmen employed in building them are bound to secrecy. The Admiralty were bound to construct some of these little craft in the Royal Dockyards, if they desired to keep a necessary check on the charges of contractors, and Chatham has been selected because all other new constructions have ceased, except that of a few barges and small craft. Apparently the work has been performed so expeditiously and cheaply, under many handicapping conditions, that their lordships have decided to build other submarines at the Medway ports, and Chatham will do the work.

At the time the C17 was one of four submarines ordered to be built at Chatham, with the C18, C19 and C20 all having been launched by the end of 1909. These 'C' class submarines were extremely small by today's standards, displacing a mere 280 tons and having a total length of only 135ft. Apart from the limited number of torpedoes that might be carried and the restricted time for which they might remain submerged, the real disadvantage of these frail craft was the petrol engine that supplied motive power whilst surfaced. This was responsible for fumes that made the submariners' life both unbearable and dangerous. In common with most later types, 'C' class submarines relied upon an electric motor which was capable of generating speeds of up to 10 knots. The later 'D' and 'E' class submarines, both of which were built at Chatham prior to World War I, were considerably improved as they were not only much larger but had diesel rather than petrol engines.

The emergence of this new role at Chatham came at a rather fortuitous moment; whilst the very largest battleships were still being built within the royal dockyards, most lesser ships, and particularly cruisers and destroyers, were being constructed in private yards. This, in turn, meant that two of the remaining government dockyards, those of Pembroke and Sheerness, were heavily underutilized. Designed from the outset as a building yard, Pembroke was especially affected with numerous 'lay-offs' and a considerable period of stagnation for the town. In 1906 alone, some seven hundrd men were dismissed who had little chance of alternative employment in a town so heavily dependent upon warship construction work. As a temporary measure Pembroke did receive some vessels in need of repair and maintenance, considerable use being made of the one dry-dock. From 1909 onwards, with the drift to war ever more apparent, Pembroke yard began receiving orders for the construction of a number of new warships, concentrating most of its resources upon 'Boadicea' and 'Active' class scout cruisers.

Despite the brief run down of Pembroke, it was clear to the Admiralty that further dockyard facilities, but of a different nature were required. Concentration, at first, was upon the foreign yards with a considerable expansion programme at Bermuda and the establishment

of a new dockyard at Simonstown Bay, South Africa. A major feature
of the improvements made to Bermuda was the positioning of a
floating dock during the year 1906. Such docks, incidentally, were to
be used increasingly over the following years, allowing refit facilities
to be created in many areas previously unable to handle the needs of a
modern navy. Dover, Portland and Harwich also received floating
docks, specifically for the repair of submarines and destroyers.

The new Simonsbay dockyard, situated to the south of Cape Town,
was originally established to meet the needs of a fleet operating in the
South Atlantic. Restricted to one dry-dock, a breakwater and various
essential buildings, Simonsbay was begun early in 1907. Substantially
completed by 1910, the dry-dock was successfully flooded on 15 June
1909.

At home, one further dockyard was also established. This was
Rosyth, planned from the outset as a major yard, and strategically
placed in the Firth of Forth, only a short distance above the famous
railway bridge. Initially recommended by a parliamentary committee
that sat during 1903, it was to be the biggest venture of the period.
Negotiations were soon in hand for the purchase of 1,200 acres of
land, together with a further 48 acres of foreshore. Owned by the
Marquis of Linlithgow and all within the area of St Margaret's Hope,
much of this land was specifically earmarked for the dockyard itself,
but with some set aside for the accommodation of numerous
workmen.

Resulting from widespread publicity given to the new dockyard, the
Garden City Association produced a pamphlet in May 1903 entitled
'The New Naval Base. A Great Social Opportunity'. The association,
recognizing that a new town would eventually be created in the
Inverkeithing/Rosyth area, hoped to influence public opinion with a
view to insisting upon an enlightened and far-sighted scheme for the
planning of the town. The history of Pembroke dockyard showed that
little thought had been given to the needs of workers, and clearly
Rosyth could repeat these errors. According to Thomas Adams, the
writer of the pamphlet:

> The growth of the new town will be accelerated because of the close
> proximity of Dunfermline in which there is a great demand for female
> labour. This will be of considerable advantage to those Sailors, Engineers,
> and Dock Labourers who desire to keep their families at home, but who are
> unable to do so except in towns or districts where there are adequate
> varieties of employment. At present over 1,000 women travel daily to

Dunfermline from Lochgelly, Cowdenbeath, and other mining villages. In these small towns, in spite of the plentiful supply of cheap land, the housing conditions are little better than in the slums of large cities, and even the presence of plenty of fresh air does little to counteract the evils of bad sanitation and uncontrolled development. In the mining villages of Scotland the sanitary conditions are most unsatisfactory, largely because of the crowding together of cottages, and the inadequacy of the space allowed for gardens. This state of affairs cannot be defended on economic grounds . . . . The need of an object lesson is therefore a local question as well as a national one, and the creation of a model town at St. Margaret's Hope will exercise a particularly beneficial influence on its immediate surroundings.

Building of the dockyard, though, did not begin immediately. It was not until 1905 that further consideration was given to the project, with the sum of £200,000 being granted by an Act of Parliament. The money was designated for clearance work whilst an additional sum would be provided for the provision of office and residential accommodation together with the building of a railway junction that would connect the dockyard with the nearby Edinburgh–Dunfermline railway.

It was not until 1908 that the government seems to have finalized its plans for the new dockyard. In that year an artist's impression of the finished yard was released, being published in the *Illustrated London News* dated 4 April. Showing a single enclosed basin of 56 acres entered through a main lock, and surrounded by cranes, internal rail system and several wharves, the dockyard was to have only one dry-dock at this stage. Additionally a factory building, smithery and pumping station were also shown. Most of these features were eventually included, although such items as an emergency entrance and several of the buildings were repositioned.

Construction of the dockyard began during the year 1909. In February Easton Gibb and Sons of Westminster won the main building contract. Much of their early efforts were directed towards the building of an electric generating station designed to power much of their own equipment and general lighting. This, together with many of the other buildings, was of stone construction with much of the required material drawn from nearby Freestone Quarry. At that time an internal railway system linked the dockyard and the quarry where a large assembly of steam cranes provided the necessary mechanical power for the removal of rock.

Another contractor soon at work within the dockyard was the

Brandon Bridge Building Company. They shared responsibility for constructing the basin, undertaking work on the walls. This basin, 56 acres in area, was to be the main feature of Rosyth dockyard, soon able to accommodate a large proportion of the ships operating within the North Sea area. Estimated to take seven years to complete, its south wall and part of the west wall consist of 120 monoliths of 1550sq ft and up to 98ft deep, each of which took several years to sink. The remaining walls were of concrete, being built either behind or in clay embankments. The basin was to be eventually completed in 1915.

Whilst the original 1908 plan had called for only one dry-dock, the Admiralty had reserved the right to order a second dry-dock at any time within three and a half years. This power seems to have been invoked sometime around 1911 when a second dry-dock was under construction, situated close to the first and leading out of the main basin. As with the first dry-dock it was 850ft long and would be able to accommodate the new Dreadnought class of battleship. Approval for the third, or No 3 dock, was given in 1913 and, again, was to be of 850ft.

Overall, work upon the new royal dockyard progressed at a rather slow and unsatisfactory pace. Poor weather, lack of positive financing and labour difficulties all seem to have contributed. Some progress, however, was certainly being made. According to the 1913 Naval Annual:

> The submarine and torpedo-boat destroyer basin is ready, and the construction of the battleship basin is progressing favourably. The work on the entrance lock is being tackled, but until it is completed the basin itself, the walls of which are almost completed, will not be available. The two graving docks, each of 1,000 feet [sic]* in length, have their entrance from the basin. They are far advanced, and the construction of a third dock has been ordered.

The estimated completion date for the dockyard at this time was thought to be about 1920, but many of the facilities would come into use before then. The torpedo boat and submarine basin referred to was a smaller tidal basin (600ft by 470ft) and standing to the west of the main basin which was non-tidal.

Accommodation for the future work-force, the factor that had led

* Presumably an extreme case of rounding up. The length of all three docks, at the time of building was 850ft with the No 2 dock later having a further 6ft added so that it might accommodate HMS *Hood* for a refit in 1920.

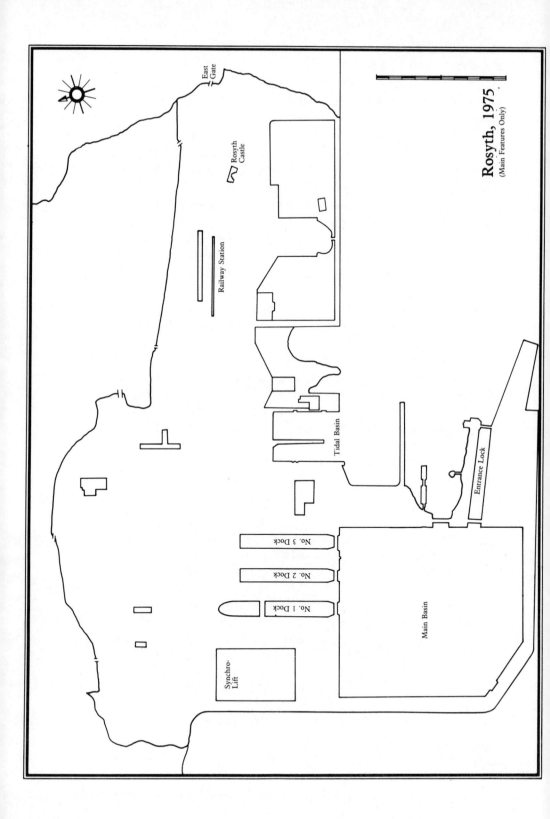

Rosyth, 1975
(Main Features Only)

East Gate

Rosyth Castle

Railway Station

Tidal Basin

Entrance Lock

No. 3 Dock

No. 2 Dock

No. 1 Dock

Main Basin

Synchro-Lift

the Garden City Association to publish its earlier pamphlet, was also under review in 1913. With an estimated 3,000 workers due to arrive at Rosyth within the next six or seven years, the government set aside 316 acres of the original land purchased from the Marquis of Linlithgow for housing. In 1911 Dunfermline Town Council extended their boundaries to include Rosyth and had undertaken to plan out the new town, whilst providing all necessary public services. By 1913 no progress had been made – all that existed was a series of shacks known as 'Tin Town'. Occupied by the civilian contract workers, it was a far cry from the noble plans of the Garden City Association.

The situation on declaration of war in August 1914 was that the new dockyard at Rosyth was far from complete. The extensive basin could not, as yet, be used whilst none of the dry-docks was ready. Large numbers of contractors were still in residence whilst the whole area appeared nothing less than a disorganized mess. This was to produce considerable problems. During the early period of hostilities, with the main theatre of operations further north than any previous war, there was no effective naval base within strategic range. Rosyth was to have been the major centre for an operational fleet, but with inadequate defences and no working facilities the Grand Fleet had initially to make greater use of Scapa Flow than originally planned. Additionally, Harwich, with its floating dock, re-entered strategic thinking, whilst Sheerness and Chatham were resorted to in emergencies. As the war developed, however, parts of Rosyth slowly came into operation and, by 1917, had become the permanent base for the Grand Fleet.

13
The World Wars

Declaration of war in August 1914 immediately placed the royal dock-yards under tremendous pressure. At each of the seven home yards there was a dramatic rise in numbers employed, a fact made necessary by the unlimited demands of a navy about to embark upon a global confrontation. Vessels which had not been at sea for a good many years were removed from their anchorages, quickly overhauled and made ready for action. Time prevented more thorough refits.

But for the various royal dockyards there was more to be done than simply preparing ships; a much expanded building programme was implemented, whilst each yard prepared for the acceptance of numerous battle-damaged warships since the Admiralty anticipated that most casualties would result from the all out naval engagements that had characterised previous wars. World War I, however, was to prove different: most of the damaged ships entering the royal yards were the casualties of two new weapons, the mine and the torpedo. Such was the case of the *Nubian* and *Zulu*, both brought to Chatham in 1916; the *Nubian* had lost most of her bow section as the result of a torpedo and the *Zulu* lacked a stern due to mine damage. As the vessels were of the same class, the two were subsequently joined between the third and fourth funnels, the new vessel being named *Zubian*.

Sheerness was typical of the three smaller yards. Recipient of a floating dock during the early part of the war, the yard was soon regularly docking four vessels simultaneously. Most were submarines and destroyers but fast minelayers were also brought to Sheerness. These particular vessels, usually requisitioned merchantmen and hurriedly converted at the beginning of the war, were used in the Channel area to restrict enemy shipping movements. Such a minelayer was the *Princess Irene*, a former Canadian Pacific liner brought to Sheerness at the time of her first commissioning. Equipped with a cargo of five hundred contact mines, the *Princess Irene* was undergoing one or two last minute repairs before sailing at the end of May 1915. By Thursday 27th, much of this work was complete, with a number of dockyard workers merely testing items of ship's gear. At exactly 11.8am, however, these shipwrights and yard labourers were among 170 men killed when a mine being primed by an inexperienced member of the crew exploded. A chain reaction resulted in a devastating explosion that ripped the entire vessel apart.

Resulting in the loss of more dockyard lives than any previous tragedy, the accident was keenly felt throughout the town. A small, close-knit community, few families were without a relative or friend killed whilst working on or near the *Princess Irene*. Equally poignant was that for many, not even a proper funeral was possible; few bodies were recovered, and of those that were, most were unrecognizable.

The explosion, as might well be expected, was heard throughout much of North Kent, whilst the huge cloud of white smoke that hung over the River Medway for a good many hours was visible for miles. At Detling, some 12 miles away, the explosion was most clearly heard; the headmaster at the village school realised that a tragedy must have occurred and called for a two minutes' silence. At Hollingbourne, about 14 miles from the explosion, the blast blew open the doors and windows of the village school.

Even closer to the explosion was the Isle of Grain where chunks of metal rained down, causing damage to naval oil storage tanks and destroying part of the Port Victoria railway pier. A metal plate belonging to the minelayer and fused on one side as a result of the tremendous heat, killed a nine-year-old girl, Ida Barten, who had been playing in her back garden. A witness at the subsequent inquest held at the Cock Inn, Isle of Grain, reported that gas and flames had risen to a height of some two miles.

Events such as the Sheerness tragedy apart, the war was not without benefits; for those fortunate enough to have a dockyard job, it was a time of rising incomes. Increased overtime allowances combined with a wartime bonus more than doubled wages, whilst a dockyard job also meant security against conscription. Large numbers of the previously unemployed were drafted into the yards, as were a good number of women. At Portsmouth, for instance, 1,750 females were employed by the end of the war, undertaking virtually every task worked by men. An account of their work appears in an immediate post-war publication entitled *Portsmouth and the Great War*:

In the Dockyard, as elsewhere, the women more than justified the highest expectations. They were entered at first for clerical duties, and then, in one shop after another, were allowed to try their prentice hand, with quite satisfactory results. . . . The adaptability of women was only equalled by their willingness; they took their places side by side with the men and performed their work to the entire satisfaction of the authorities. The character of that work will be seen from the following record: In the factory they were employed in the working of lathes, planing, shaping, milling, engraving, buffing, auto and slatting machinery; in cleaning, cutting, and testing condenser tubes, making condenser ferrules, cleaning air bottles for submarines and ships; in general bench work and assisting the mechanics in cutting blades for condenser turbines. In the Boiler shop they were engaged in acetylene welding, in cleaning, picking, galvanising, testing boiler tubes. Here also they were employed at lathes, drilling, screwing, punching and shearing machines. They also did small work on forges and assisted the mechanics on the automatic machines for bolts and nuts. In the Gun Mounting Shop, in addition to general bench work, they were employed on drilling, shaping, screwing, and engraving machines, and also in fitting, adjusting etc., on range finders. In the Coppersmiths' Shop they did acetylene welding, cleaning and picking tubes, the repair of lamps for ships, and general work in assisting the mechanics. In the Pattern Shop they were employed in making packing cases, painting patterns, turning wood plugs for boiler tubes, and rollers for drawings, and also on the band saw machines. In the drawing office they did the tracing of drawings and worked the sun printing apparatus. . . . The payment of their work was fixed at 20s. a week when first they were employed, and this was gradually advanced to a flat rate of 35s. The best feature of this employment was the camaraderie which was established with the men. At first they were kept at work by themselves, and they left the Yard in advance of the men; but before many months had elapsed no distinction was shown. They entered with the men, worked with the men, and left together when the bell rang; whether it was light or dark, wet or fine, they went cheerfully to their daily task, and wended their way homeward with a happy consciousness of duty done.

In respect of shipbuilding, the emphasis moved to smaller vessels, with a large number of cruisers and submarines emanating from the royal yards. Chatham, having already developed an expertise in the realm of submarines, was joined by Devonport, Pembroke and Portsmouth. Between them, these last three yards built all seven 'J' class and a small number of 'K' class submarines. Chatham, on the other hand, continued to concentrate on 'E' class and the later 'G' class boats.

That an entire class of submarine should be built within the royal dockyards possibly related to the role for which 'J class' submarines were designated. Much larger than any earlier design, they were initially planned to operate with the fleet, but to do so a surface speed of 21 knots was needed. To achieve this, each of the newly built submarines possessed three of the engines fitted to the earlier 'E' class. Even so, the design was a failure; the craft rarely reached 19 knots and were therefore unable to keep pace with the fleet. In many ways, though, this was to prove fortunate. Heavy ships and surfacing submarines do not really mix, and their introduction to a fleet on manoeuvres might well have been hazardous. Instead, however, this particular class of submarine eked out a fairly successful career in the Baltic and North Sea.

Successor to the 'J' class was the much more ambitious 'K' class. Again, it was designed to operate with the fleet; this time the hoped-for surface speed was 24 knots. To gain the extra speed this new class of submarine, instead of being fitted with a diesel engine, had nothing less than a steam engine that could be quickly extinguished once the craft was required to submerge. Astonishingly funnels were built into the design, these being hinged and supposedly watertight. As might be expected, the final product fell short of requirements. 'K' class submarines continually found themselves subjected to major and minor difficulties, the five constructed within the royal dockyards being no exception. At Portsmouth, trials of the K1 were far from satisfactory whilst the K2 suffered a fire during her first dive. The K6, built at Devonport, successfully submerged in the non-tidal basin of Keyham yard, but refused to surface again; the fault was traced to a faulty compressed air system and the craft subsequently forced to the surface. Thereafter dockyard workers were most reluctant to board such vessels, and shipwrights from outside the dockyard had to be employed. It was also the 'K' class submarine that put an end to the myth that such craft can safely operate in close proximity to the fleet. In what became known as the Battle of May Island, an event that occurred one night in January 1918, no less than five submarines were involved in major collisions of which two were permanently lost.

The wartime emergency naturally precluded any general improvements to dockyard buildings, although efforts to complete Rosyth dockyard became a priority. Designed as a first-class naval base within striking distance of the new North Sea battlegrounds, Rosyth was in a totally unusable condition at the outbreak of war. By August 1914 only the tidal basin was complete, with several months' construction work still required upon the non-tidal basin, entrance locks, pumping station, electricity generating station and dry-docks. Whilst the generating station – a three-storey stone building with a boiler house, battery room and coal store – was fairly close to completion, the pumping station was little more than a shell bereft of any boilers. Completion of both units was essential before any of the dry-docks could be used.

Shortly after the outbreak of war, large numbers of additional building workers were brought from the south to help progress at Rosyth. Completion of Rosyth yard was considered so important, that at one time two thousand able seamen were employed upon construction of the main basin. Plans for the future garden city were placed on one side for the time being, accommodation for the next few years consisting of the original timber-framed, corrugated bungalows of 'Tin Town'. Throughout 1915, work continued at the newly accelerated pace. In October the all-important power station and pumping station were complete, with many other key facilities due to be finished the following spring. In March 1916 warships first entered the semi-complete but usable dockyard. On the 17th, for instance, the *Crescent*, a 7,700-ton cruiser, became the first ship to enter the basin by means of the emergency entrance. She was towed in by the recently purchased dockyard tug *Conqueress*. A few days later, the 27th, the *Zealandia* also entered the main basin, this time by means of the completed entrance lock. On the following day this same vessel entered the No 1 dock, being the first vessel ever to do so. The first ship to enter the No 2 dock was the *New Zealand*, being brought in during April 1916, with the *Canada* entering the No 3 dock on 9 September, 1916.

Despite the fact that much work still had to be done at Rosyth, the dockyard was soon undertaking a full refit and repair programme. From 1916 until the end of the war in November 1918, a total of 197 vessels were docked, of which the great majority were cruisers and battleships. The weeks after Jutland perhaps proved the busiest, with a large proportion of the battle-damaged ships being brought to the yard. Many of these ships, such as the *Onslow* and *Acasta*, were so badly damaged that they had to be towed all of the way, whilst the *Warspite* was still on fire in seven places and had to be docked immediately.

Of the foreign yards during World War I, Malta was probably the busiest with a permanent squadron of cruisers and destroyers based there. Additionally, facilities at this dockyard were being used by ships of other nationalities, including France, Japan, the United States and

Italy. The dry-docks at Malta, therefore, were in constant use, with capital ships of two nations invariably undergoing major refits. Employing a work-force of 3,500 in 1914, the yard was eventually to employ well over 10,000.

Harwich, on the other hand, was one of the older home yards making something of a revival. Having ceased to provide refit facilities since the seventeenth century, a floating dock had been brought into the harbour, whilst a force of destroyers, light cruisers and submarines was based there. Like Rosyth, it was better placed for the provision of repair facilities when hostilities were conducted in the Baltic area.

The inter-war period brought a number of dramatic changes to the royal dockyards: the status of Pembroke and Rosyth was reduced to that of care and maintenance, and Haulbowline was transferred to the newly created Irish Free State. Rather more unsatisfactory was the treatment of the work-force following the infamous economies initiated by Sir Eric Geddes. A businessman who was brought into top-level government during the war, Sir Eric was later responsible for streamlining public expenditure by means of severe economies that have gone down in history as the 'Geddes axe'. The dockyards were an easy target and were treated ruthlessly, with a great number of men thrown on to the ever increasing dole queues. Many were not to find employment until the re-armament phase of the 1930s; others would never return to the dockyards.

It was during the 1920s that the dockyards reached an all-time low. With most of the navy held in reserve and few ships released for foreign service, the once busy dry-docks were empty and the decade brought only a few orders for new ships. Devonport provides a typical example: during four years of war the yard launched five submarines, one cruiser and a Dreadnought, but in ten years of peace the construction rate was reduced to that of three cruisers (one of which had been laid down during the war), a minelayer and two oilers. At Chatham, the situation was worse if anything. At one time, the only work in hand was the completion of a cruiser and the painting of one or two oilers by highly skilled shipwrights. The waste of resources was being repeated at Sheerness and Portsmouth, the only other home yards remaining open in this period.

It was not until the 1930s that things began to improve. Increased orders were received, more shipwrights were employed and some of the dockyards witnessed a little rebuilding work, such as the enlargement to the No 10 dock at Devonport. Although minor in comparison with former programmes, it is perhaps the various electrification programmes that need be considered. At Portsmouth £¼ million was spent on such a project, and a new electrical shop was built at Devonport. The need for an increase in the provision of electricity resulted from changing shipbuilding techniques and the arrival of electro-welding combined with the greater use of machine tools worked by compressed air.

The declaration of war in 1939 immediately saw the re-establishment of Pembroke and Rosyth dockyards and expansion in the work-force of all other yards. Over the next five and a half years, the royal dockyards were to maintain a pace of work that had never previously been witnessed. Throughout the entire war, the various home and foreign yards carried out some 97,000 refits, laid down 1 aircraft carrier, 4 cruisers, 4 sloops, 22 submarines and 6 floating docks. Moreover, a good many demands placed upon them by the Army and Air Force were also executed. For instance, Portsmouth undertook the construction, wiring and communication work of SHAEF (Supreme Headquarters Allied Expeditionary Force) at Fort Southwick from where the D-day landings were principally directed. Similarly, the staff at Devonport helped plan and equip many of the decoy sites established to lure enemy aircraft from more important targets, whilst at Chatham the dockyard supplied stud welding equipment for tanks and other fighting vehicles and also fitted 2,000 shore establishments. Through this broader function of the yards, work contributing to each stage of the world-wide conflict can be traced.

The first major naval engagement of the war, culminating in the scuttling of the *Graf Spee*, brought the *Exeter* to Devonport and the *Ajax* to Chatham. The *Exeter* remained in dockyard hands for nearly a year, receiving a complete repair to extensive battle damage. Whilst under repair at Chatham, the *Ajax* became the object of several German air raids. Following one such raid, from which the *Ajax* survived unscathed, her position alongside the Upnor wall was taken by a C-class cruiser then undergoing conversion to an anti-aircraft gun ship. With upper decks burnt away, this cruiser looked a complete wreck. Fortunately upon the return of a German reconnaissance plane this ship was mistaken for the *Ajax*, resulting in a jubilant claim about her complete destruction.

In April 1940, Rosyth became the main assembly point for the ill-fated Norwegian expedition, the dockyard preparing something like 1,200 vessels. Further south, the retreat from Dunkirk was partly co-

HMS *Hood* being berthed at Rosyth in January 1920. She was later to enter No 2 dock which had been lengthened for this very purpose

Launched at Chatham in June 1910, C.34 was one of the earliest submarines to be built in the royal dockyards (*MoD Photo*)

Last of the Chatham submarines was the *Okanagan*, launched from No 7 slip in September 1966 (*Courtesy Mr A. Morris*)

ordinated at Sheerness with many of the small evacuation craft
assembling and later being repaired at that yard. The larger vessels
sent to Dunkirk, such as destroyers, generally converged upon
Chatham. Here, often on the verge of sinking, they were quickly
repaired by means of the simple expediency of covering gaping great
holes with a few metal plates.

The Spitfire summer of 1940 and the dark winter that followed, saw
numerous air raids upon Chatham, Portsmouth and Devonport, but
none of the dockyards was put out of action. Chatham received a
direct hit on the factory, with the loss of twenty-three lives, but the
sufferings at Devonport were undoubtedly the most severe. German
bombers were frequently directed towards the Plymouth area, the
intention being the complete destruction of the dockyard. An easy
target, the original south yard was completely devastated. The Keyham
end escaped such destruction, but only at the expense of nearby
suburbs where whole streets were erased. Within the south yard many
of the eighteenth-century buildings were destroyed, including the
original dockyard church, several workshops, parts of the terrace and
east and west rope-houses.

It was also at Devonport that HMS *Campbeltown* was prepared for
the raid upon the Normandie dock at St Nazaire, an important
Channel base for the larger ships of the German navy. The eventual
destruction of the dry-dock was an important landmark of the war.
Conducted on 27 March 1942, *Campbeltown* was crashed into the
dock gates, allowing a number of commandoes to carry out demolition
work. The main damage, however, was inflicted during the following
morning when explosives on board the vessel detonated and put the
dry-dock completely out of action. Devonport's role was that of
reducing the *Campbeltown*'s draught by 3ft, adding ¼in armour-plate
shielding to her bridge structure, armoured bulkheads to the main
deck and removing upper deck armaments, torpedo tubes,
ammunition lockers, stores and lifeboats. Her smoke stacks were also
altered so that she might resemble one of the Moewe class destroyers
then being used by the German navy in that area of the Channel.

The Italian and North African campaigns were the province of three
Mediterranean dockyards – Gibraltar, Malta and Alexandria. Malta,
of course, was continually subjected to air attacks, with thirty-four
ships sunk in the harbour alone. By April 1942 all five dry-docks were
out of action and it was because of this situation that naval facilities
were established at Alexandria. Provided with a floating dock and the

rapidly acquired Gabbari graving dock, then the property of the Egyptian authorities, Alexandria became a very useful adjunct, repairing some three thousand vessels before the war was out.

Another royal dockyard created in these years was Kilindini, close to Mombasa in southern Kenya. Developed in response to the Japanese threat, much of the work upon Kilindini was carried out in 1942. An old, commercially built slipway was utilized, whilst repair work upon ships of the Indian Ocean fleet was conducted through extensive use of the two depot ships *Adamant* and *Maidstone*. Kilindini never received a dry-dock, only a floating dock. In all other respects, however, it was a miniature royal dockyard with all the necessary workshops and stores. Only in use for a limited period, it was fully dismantled before the war had finished, the fleet returning to Ceylon once the Japanese threat had subsided.

At this point reference should be made to Singapore; a product of the 1920s, it was the last of the major dockyards to be constructed, being designed to counter a perceived Japanese threat in the Pacific. Land was first selected in 1922, but construction proceeded hesitantly. Indeed, on at least one occasion work ceased altogether, when thinly stretched resources were directed to other areas of the failing British national economy. As planned, the new dockyard and naval base at Singapore would cost approximately £11 million, and would provide docking facilities for the largest battleships afloat.

It was on 15 February 1938 that Sir Shenton Thomas formally opened what had become the £20 million dockyard at Singapore. Some eleven thousand people were in attendance, including high-ranking naval officers, the Duke and Duchess of Sutherland and a good many Indian and Chinese labourers who had been responsible for its construction. For many, the most memorable event must have been an impressive display of British warships, combined with a fly-past of aircraft from the carrier HMS *Eagle*. At the time, a misguided British government assumed that the East was now secure, a fact from which they were to be rudely awoken only four years later when the dockyard at Singapore was captured by the Japanese.

The naval base at Singapore, designed for the protection of Australia, New Zealand, Hong Kong and other British dependencies in the area, was most impressive. Within the dockyard, an area of 4 square miles ringed by high walls and iron gates, stood a bomb-proof underground headquarters, elaborately ventilated stores, canteens, cinemas and a church. The dry-dock, built at a cost of £1 million, was large enough to accommodate the *Queen Mary* passenger liner, whilst an equally impressive floating dock had been brought out from England. The only thing lacking at the naval base was an adequate defence, the result of the current belief that in the event of an emergency the fleet, rapidly reinforced by ships from Europe, would be quite sufficient.

Apart from Singapore, the only other naval facilities available in this area were those at Hong Kong and Trincomalee. Neither, however, were of true dockyard status, being no more than naval yards. At Hong Kong, however, a dock had been laid down in 1902, but at Trincomalee the main facilities were those of oil tanks and magazines. Much expanded in 1942, when residences, a hospital, a storage depot and wharfage in China Bay were added, Trincomalee was used as a base for the reconquest of the Pacific.

Emphasis in the European theatre of operations during the later years of war moved towards preparation for the invasion of France. Chatham dockyard undertook some of the work upon PLUTO (Pipe Line Under the Ocean), whilst part of the invasion armada was assembled at Devonport. It was at Portsmouth, however, that the greatest contribution was made, nearly a thousand miscellaneous assault craft being prepared. Nor did the work of this particular yard cease once the fleet had sailed; during the months of June and July 1944, no less than 418 ships were brought back to Portsmouth, repaired and returned to service.

The final mammoth task of the dockyards, and one that was never completed, involved the preparation of a final battle fleet destined for the invasion of Japan. Very few of these ships were needed, being pre-empted by the surrender of Japan.

The achievements of the dockyards during the six years of war were prodigious. Employing a considerably increased personnel, including over 7,000 women, the dockyards completed all that was demanded of them. Despite the hardships of bombing, material shortages and a heavily diluted labour force, the dockyards ended the war with outstandingly high levels of output. With the return of peace the need for such productivity ended, and cuts would soon be made so that capacity could be aligned with post-war requirements.

14
Retrenchment

The first post-war economies came in the form of cancelled construction orders, with five submarines and two sloops never reaching completion. At Devonport the already launched 'A' class submarines *Ace* and *Achates* were scrapped as were the *Abelard* and *Acasta* at Portsmouth. Whilst the two Portsmouth submarines had reached the slipway, the *Adept* at Chatham did not even progress that far, being cancelled in October 1945. Chatham also saw two sloops, *Nonsuch* and *Nymphe*, cancelled whilst on the slipway.

The warship cancellations led to a considerable reduction in overtime and a series of dismissal notices were handed to a large proportion of temporary workers. Hardest hit were women: employed for the duration of hostilities only, the rapidly trained female labour force was thanked with no more than a handshake and a hurried goodbye. The dockyards were being returned to peace-time conditions in which women were not considered the equal of men. It was not until the 1970s that this particular trend was to be reversed.

A number of dockyards came under threat of closure, with Pembroke and Rosyth most at risk. Neither wished to be returned to their former 'care and maintenance' status, and the work-force at both yards campaigned vigorously. Amongst the arguments used for the retention of Rosyth was that it served as Scotland's only real connection with the navy, and that the strengthening of this tie would be in the general interest of the entire nation.

Eventually the axe fell upon Pembroke. In 1947 the gates were finally closed, the more experienced workers being transferred to other yards. The site remained in Admiralty hands until 1964 when a large portion was acquired by Pembroke Properties Ltd to develop as an industrial site. The project, however, was only partially successful with few firms moving into the area. In 1974, the outlook improved when a number of oil companies chose to base themselves on the site.

The Admiralty itself still possesses an oil fuel depot at Pembroke, but this is to be axed following the 1981 Defence White Paper.

That Rosyth avoided closure was due almost entirely to the recent experience of war. Virtually immune from air attack, war work had been undertaken with the work-force safe in the knowledge that high ground to the north afforded perfect shelter and concealment for workshops and oil storage tanks. Rosyth had other advantages: it was the only dockyard in the United Kingdom which could accommodate the entire home fleet at any state of the tide, whilst the approach channels could be totally secured against submarine attack.

For the dockyards as a whole, the immediate post-war years were a particularly difficult time. Order books remained empty, and only a number of smaller vessels were brought in for refits. Along the Medway the situation was particularly bad, with both Sheerness and Chatham under the threat of closure. At Devonport, however, certain improvements and general repairs to extensive wartime damage were made. Many buildings were replaced at this time, whilst the yard itself was increased by 48 acres. Much of the newly enclosed land included parts of old Devonport that had been totally destroyed. According to the Devonport dockyard historian, George Dicker, 'The extension brought inside the walls much of what was once the pride of Devonport including the famous Fore Street. Devonport Yard gathered within its walls at least 3 nationally known stores, a school, a number of hotels, 2 banks, a large Salvation Army Hostel, the Devonport Market and any number of miscellaneous buildings in varying degrees of war damage.'[22]

The rebuilding of Devonport dockyard was not to be completed for at least a decade, with one particular landmark, the dockyard wall, being finished in 1962. Devonport was also one of the first yards to begin refit work upon the larger ships of a much depleted post-war navy. In 1956, for instance, the aircraft carrier *Centaur* entered dry-dock for what was to become the largest single task until then undertaken at the yard. With 2,000 men engaged in the installation of much new equipment, a local newspaper was later to record that 110,000sq ft of linoleum, 100,000 tiles, 60 miles of piping, 450 miles of electric cable with 10,000 gallons of paint had been used.

Apart from an increase in refit work, the 1950s also witnessed a recommencement of shipbuilding work at Devonport. In 1952 the name class frigate, *Salisbury*, was laid down, being the prototype vessel of a genuine post-war design. Built on the prefabricated

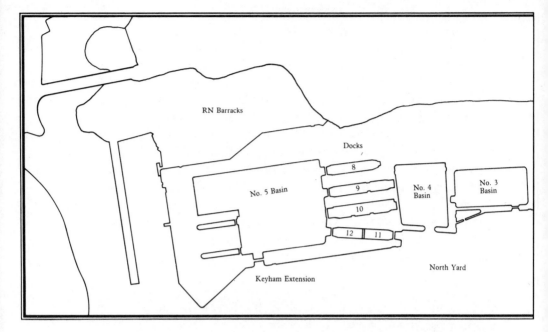

principle, the *Salisbury* was of all-welded construction. It was not, however, until 1958 that a second new warship was laid down – the *Plymouth*, a Rothesay class frigate. Later the *Tartar*, *Cleopatra* and *Danae* were to be launched at Plymouth, helping to ease further cut-backs of the mid-1960s. Additionally two aircraft carriers, the *Eagle* and *Ark Royal*, were brought to Devonport for modernization programmes whilst the *Blake* was converted from a cruiser to her helicopter-cruiser role.

Portsmouth was to remain by far the busiest of the post-war dockyards, undertaking much refit work upon all types of vessels, ranging from aircraft carriers and cruisers to patrol submarines and minesweepers. The largest single task was a rebuild of the aircraft carrier *Victorious*, a task which took eight years to complete. Additionally several cruisers and carriers were refitted prior to their sale to overseas navies. Ships built at Portsmouth in this period were the frigates *Leopard* (1951), *Rhyl* (1959) and *Nubian* (1960).

Work at Chatham, on the other hand, continued at a very much reduced pace, with closure appearing all but inevitable. Very few vessels, usually of destroyer size or less, were sent to Chatham, with the greater part of the yard's work appearing to be the maintenance of a huge ghost fleet of moth-balled warships that littered the entire length of the Medway. Most of these were subsequently scrapped. A

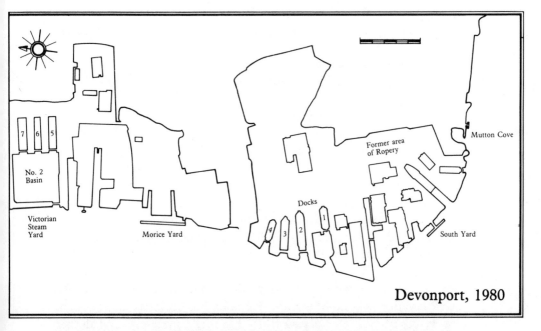

Labels on map: No. 2 Basin · Victorian Steam Yard · Morice Yard · Former area of Ropery · Docks · Mutton Cove · South Yard · 7 6 5 · 4 3 2 1

Devonport, 1980

dramatic improvement in the Chatham situation was not to occur until 1957 when a conventionally powered submarine, later to be named *Oberon*, was laid down. The first of a new class, six were subsequently built at Chatham with three, *Ojibwa, Okanagan* and *Onondaga*, destined for the Royal Canadian Navy. The building of these submarines was to keep Chatham busy for the next ten years, by which time the new refit complex had been announced.

Although the royal dockyards continued to build warships, it was a policy much under review. Most new construction work was being directed towards the private yards, with only an occasional lead vessel being launched at Portsmouth, Devonport or Chatham. Eventually, however, the whole concept of building ships in the royal dockyards was to disappear with the currently nationalized 'British Shipbuilders' taking on the entire operation. At Portsmouth the last vessel to leave the slipway was the *Andromeda*, a Leander class frigate launched in 1967. It was during the following year that Devonport launched its final warship, also a Leander class frigate, the *Scylla*. At Chatham the last new launching was the already mentioned *Okanagan*, a vessel finally completed in June 1968.

It was on 31 March 1960 that Sheerness dockyard finally relinquished its Royal Navy connection. Since the end of World War II the yard had been engaged in the repair of small warships and yard craft, tasks that could easily be transferred to an underutilized Chatham. The resulting closure created much local unemployment since only a small proportion of the thousand-strong work-force could find alternative jobs. The ceremony accompanying the closure was a simple but moving affair led by the band of the Royal Marines. Part of the ceremony included the presentation of a wooden replica key to Mr David Finnie, chairman of the new Sheerness Harbour Company which from sunset onwards, became owners of the former naval dockyard.

The immediate effect upon Sheerness Town was one of despondency. Numerous families left the area: the population of Blue Town, for instance, the part of Sheerness which lay closest to the dockyard, fell from 700 to 330. The new owners, a civilian company determined to create a trade port and industrial estate, did much to alleviate the most immediate problems, eventually creating a highly successful commercial venture. Now owned by the Medway Conservancy Board, Sheerness Harbour has facilities for handling many types of cargo, ranging from fruit to Japanese cars and timber. Part of the former dockyard has also been turned into a separate industrial estate for the manufacture of iron and steel. Despite these changes, many of the former dockyard buildings have been retained, with a fine collection of eighteenth-century residential and administrative buildings standing close to the main gate. Additionally, Rennie's early nineteenth-century extension remains virtually untouched as does the four-storey boat-house dating to 1859.

The decision, first announced in June 1963, to make Rosyth dockyard into a nuclear refitting base, was one of several such decisions to update the four remaining royal dockyards. Designed for repairing and refuelling the Resolution class submarines, Rosyth is the only yard capable of handling these Polaris carrying warships. Locating the multi-million pound refit centre at Rosyth naturally ended fears that closure was imminent. Nowadays an extremely important naval base, Rosyth also carries out refit work upon frigates, patrol craft and auxiliary vessels.

The building of a second nuclear complex, at Chatham, was announced in March 1965, when the last of the Oberons were nearing completion. Constructed between the old Nos 6 and 7 docks, the nuclear complex was designed for the refit and refuelling of the non-Polaris-carrying Fleet class submarines then being built at Barrow. Eventually opened in June 1968, the complex consisted of two dry-docks, a huge cantilever crane for the removal of used reactor cores, an office block, underground workshops and a health physics building. In the light of more recent developments it is interesting to note the remarks of Vice-Admiral Sir Horace Law at the time the complex was opened:

Nuclear power has given submarines an entirely new dimension – something they have always wanted – the ability not to come to the surface for air. The Royal Navy is extremely proud of its nuclear fleet submarines, they are the capital ships of the future, and it will not be lost on those present that Chatham is really well in on the support of the navy in years to come. It was an obvious choice to put these facilities on the Medway.

Devonport was the next yard to receive the attention of the planners, with much new plant and equipment being installed during the mid-1960s. In 1966, for instance, a £½ million central office block was completed, whilst in 1969 it was announced that Devonport would become an operational base for nuclear-powered fleet submarines. Subsequently plans were put in hand for extensive refit facilities, with work beginning in 1973. The actual site of the Submarine Refit Complex (SRC) was the old Keyham dockyard extension, originally opened at the north end of the yard in 1907. Initially the site had to be extended and strengthened with work beginning on the main support buildings in 1975. As finished in 1981, the complex has two dry-docks, a wet berth and all the workshops and other necessary support facilities. Unlike Chatham, which specialises in the Valiant class submarines, the Devonport SRC is designed to cater for the needs of the new Swiftsure and Trafalgar classes which are currently entering service with the Royal Navy.

Before completion of the submarine complex, Devonport also witnessed the opening of a frigate complex in 1977. Announced in 1970 it was part of a £600,000 modernization programme that would allow Devonport the ability to take a lead role in the refitting of Leander general-purpose frigates. As such it would mean that all Leanders and their replacements would automatically be directed to Devonport for any major refits. An enclosed, roofed structure, the frigate complex was built out of the Nos 5, 6 and 7 docks which date from the mid-nineteenth century. At the time the complex was announced, the No 7 dock could already accommodate Leanders, but the other two docks needed lengthening. Alterations were also made to the No 2 wet basin, subsequently improving berthing facilities

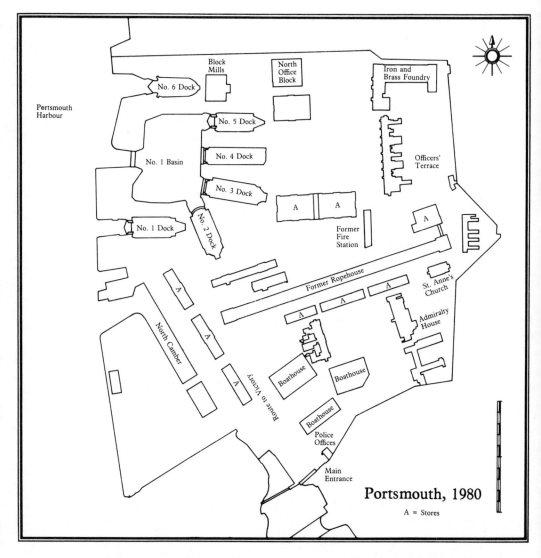

Portsmouth, 1980

A = Stores

together with nearby stores and workshops.

Now functioning, Devonport's frigate complex allows for a much faster refit time, with the work-force unhindered by weather conditions. Organized on a three shift, twenty-four hour day, the complex is a production shop organized on factory lines, with everything on hand for an uninterrupted programme of work. At the time of the author's visit to Devonport during the spring of 1981, only two frigates were docked with the *Scylla* in No 5 dock receiving Exocet and

Sea Cat missile systems, whilst the *Amazon* was being refitted in the
No 6 dock. When all three docks are in use, a total force of 1,500 men
(including Royal Navy personnel) are at work.

Portsmouth, long neglected, had a £60 million modernization
programme announced during the early summer of 1970. Part of the
plans included the erection of a heavy plate and pipe shop and the
replacement of armament storage facilities. General improvements
were made to the docks, so allowing Portsmouth to specialize in Type
42 destroyers. A covered refit centre was also proposed, but little
progress has so far been made in this particular area.

Naturally improvements and changes to the dockyards continue;
at Rosyth, where it is likely that Trident-carrying submarines will
eventually be refitted, a new synchro-lift was brought into operation
during the autumn of 1980. This has the ability to physically remove a
smaller patrol vessel right out of the main basin prior to transfer
ashore; the vessel is then brought inside a covered factory. This has
resulted in a considerable improvement to working conditions since
previously all small ship refits had to be undertaken on one of three
floating docks. The largest vessels able to use the synchro-lift complex
are the 1,000-tonne Island class patrol vessels and the Ton class
minesweepers of 370 tonnes.

Perhaps the most dramatic change came as a result of the White
Paper issued in June 1981. Entitled 'The Way Forward', it announced
not only the closure of Chatham yard in 1984 but also 'a very sharp
reduction in the scope and volume of dockyard work at Portsmouth'.
Although the Falkland crisis of 1982 earned a temporary reprieve for
Portsmouth, this was not the case at Chatham. If and when this yard
does close, it is difficult to see how the Valiant class submarines will be
refitted during future years. Devonport, the most obvious alternative
yard, is already fully committed and has neither the room nor facilities
for the refitting of all Fleet class submarines.

Of the foreign yards, only Gibraltar continued into the 1980s*; all
others have either been closed or handed over to the new governments
upon the granting of independence. Malta, for instance, completely
repaired and updated following its partial destruction during the war,
was eventually closed down in 1958 following the run-down of the

---

*As previously indicated Hong Kong, currently a naval base supporting a small force of patrol
vessels, has not been classified a royal dockyard.

Mediterranean fleet. Facilities at Malta were taken over by the civilian authorities with a number of British ship companies agreeing to run it on behalf of the island government. In 1971, however, the Malta Dry Dock Company was formed, a nationalized concern which ran the yard as a direct venture. Since then it has proved a highly profitable enterprise, undertaking numerous repairs upon commercially owned shipping. Indeed two of the old dry-docks have been lengthened so that bulk carriers could be docked, whilst a sixth dock has been added for the use of supertankers.

Gibraltar, despite its past importance to the Royal Navy, is now threatened. Together with Chatham and Portsmouth its demise was heralded by the 1981 Defence White Paper which suggested that naval work on the island may not be continued 'indefinitely'. Later during that year, its closure was officially announced for 1983, with the loss of some 900 jobs. Taking responsibility for maintaining a good portion of all Royal Navy and Royal Fleet Auxiliary ships that entered the Mediterranean, Gibraltar was extremely well equipped, still containing a great number of back-up facilities with the largest dry-dock in that area of the Mediterranean. Additionally, Gibraltar was a major port of call for many NATO ships, though some countries, for political reasons, preferred not to make use of its numerous advantages.

Great Britain, then, currently possesses five royal dockyards, four at home and one abroad. With several of these under threat of closure or severe reduction in the scope of work undertaken, the future will see most maintenance work being centred upon Devonport and Rosyth. A certain logic obviously prevails as the two home yards most at risk are the ones that have been least modernized over the years. Despite its submarine refit complex, Chatham has very little else that is modern and many essential items of equipment are of pre-war design. The work-force, on the other hand, is extremely experienced, and its loss to the navy will be quite incalculable. What is a little more difficult to appreciate is how a government can justify the expense of a modern refit centre, only to close it down long before its usefulness has ended.

With the projected closure of Chatham, consideration must be given not only to the future of the work-force, of which only a small proportion can be transferred, but also to the dockyard's historic enclave. In common with Portsmouth and Devonport, the yard at Chatham has a great many listed buildings, many of which still perform the tasks for which they were originally designed. Close to the main gate, for instance, stands the rope-house, a massive building which still spins rope for all naval requirements. Nearby stand the sail and colour lofts, several mould lofts and a mast house, all of which date to the eighteenth century and require careful preservation in a sympathetic background. Plans for the National Maritime Museum to take over these architectural gems exist, but it may be necessary for local preservation groups to become more directly involved.

The historic enclaves at Portsmouth and Devonport are almost certainly in safer hands. At Portsmouth a well-established naval museum already exists, whilst many thousands of visitors are annually attracted to Nelson's flagship, the Chatham-built HMS *Victory*. What some of these visitors probably miss, however, are a number of the extremely old dockyard buildings that line the route to *Victory*. On passing through the main gate there is a seventeenth-century mast pond, some nineteenth-century boat-houses and several sets of eighteenth-century stores. Elsewhere within the dockyard are to be found various residences, the original rope-house, block mills, storehouses, dry-docks and basins, all of which have very long histories. Sadly, most are not open for public inspection.

Devonport also has an historic enclave backed by a dockyard museum. Guided tours of the enclave include visits to the ropery, several of the old dry-docks, the covered slipway and King's Hill. All are to be found in the south yard, well away from the bustling Morice* and Keyham yards. Whilst plans exist for this area to be fully open to the public at some time in the near future, visits at the moment are restricted and must be planned beforehand.

One other dockyard, or rather former dockyard, is also worth a visit. This is Woolwich which, although closed in 1869, remains partially intact. Surrounded by a modern council estate, two of the former dry-docks are preserved, as is the original clock-tower office block that was built during the eighteenth century. For those who do not know Woolwich, the dockyard lies about a mile to the west of the town centre and close to the River Thames. By train Woolwich Dockyard station makes an obvious alighting point.

Although retrenchment is clearly the current trend, it is not one that can last for ever. Britain needs a navy and therefore needs the royal dockyards for repair and maintenance. Portsmouth will continue in

---

*The Morice Yard is the central area of the Devonport dockyard complex, being a former gun-wharf and added to the dockyard during the late 1930s. In 1963 the Morice Yard was linked to the South Yard by means of a flyover, with a second flyover, built in 1964, linking the Morice and the Keyham (North) Yard.

use, as a navy base with repair facilities for certain types of destroyers and any diesel-electric submarines remaining in service. Devonport will concentrate on frigate work and the refitting of nuclear attack submarines, leaving Rosyth the nuclear ballistic submarines and smaller vessels required for the North Sea area. However, it is possible that current Royal Navy needs may prevent a full implementation of the 1981 defence review.

However the royal dockyards continue to change, what will not alter is the faith of each dockyard worker in the abilities of a particular yard. Be it Chatham, Devonport, Portsmouth or Rosyth, the story is always the same – each worker always declares his particular dockyard the best. Long established and firmly part of the community, they are the pride of the local population. Without them employment opportunities would have been limited, certain towns non-existent and our nation state would have been ill-equipped to defend its shores.

Appendix

BUILDINGS OF HISTORIC INTEREST: The Original Yards

The following is a list of the most interesting buildings to be found either in the remaining royal dockyards or on the site of former dockyards. In most cases the buildings are listed. Whilst the list applies only to the home yards, it should be noted that a great array of such buildings can also be found in former foreign yards. English Harbour, Antigua, has a particularly good collection, but Malta, Bermuda, Minorca and Gibraltar should not be ignored. The names of buildings relate to their original use. Building dates refer to completion.

Chatham

Most of the buildings of interest are to be found within the historic enclave which is sited near the main gate. Here, for instance, is the ropery, still in use to this day. Other buildings of note are the saw mill, designed by Marc Brunel, but now a laundry, whilst the clock tower, with its upper storey mould loft, probably had the lines of *Victory* scribed upon its floor.

Medway House, former accommodation of resident commissioner (1703)
Main Gate (1720)
Officers' Lodgings (c1720)
Clock Tower Store (c1725)
Stables (c1730)
Sail Loft (1735)
Mast House and Mould Loft (1753)
Timber seasoning sheds (1772)
Hemp Store (c1780)
Spinning House (c1780)
Tarring House (c1785)
Double Rope-house (1787)
Storehouses (1783 and 1796)
Dockyard Church (1808–11)
Cashier's Office (1811)
Admiral's Office (1813)
Saw Mill (1813–14)
Lead and Paint Mill (1819)
Smithery (1850)

Deptford

The former area of Deptford dockyard has been fully redeveloped as part of a modern industrial complex. Consequently very few structures connected with the former dockyard remain. However, some terraced houses (1780), the former residence of the master shipwright and two covered slipways have been preserved.

Devonport (Plymouth)

Devonport probably has the widest range of buildings to be found in any one dockyard. Amongst other features it has the earliest of officers' lodgings, a rope-house predating those at Portsmouth and Chatham and the earliest covered slipway. Also, with regard to the Victorian period, it has in the Quadrangle the finest and most complete group of buildings designed to service the steam navy.

The Terrace, South Yard (1692)
The Terrace, Morice Yard (1720)
Morice Gate (1720)
Stores, Morice Yard (1722, 1730, 1750, 1776, 1777, 1790 and 1812)
Joiners' Shop (1760)
The East Ropery (1766)
Stores, South Yard (1766)
Tarred Yarn House (1766)
Colour Loft, Morice Yard (1810)
Sail Loft, Morice Yard (1811)
Covered Slip, South Yard (1814)
Gazebo, King's Hill (1822)
The Swing Bridge, South Yard (1838)
South Sawmills, South Yard (1847)
The Quadrangle, North Yard (1850)
Fire Station, South Yard (1851)
Main Dock Pump, South Yard (1851)
The Smithery, South Yard (1857)

Harwich

Of the former royal dockyard at Harwich little or nothing remains – hardly surprising as it ceased to function as a full dockyard during the seventeenth century. Nevertheless a tread-wheel crane built in 1667 and used within the dockyard can be seen on Harwich Green. Additionally, the old dockyard bell, cast in 1666, also exists.

Portsmouth

Portsmouth boasts a great mass of buildings, several of which are open to the public. Others can be viewed during the walk from the main gate to *Victory*. Of particular note are a number of iron-framed buildings that date from the late eighteenth and early nineteenth centuries, such as the dockyard pay office, possibly designed by Sir Samuel Bentham. Another important building is the block mill in which the mass production of pulley blocks was pioneered under the guidance of Marc Brunel.

Porter's Lodge (1708)
Main Gate (1711)
Officers' Lodgings (1717)
Royal Naval Academy (1729)
Stores (1763, 1776, 1782)
Great Rope-house (1770)
Hatchelling House (1771)
Hemp House (1771)
Hemp Tarring House (1771)
South-west Building (1782)
South-east Building (1783)
Short Row (1787)
South Office Block (West, 1786; East, 1789; Central, 1840)
Smithery (1791)
Block Mills (1802)
School of Naval Architecture (1816)
Old Fire Station (1843)
Mast House (1845)
No 2 Ship Shop (1849)
The Round Tower (1858)

Despite its outward appearance, the four-storey Sheerness dockyard boat store dates to 1859. The 200ft building is the earliest multi-storey iron-framed building in existence

HMS *Princess Irene*, destroyed by accident in 1915. An internal explosion killed a number of Sheerness dockyard workers

One of three dry-docks at Sheerness. Still in use for the maintenance of tugs, the dock dates to the early nineteenth century

A view of Devonport's huge frigate complex. Originally opened in 1977, it specialises in Leander and Type 21 refits. With a production shop organised on factory lines, everything is on hand for an uninterrupted programme

Sheerness

A busy container and passenger port, the Medway Port Authority has
undertaken an extensive clearance project within the area of Sheerness
dockyard. Despite this, a number of interesting buildings remain, not least of
these being the four-storey, iron-framed boat store.

Storehouse (1824)	Foundry (1857)
Garrison Church (1828)	Ship Fitting Shop (1857)
Captain's House (1830)	Boatstore (1859)
Smithery (1856)	

Woolwich

Woolwich ceased to operate as a dockyard during the mid-nineteenth century
but the area was not fully redeveloped until the early 1970s. Immediately
prior to this, however, an extensive archaeological investigation was
successfully carried out. Only a few structures survived the redevelopment
programme, these being the eighteenth-century clock house, two graving
docks, Hill Gate and Colonnade. All have been successfully incorporated into
a combined housing and recreation area.

Glossary

Apron The ledge found at the entrance of a dry-dock. Helping to ensure water tightness, it was upon this that the gates rested

Ballast Additional weight added to a vessel in order to achieve stability. Warships during the age of sail were normally ballasted with quantities of gravel brought into the various royal dockyards by a local contractor. It was normal for such ballast to be removed prior to dry-docking and reballasting after being refloated

Breaming The cleaning of a ship's bottom with a lighted faggot. The flame, burning with the pitch previously placed upon the hull, immediately loosens such adhering matter as grass, ooze and seaweed. Once the task is complete wooden sailing vessels were then recaulked

Camber An enclosed dock which was used either for the seasoning of masts and yards or harbouring of small boats

Capstan Mechanical apparatus found on seagoing and other vessels, used for the raising of the anchor

Careening A commonly performed operation which consisted of heaving a sailing warship down on one side by applying tackle to the upper masts. Frequently adopted when the underside of a vessel needed cleaning and there was no dry-dock available. Many of the foreign yards, when not endowed with dry-docks, had special careening pits and careening capstans

Careening Capstan One of a set of capstans, set in the side of a wharf or dock and used to heave down a sailing warship prior to cleaning. Such yards as Bermuda, where no proper dry-docks existed, had several such capstans which worked in association with a careening pit

Careening Pit A ditch dug in the side of a wharf and so situated that the lower yard arms of a ship could be comfortably accommodated. This meant that the yardarms themselves would not have to be lowered. For a diagram of the entire operation Lt Cdr Ian Stranack's *The Andrew and the Onions* should be referred to

Caulking The sealing of a ship's bottom by means of hot melted pitch and old rope which, prior to the application of pitch, is pushed into the seams of a timber hull. A skilled job, it was a task that at one time was undertaken by gangs of caulkers, each of whom would have had to serve a seven-year apprenticeship

Chain Moorings The normal means of establishing a series of permanent moorings. Anchors are fixed on either bank of a suitably sheltered river and connected by chain. In the middle of the chain is a square link attached to a cable which was then used to retain a ship at anchor. More efficient than use of a ship's anchor, such moorings were once sited adjacent to each of the royal dockyards during the era of sail

Commission The assigning of a naval vessel to a period of service

Cruiser During the days of sail a general name given to any vessel capable of being detached from the fleet for purposes of searching out the enemy. Usually a fourth rate or above. In the days of steam, a cruiser referred to a particular type of warship, and one that could remain in more distant waters for long periods of time

Dry-dock Often referred to as a graving dock, such docks are designed to accommodate vessels when it is necessary for the hull to be inspected, cleaned or repaired. Whilst the earliest dry-docks were made of mud, timber and stone docks were more common during the age of sail. Once a vessel had entered the dry-dock, usually at high tide, the dock would either empty naturally, or be pumped free of water. A watertight gate would then be closed

Dunnage Loose blocks used to secure cargo in the hold of a vessel

Floating Dock Developed in the nineteenth century, a floating dock consists of a number of watertight compartments which, once flooded, immerse the dock and so allow a vessel to enter. Once pumped out, the dock will bring the hull of the ship above water. Its main advantage is that it can be towed considerable distances and established where permanent docks cannot be built

Hulk An old or rotting warship. Hulks were found close to all of the royal dockyards and used to accommodate certain workmen, prisoners-of-war and crews of a ship in dry-dock. Their usefulness for the last purpose disappeared with the establishment of proper naval barracks towards the turn of the present century. Some dockyard hulks in former times were supplied with sheer legs for the stepping of masts

Jury Rigged Temporary rigging used in the case of a few dockyards, such as Chatham, Deptford and Woolwich, for navigating vessels the length of the Thames and Medway, prior to receiving a set of full sails and crew

Keel The principal timber of any vessel, and laid down prior to its construction. Used to hold the bottom of the vessel together. As it runs the entire length of the ship, several very large timbers are **scarph jointed**. In building the *Victory*, laid down at Chatham in 1759, seven such keel timbers, each measuring 150ft by 20ft had to be used

Keelson A piece of timber running parallel to the keel but placed inside the vessel and mounted over the floor timbers. Designed to give additional strength

Lighters A barge, or other small vessel, used for the conveyancing of cargo between the shore and loading vessels

Ordinary The name given to those vessels laid up in harbour and without a commission

Rates The classes into which warships were divided during the age of sail. In all there were six separate rates, ranging from a first rate of 100 guns or more, to that of a sixth rate with less than 18 guns. Amongst the most common of fighting ships were the 74-gun third rates which came to dominate the line of battle during the late eighteenth century

Scarph Joint A joint used by shipwrights for bonding two timbers so that they overlap without increasing thickness

Sheathing Board A means of protecting ships against *Teredo navalis*. Originally sheathing boards were no more than planks of fir placed over the hull. Proving quite inadequate, they were discontinued with the adoption of copper sheathing

Sheer Hulk A dockyard hulk fitted with lifting gear that consisted of a central pole incorporated into the hulk, with a second pole attached to this at a point near the top. Known as sheer legs, partly because they resembled a pair of shears, they were used for stepping the masts into great ships

Teredo Navalis A small boring mollusc which has the ability to convert timber into food. Found in warmer seas, hundreds of these attached to a ship's hull would eventually reduce it to a worthless hulk

Wet-Dock (or basin) A large area of water, artificially contained at high-tide level, in which vessels can be fitted and refitted in a much safer and more convenient situation. As with a dry-dock, ships enter at high tide, a process which allows the water inside to be maintained at the correct level. The enclosing gate is known as a caisson

References

1 Monson
2 Kings 43. British Library
3 Ibid
4 Ibid
5 Stephens, A. E. *Plymouth Dock* (London University thesis, 1940)
6 Kings 44. British Library
7 PRO ADM 7/658. 12 August 1749
8 Kings 44. British Library
9 PRO ADM 7/660. 13 July 1773
10 Barnes and Owen, *The Sandwich Papers*, Vol IV, p287
11 Ibid
12 PRO ADM 7/659
13 National Maritime Museum CHA/L/35. 24 March 1801
14 National Maritime Museum POR/N/1. 7 August 1689
15 PRO ADM B/185
16 Kings 44. British Library
17 Ibid
18 Ibid
19 Considerable confusion exists as to the correct spelling of Widley. I have adopted the spelling later used in Rennie's *British and Foreign Harbours* (1854)
20 Rennie, J. *British and Foreign Harbours* (1854)
21 Ibid
22 Dicker, George. *A Short History of Devonport Royal Dockyard*

Bibliography

A Note on Primary Manuscript Sources

Of primary sources used in the writing of this book, undoubtedly the most important were a wide range of documents held at the National Maritime Museum, the Public Record Office at Kew and the British Library. Within the Maritime Museum, perhaps the most important source of information, is a great mass of letter volumes relating to the Admiralty in general and more specifically the dockyards of Chatham and Portsmouth, together with some foreign yards. Apart from such manuscript material, however, the museum also possesses numerous paintings, maps and a collection of models, dating to 1774, showing an exact layout of each home yard.

At the Public Record Office a further wide range of material is available, with both Admiralty and Navy Board letter books open to inspection. Particularly useful were various accounts relating to eighteenth-century dockyard visits, a collection of photograph albums depicting building progress and a considerable array of maps. For those wishing to research further into the dockyards, the reader is recommended to peruse the 'Guide to the Contents of the Public Record Office' Volume II (HMSO).

Within the British Library, Kings 43 and 44 proved of particular value. Kings 43 provides a complete record of the dockyards for the period 1688 to 1698. All buildings, dry-docks and slipways are described, together with expenses incurred. Kings 44 is rather similar, providing a description of each dockyard for the year 1774. A very handsome book, it was produced as a birthday present for King George III. It should be used in conjunction with the dockyard models held at the National Maritime Museum.

A further source of information, though used less frequently for the writing of this book, is the respective county record office. The one at Plymouth is without doubt the most useful, possessing a number of letter books relating to Devonport. Other county record offices, such as the one at Maidstone, hold a number of early maps and parish registers, which help indicate the rapid growth of dockyard towns following the establishment and expansion of each dockyard.

Printed Sources

General

Abell, Sir W. *The Shipwright's Trade* (London, 1981)

Barnes, G. R. and Owen, J. H. (ed) *The Private Papers of John, Earl of Sandwich* (Navy Records Society, 1938)

Baugh, D. *British Naval Administration in the Age of Walpole* (Princeton, 1965)

Baugh, D. *Naval Administration* (Navy Records Society, 1977)

Browne, D. G. *The Floating Bulwark* (London, 1963)

Brenton, E. P. *Life and Correspondence of the Earl of St Vincent* (1838)

Dougan, D. *The Shipwrights* (Newcastle upon Tyne, 1975)

Ehrman, J. *The Navy in the War of William III* (Cambridge, 1953)

Gardiner, L. *The British Admiralty* (London, 1968)

Haas, J. M. 'The Introduction of Task Work in the Royal Dockyards, 1775', *The Journal of British Studies* Vol VIII:2 (1969)

Hasted, E. *The History and Topographical Survey of the County of Kent* Vol IV (Canterbury, 1797–1801; republished Wakefield, 1972)

Horsley, J. E. *Tools of the Maritime Trade* (Newton Abbot, 1978)

Holland, A. J. *Ships of British Oak* (Newton Abbot, 1971)

Johns, A. W. 'Phineas Pett', *Mariner's Mirror* Vol XII:4, p432

Knight, R. J. B. 'Pilfering and Theft from the Dockyards', *Mariner's Mirror* Vol LXI:3, p215

Landstrom, B. *Sailing Ships* (London, 1978)

Longridge, C. N. *The Anatomy of Nelson's Ships* (London, 1961)

Macleod, N. 'The Shipwrights of the Royal Dockyards', *Mariner's Mirror* Vol XI:2, p276

Macleod, N. 'The Shipwright Officers of the Royal Dockyards', *Mariner's Mirror* Vol XI:3, p355

Merriman, R. D. (ed) *Queen Anne's Navy* (Navy Records Society, 1961)

Merriman, R. D. (ed) *The Sergison Papers* (Navy Records Society, 1960)

Morris, C. (ed) *The Journey of Celia Fiennes* (London, 1947)

Morriss, R. A. 'Labour Relations in the Royal Dockyards' *Mariner's Mirror* Vol LXII:4, p337

Oppenheim, M. *A History of the Administration of the Royal Navy* (London, 1896)

Oppenheim, M. *The Naval Tracts of Sir William Monson* (Navy Records Society, 1914)

Perrin, W. G. *The Autobiography of Phineas Pett* (Navy Records Society, 1918)

Ranft, B. McL. 'Labour Relations in the Royal Dockyards 1739', *Mariner's Mirror* Vol XLVII:3, p281

Ranft, B. McL. (ed) *The Vernon Papers* (Navy Records Society, 1958)

Richardson, H. E. 'Wages of Shipwrights in HM Dockyards, 1496–1788', *Mariner's Mirror* Vol XXXIII:3, p265

Chatham

Bugler, A. *HMS* Victory: *Building, Restoration and Repair* (London, 1966)

Coad, J. G. 'The Chatham Mould Loft and Mast House', *Mariner's Mirror* Vol LXI:2, p127

Coad, J. G. 'Chatham Ropeyard', *Post Medieval Archaeology* (1969)

Cull, F. 'Chatham Dockyard: Early Leases and Conveyances', *Archaeologia Cantiana* Vol LXXIII (1959)

Cull, F. 'Chatham – The Hill House', *Archaeologia Cantiana* Vol LXXVII (1963)

Grace, J. G. *Some Notes on the History of Chatham Dockyard* (Chatham, 1946)

Harris, E. *History of Chatham Dockyard* (Rochester, 1911)

Harris, E. *History of Chatham* (Rochester, 1912)

Harris, E. *History of the Chatham Chest* (Rochester, 1915)

MacDougall, P. 'Chatham Dockyard – A Living Museum', *Coast and Country* Vol 8, No 6, p8

MacDougall, P. *The Chatham Dockyard Story* (Rochester, 1981)

MacDougall, P. 'The Chatham Gun Wharf', *Bygone Kent* Vol 1:12, p738

MacDougall, P. 'The Victorian Extension to Chatham Dockyard', *Bygone Kent* Vol 2:4, p234

Presnail, J. *The Story of Chatham* (Chatham, 1952)

Preston, J. M. *Industrial Medway* (Rochester, 1977)

Deptford and Woolwich

Courtney, T. 'Excavations at the Royal Dockyard Woolwich, 1972', *Transactions of the Greenwich and Lewisham Antiquarian Society* Vol VIII:1, p27

Courtney, T. 'Excavations at the Royal Dockyard Woolwich, 1973', *Transactions of the Greenwich and Lewisham Antiquarian Society* Vol VIII:2

Dews, N. *The History of Deptford* (Deptford, 1884)

Grinling, W. H. *A Survey and Record of Woolwich and West Kent* (Woolwich, 1909)

Illustrated London News (various but especially 1859 to 1869)

Jefferson, E. F. E. *The Woolwich Story 1890–1965* (Woolwich, 1970)

MacDougall, P. 'Deptford: Former Royal Dockyard', *Bygone Kent* Vol 2:11, p642

MacDougall, P. 'Woolwich Dockyard', *Bygone Kent* Vol 2:10, p579

Pembroke

Carradice, P. 'The Rise and Fall of a Welsh Dockyard' *County Quest* April 1981, p12

Findlay, J. A. *Handbook of Pembroke Dock* (Pembroke, 1875)

John, B. S. *Old Industries of Pembrokeshire* (Pembroke, 1975)

Mason, G. *Pembroke Dock* (Pembroke, 1905)

Peters, S. *History of Pembroke Dock* (Pembroke, 1905)

Plymouth/Devonport

Burns, K. V. Lt Cdr *Devonport Built Warships Since 1860* (Liskeard, 1981)

Burns, K. V. Lt Cdr *Plymouth's Ships of War* (Greenwich, 1972)

Dicker, G. *A Short History of Devonport Royal Dockyard* (Devonport, 1969; revised, 1980)

Fenton, A. C. 'Story of Devonport Dockyard', *Periscope* (March 1968 to August 1968)

Gill, C. *Plymouth: A New History* (Newton Abbot, 1979)

Merrett, L. H. 'The Building of Plymouth Breakwater', *Maritime History* Vol 5:2, 1977

Worth, R. N. *History of Plymouth* (Plymouth, 1890)

Portsmouth

Defoe, D. *Journal of a Tour Through England and Wales* (Harmondsworth, 1971)

Gates, W. G. *History of Portsmouth* (Portsmouth, 1900)

Geddes, A. *Portsmouth during the Great French Wars 1770–1800* (Portsmouth, 1970)

Gilbert, K. R. *The Portsmouth Blockmaking Machinery* (London, 1965)

Hoad, M. J. *Portsmouth – As others have seen it Part 1 1540–1790* (Portsmouth, 1972)

Hoad, M. J. *Portsmouth – As others have seen it Part 2 1790–1900* (Portsmouth, 1973)

Kitson, Sir H. K. 'The Early History of Portsmouth Dockyard, 1496–1800', *Mariner's Mirror* Vol XXXIII, p256; Vol XXXIV, p3, 87 and 271

Lloyd, D. W. *Buildings of Portsmouth and its Environs* (Portsmouth, 1974)

MacDougall, P. ''Twas Impossible to Save', *Coast and Country* Vol 10:5

Marsh, A. J. *The Story of a Frigate* (Portsmouth, 1973)

Patterson, A. Temple *Portsmouth* (Bradford-on-Avon, 1976)

Patterson, A. Temple *The Other Armada* (Manchester, 1960)

Portsmouth Reference Library *Public Monuments in Portsmouth* (Portsmouth, 1975)

Riley, Dr. R. C. *The Growth of Southsea as a Naval Satellite and Victorian Resort* (Portsmouth, 1972)

Sparks, H. J. *The Story of Portsmouth* (Portsmouth, 1921)

Washington, E. S. *Portsmouth in the Age of the Armada* (Portsmouth, 1972)

Webb, J. *An Early Nineteenth Century Dockyard Worker* (Portsmouth, 1971)

Rosyth

Adams, T. *The New Naval Base. A Great Social Opportunity* (London, 1903)

Dunfermline, City and Royal Burgh of *Rosyth Dockyard* (Dunfermline, 1947)

Harrison, G. *Alexander Gibb* (London)

Rosyth Naval Base Development Plan, Vol 1, 1980

Sheerness

Bentham, Sir S. *Improvements of the Naval Arsenal at Sheerness* (London, 1814)

Fellowes, J. 'Shipbuilding at Sheerness, 1750–1802', *Mariner's Mirror* Vol 60:1, p73

Goodsall, R. H. *The Widening Thames* (London, 1965)

Little, B. D. G. 'A Relic from the Age of Sail: the Dockyard at Sheerness', *Country Life* 1958

MacDougall, P. 'Sheerness Naval Dockyard', *Bygone Kent* Vol 1:10, p610

Taylor, J. 'John Rennie's Reconstruction of Sheerness Dockyard', *Kent*

Archaeological Review No 43, Spring 1976

Woodthorpe, T. J. *A History of the Isle of Sheppey* (Sheerness, 1951)

Other Dockyards

Cary, L. H. St C. 'Harwich Dockyard', *Mariner's Mirror* Vol XIII:2, p167

Cary, L. H. St C. 'Trincomalee', *Mariner's Mirror* Vol XVII:1, p20

Elliott, P. *The Cross and the Ensign* (Cambridge, 1980)

English Harbour, Friends of *The Romance of English Harbour* (Antigua, 1972)

Harwich Society *A Walk Around Old Harwich* (Harwich, 1973)

Howes, H. W. *The Story of Gibraltar* (London, 1946)

Hughes, B. Carlyon *Harwich Harbour* (Harwich, 1939)

Johns, A. W. 'Sir Anthony Deane', *Mariner's Mirror* Vol XI:2

Laker, J. *History of Deal* (Deal, 1921)

Leasor, J. *Singapore* (London, 1968)

Lindsey, W. H. *A Season at Harwich* (Harwich, 1851)

McSwiney, Rev. P. 'Eighteenth Century Kinsale', *Journal of Cork Historical and Archaeological Society* Vol XLIII, No158 (1938) p75

O'Neil, B. H. St J. 'Notes on the Fortifications of Kinsale Harbour', *Cork Historical and Archaeological Society Journal* Vol XLV, (1940) p110

Palao, G. *Gibraltar: Our Forgotten Past* (Gibraltar, 1977)

Palao, G. *Gibraltar: Our Heritage* (Gibraltar, 1979)

Pritchard, S. *The History of Deal* (Deal, 1864)

Stranack, Lt Cdr I. *The Andrew and the Onions. The Story of the Royal Navy in Bermuda, 1795-1975* (Bermuda)

Vaughan, H. R. H. 'The Old Dockyard at English Harbour, Antigua' in *Mariner's Mirror* Vol XI, p301

Page, W. and Round, J. H. (ed) *Essex* (Victoria County History) Vol II, p259 (London, 1907)

Acknowledgements

In the writing of this book, as with any non-fiction book, a considerable amount of help was solicited from a great many people. I would like to indicate my gratitude and appreciation to all concerned. First and foremost, I must thank the Ministry of Defence, Press Facilities Section (Navy) whose personnel were kind enough to arrange a visit to each of the home yards. For help at each of these yards I would like to thank Tim Hunt and Peter Ridolfo (Devonport), Michael Hill (Portsmouth), Maureen Ferrier and Dan Patterson (Rosyth). At Sheerness, now a commercial port, I would also like to thank Mr A. Howard, Assistant Dock Manager to the Medway Port Authority, for arranging a similar visit.

Others who helped in the writing of this book were John Jenkins, MBE, The Friends of English Harbour, Antigua, the Harwich Society and the staff of the following public libraries: Chatham, Cork, Dunfermline, Gillingham, Harwich, Haverfordwest, Plymouth, Portsmouth and Rochester. Help was also given by the staff of the Greenwich Local History Library, the Imperial War Museum, the National Maritime Museum, the Public Record Office and the Royal Engineers Library, Brompton. An especial thanks must also be given to George Dicker, author of 'Devonport Royal Dockyard' for allowing me to quote a short passage from this booklet.

Index

to care and maintenance, 179; re-established, 180
Penlee Point, 134
Pepys, Samuel, 49, 53–65
Pett, Christopher, 49, 57, 59, 60
  Joseph, 49
  Peter, 36, 40, 49–50, 53, 58, 60, 64
  Phineas (senior) 36, 40–9
  Phineas, 65, 70
Plymouth, 35, 140
  dock *see* Devonport
  dockyard *see* Devonport dockyard
Port Antonio
  dockyard, 83
Portland, 169
Port Mahon
  dockyard, 82, 139
Port Royal
  dockyard, 10, 82, 139
Portsea, 100
Portsmouth, 100, 140
  dockyard, 7–8, 9, 12, 13, 16, 17, 18–24, 30–1, 34, 36, 45, 50–1, 57, 58, 65, 66, 84, 94, 95–6, 99, 123, 179, 188, 193, 194, 196; administration of, 53; chapel, 123; dispute over task work, 108; expansion under William III, 78–9; facilities, 70; fires, 112–22, 124; Great Basin, 90; historic build-ings, 198; Long Row, 90; merits of, 129; No 2 Ship Shop, 148; No 3 Ship Shop, 148; No 6 Boat House, 141; numbers employed, 90, 155; Old Fire Station, 141; Pay Office, 141; resident commissioner, 70; role of, 87, 90, 155; ropery, 70, 79, 112–23, 124, 129; Short Row, 123; Steam Basin, 144; steam power, use of, 133; Victorian extension, 154; wet docks, 125, 132; World War II, 185
  Gun wharf, 86
  Hard, 119
  St George's church, 100

Raleigh, Sir Walter, 76
Rennie, John, 134–6, 143
Riggers, 15, 104
Rochester, 101
Rodney, Admiral, 15
Rolling mills, 11, 16
Rope-making process, description of, 14
Rosyth
  dockyard, 7, 10, 16, 190; completion, 177–8; established, 169–73; reduced to care and maintenance, 179; re-established, 180; World War II, 180
Royal dockyards (*passim*)
  administration of, 53

corruption in, 59–61, 87, 104
criticisms of, 131–3, 136
definition of, 7
design of, 131
electric power, 16
fires in, 112–121
function of, 12–15, 79, 81
security, 144
steam power introduced, 134
Royal Marine Police, 144
Ryswick, Peace of, 81

Sailmakers, 14, 104
Sandwich, Earl of, 97–8
Saw mills, 11, 133
Sawyers, 13
Scavelmen, 14, 15
Sheerness, 101, 140
  dockyard, 7, 9, 65, 69, 79, 88, 116, 147, 173, 175, 179; boathouse, 141; closure, 189–90; conditions, 72, 90; description, 158; extension, 143–4; historic buildings, 201; World War II, 181
  gun wharf, 86
Ships
  A-class submarines, 186
  Acasata, 178
  Achilles, 149–50, 151–2
  Ajax, 180
  Amazon, 193
  Andromeda, 189
  Anne, 58
  Ardent, 96
  Ariadne, 140
  Ark Ralegh, 34, 40, 41, 43
  Arrogant, 157
  Bedford, 80
  Bellerophon, 166
  Blake, 188
  Bonavolia, 32
  Britannia, 65, 68
  Brunswick, 94
  C-class submarines, 167–8
  Caledonia, 152
  Campbeltown, 183
  Canada, 178
  Canopus, 156
  Centurion, 77
  Charles (1662), 58
  Charles (1668), 64
  Cleopatra, 188
  Comet, 144–5
  Commerce de Marseilles, 96
  Conqueress, 178
  Cornwall, 96
  Discovery, 130
  Dreadnought, 161–6